INSIGHTS & OUTCOMES

Assessments
for Great Explorations
in Math and Science

by
Jacqueline Barber, Lincoln Bergman, Jan M. Goodman,
Kimi Hosoume, Linda Lipner, Cary Sneider, Laura Tucker

LHS GEMS

Great Explorations in Math and Science (GEMS)
Lawrence Hall of Science
University of California at Berkeley

Lawrence Hall of Science
    Chairman: Glenn T. Seaborg
    Director: Marian C. Diamond

Initial support for the origination and publication of the GEMS series was provided by the A.W. Mellon Foundation and the Carnegie Corporation of New York. Under a grant from the National Science Foundation, GEMS Leader's Workshops have been held across the country. GEMS has also received support from the McDonnell-Douglas Foundation and the McDonnell-Douglas Employees Community Fund, the Hewlett Packard Company Foundation, Join Hands Educational Alliance, and the people at Chevron USA. GEMS also gratefully acknowledges the contribution of word processing equipment from Apple Computer, Inc. This support does not imply responsibility for statements or views expressed in publications of the GEMS program.

For further information on GEMS leadership opportunities, or to receive a publication brochure and the *GEMS Network News*, please contact GEMS at the address and phone number below.

COMMENTS WELCOME

Great Explorations in Math and Science (GEMS) is an ongoing curriculum development project. GEMS guides are revised periodically to incorporate teacher comments and new approaches. We welcome your criticisms, suggestions, helpful hints, and any anecdotes about your experience presenting GEMS activities. Your suggestions will be reviewed each time a GEMS guide is revised. Please send your comments to:

    GEMS Revisions
    Lawrence Hall of Science
    University of California
    Berkeley, CA 94720-5200

Our phone number is (510) 642-7771.
Our fax number is (510) 643-0309.

WHAT IS GEMS?

Great Explorations in Math and Science

*T*he basis for the GEMS approach is that students learn best by doing—an approach backed by overwhelming educational evidence. Activities first engage students in direct experience and experimentation, before introducing explanations of principles and concepts. Utilizing easily obtained and inexpensive materials, GEMS activities allow teachers without special background in science or mathematics to successfully present hands-on experiences.

*D*eveloped at the University of California at Berkeley's Lawrence Hall of Science, and tested in thousands of classrooms nationwide, more than 40 GEMS teacher's guides offer a wide spectrum of learning opportunities from preschool through tenth grade.

*E*mphasis on teamwork and cooperative learning, the use of a wide variety of learning formats, and reliance on direct experience rather than textbooks makes GEMS highly appropriate for use with populations that have been historically underrepresented in science and mathematics pursuits and careers. In GEMS activities, students are encouraged to work together to discover more, explore a problem, or solve a mystery, rather than fixating on the so-called right answer, or engaging in negatively competitive behavior. Cooperative (or collaborative) learning is one of the most effective strategies for bridging and appreciating differences

and diversities of background and culture. It is also one of the most effective ways to help prepare students for the workplaces of the future.

*T*he GEMS series interweaves a number of educational ideas and goals. GEMS guides encompass important learning objectives, summarized on the front page of each guide under the headings of skills, concepts, and themes. These objectives can be directly and flexibly related to science and mathematics curricula, state frameworks, and district guidelines.

*T*he GEMS handbook *To Build A House: GEMS and the Thematic Approach to Teaching Science* provides concrete examples from the GEMS series to illustrate the latest approaches in science education. Other handbooks include a *Teacher's Handbook*, a *Leader's Handbook*, *A Parent's Guide to GEMS*, and *Once Upon A GEMS Guide* (a literature connections handbook).

*S*ince classroom testing began in 1984, more than 400,000 teachers and at least five million students have enjoyed GEMS activities. A national network of teachers and educators take part in GEMS Leadership workshops and receive a regular newsletter, the *GEMS Network News*. GEMS is a growing series. New guides and handbooks are being developed constantly and current guides are revised frequently.

Acknowledgments

Taking on the subject of assessment for the entire GEMS series has been a mammoth task. While all the contributing authors played an important role throughout the origination, development, testing, and writing of this handbook, we would like to especially acknowledge the efforts of **Jan M. Goodman**, who served not only as one of the primary authors, but coordinated the writing and rewriting process with insight, humor, and energy—making it possible for this ambitious and complex work to become a reality.

In addition to the main authors of this handbook, the following people provided invaluable assistance and advice: From the GEMS staff and from the Lawrence Hall of Science, we are indebted to **Katharine Barrett, Gerri Ginsburg, Jaine Kopp, Jean Stenmark**, and **Carolyn Willard** for their thoughtful contributions to and critical review of this manuscript or portions thereof.

We would especially like to thank the following educators who advised us, assisted us in devising and trial testing the assessments featured in the Insights section, allowed us to use their classrooms to explore these assessments, reviewed portions of the manuscript, or in other ways brought their special expertise to this modest milestone in the continuing pursuit of excellence in science and mathematics educa-tion: **Ray Adams, Dr. Eloise Appel, Donna Baines, Debbie Baldwin, Laura Brown, Joe Brulenski, Susan Butsch, Kathy Comfort, Mark Edwards, Mark Endsley, Laurie Fregian, Liz Fuentes, Stefan Gair, Susan Hodge, Elaine Ikeda, Christine King, Carol Olson, Steven Rutherford, Jeanne Vetter**, and **Eric Watterud**. Among the California schools and school districts they represent are Albany Middle School in Albany; numerous public schools in Pittsburg; Lawrence and Lockeford schools in Lodi; Bancroft Middle School in San Leandro; Kent Middle School in Kentfield; and, in Berkeley, the Emerson, Oxford, and Thousand Oaks elementary schools, and the Bancroft Cooperative Kindergarten.

Last but far from least we thank the hundreds of students whose participation in these assessment activities helped all of us learn more about effective and exciting ways to assess their understandings and our own teaching.

LHS GEMS

Cover
Carol Bevilacqua

Photographs
Richard Hoyt
and
Jacqueline Barber, Jane Callaway,
Elizabeth Crews, Elizabeth Curtis,
Leslie Cusick, Saxon Donnelly,
Kay Fairwell, Jack Fishleder,
Jan Goodman, Jadin Hawkins,
Lawrence Migdale, Cary Sneider

Illustrations
Lisa Haderlie Baker, Carol Bevilacqua,
Rose Craig, Lisa Klofkorn

INTRODUCTION

Assessment is a highly charged word in educational circles—and that's an understatement! It is a complex, changing, and controversial subject that overlaps with major societal issues regarding quality of education, diversity and equality of access, the implementation of district and state guidelines, the efforts to evolve national standards, and many other aspects of our current educational crisis. At its heart, and at its best, assessment, as we see it, speaks to the continuing dedicated struggles of teachers and educators nationwide to improve instruction, to reach out to all students in effective and stimulating ways.

In the specific area of activity-based science and mathematics, thinking and practice related to assessment have undergone and continue to undergo many exciting transformations. All the authors of this handbook have had long and creative involvement in math and science education and the GEMS series, and some have considerable expertise in areas of assessment and evaluation. We must stress, however, that this handbook, like all GEMS publications, is written in the spirit of inquiry.

As we worked on this handbook and pondered the ways the GEMS series encourages and stimulates inquiring minds, we learned an incredible amount about assessment and the multilayered potential of GEMS activities, but we are very well aware that what we have learned is only the beginning of the journey.

This handbook is therefore presented with all due modesty. The ideas expressed are not intended to be taken as absolute truth, or to be applied mechanically. On the contrary, as with GEMS activities in general, flexibility, creativity, and your own judgment and experience are needed for the ideas to take root and blossom in your classroom. We very much welcome your comments and suggestions.

Our efforts are intended to ensure that a coherent assessment component is in place for the entire GEMS series. Through this handbook, we seek to provide ready-made assessments for those who want them, and to inspire and support the creation of new outcomes and assessments for those who need or want to generate their own. It is our hope that this handbook will not only be helpful to teachers who present GEMS activities, but will also encourage new and creative efforts by all teachers in integrating assessment strategies and techniques, as appropriate, within their presentation of activity-based math and science units, as well as in other subject areas.

A Word About Terminology

In the rapidly changing area of assessment, various terms have risen to the fore to differentiate the newer forms of assessment from more traditional methods. Among these terms are "alternative assessment," "authentic assessment," and "performance-based assessment." Rather than overusing one of these adjectives, choosing one of several others vying on the horizon, or coming up with our own, we decided instead to speak of assessment in a more generic way, as it applies to activity-based science and mathematics. As can be seen in this handbook, there are many and various approaches to such assessment, and no one label says it all. We have also attempted to avoid excessive use of the highly developed special vocabulary of assessment/evaluation expertise, and to rely instead on clearly describing learning goals and assessment methods in the context of and with numerous examples from the GEMS series.

The detailed Table of Contents that follows is intended to assist you in finding what you need. There are three main sections in the handbook:

➤ **Pearl's Journal**
This fictional teacher's journal is interspersed with comments to provide an overview of assessment issues as well as some ideas about how to use this handbook.

➢ Insights

These descriptions of major assessment strategies, with case studies from GEMS, use actual student work, analyze the insights gained from these case studies, and list other opportunities in the GEMS series for using each strategy.

➢ Outcomes

This alphabetical list and brief summary of all GEMS teacher's guides highlights selected student learning outcomes for each guide, and describes both built-in and additional assessments.

In order to make a sometimes intimidating and admittedly complex subject accessible and relevant to the classroom, we decided to build the first portion of this book around a fictional teacher's journal, as she works with another teacher to present and assess GEMS activities. The journal seemed a practical way to interweave some of our basic ideas about activity-based assessment while emphasizing what we see as the basic goals of such assessment. We realize that for many overworked, overcommitted teachers with no-time-to-even-write-a-postcard, such a journal may seem unrealistic. Yet the challenges—and successes—these two teachers achieve are quite real. They are drawn from the real-life experiences of many everyday heroes: teachers who are committed to enlivening the limitless potential of their students through activity-based math and science, and to creating innovative and effective assessment methods to help learners learn and teachers teach. It is to teachers like Pearl and Maria Rosa—and especially to all their bright-eyed students—that this handbook is dedicated.

Mystery Festival

Color Analyzers

TABLE OF CONTENTS

An imaginary teacher's yearlong journal (with our narration) highlights the characteristics of effective assessment for activity-based mathematics and science; discusses issues and concerns; provides suggestions about how to develop and evaluate assessment tasks; and explains how to use this handbook.

Thirteen **assessment strategies** with 17 detailed **case studies** show how these strategies can be used to evaluate student performance on specific GEMS activities. Each assessment strategy relates to real-life activities. Each case study shows a range of student responses and describes how these responses were analyzed in light of the goals for each assessment and usefulness to teachers. A list of **additional assessment opportunities**—natural opportunities to use each assessment strategy in other GEMS guides—is also provided. The object: to gain new **insights** into learning and teaching.

TABLE OF CONTENTS

TABLE OF CONTENTS

Four to six key **student learning outcomes** (learning objectives) for each GEMS teacher's guide are described. GEMS guides are listed alphabetically by title. For each guide, the student learning outcomes are followed by descriptions of **Built-In Assessment Activities** and **Additional Assessment Ideas** keyed to each outcome.

A brief bibliography of **assessment resources**.

In our terrarium I can see alot of roots. When I look through my glass I can see the roly polys hiding in the leaves. The sow bugs haven't been coming out the worms haven't either. And now my groups terrarium has a flower growing. The potatoes have teeny tiny holes in them.

This student writing and drawing sample is from a story-writing assessment given to students who were learning about Terrarium Habitats. A detailed case study using story writing as an assessment strategy from this GEMS Teacher's Guide is on page 35. Terrarium Habitats is also one of the GEMS guides our fictional teachers in the next section use in their classroom.

Pearl's Journal

or

A Year in the Life of...

This section features a fictional teacher's journal interspersed with general commentary on assessment.

The assessment adventures of Pearl and Maria Rosa provide practical examples of ways for you to use this handbook. While any resemblance to actual individuals is purely coincidental, all efforts to bring this subject alive in the classroom are purely intentional.

The accompanying commentary seeks to clarify the need for, the thinking behind, and the multi-purposes of assessment of GEMS and other activity-based science and mathematics units.

Pearl's Teaching Log September

GOT A MATCH?

September 1

I'm excited and nervous about this school year! When I arrived, there was a stack of five GEMS guides, selected especially for fifth grade. This past summer a team of teachers made kits of needed materials to go with the guides. That helps!!! Maria Rosa, my grade level partner, plans to work with me so we can support each other and the curriculum will be consistent. We start *Terrarium Habitats* next week. Now, our science program will be truly hands on!

September 15

Both classes are thrilled with *Terrarium Habitats!* As we set up our terrariums, our students learned that soil is more than dirt! Our habitats now contain soil, plants, seeds, leaf litter, and moisture. The students can't wait until next week, when we'll add earthworms and isopods. They are fascinated by the terrariums and are developing keen observation skills. I plan to continue for an entire month, so students can see changes in the habitats. What a great way to start off the school year!

September 27

Our students' enthusiasm is evident to everyone who visits the school. I was thrilled at Back-to-School Night. Many of the parents had already heard detailed reports of the terrariums, knew all about their child's isopods, worms, and snails, and told me how excited their children were about science this year. In fact, I was on Cloud 9 until today's staff meeting, when we met in grade level teams to discuss report cards. "How are we going to grade our students in science?" Maria Rosa asked. "I don't know," I said. "With our textbooks, there were always questions to answer and end-of-chapter tests that we could turn into report card grades. How <u>DO</u> we know what students have learned through activity-based math and science programs like GEMS?"

"I know my students are learning because I can see huge improvements in what they know and in the quality of their thinking," said Maria Rosa. "But I don't know how I can measure this progress. What we need is a match between how we teach with GEMS and how we assess our students!" "Got a match?" I joked.   But the dilemma we faced wasn't humorous.

The dilemma faced by Pearl and Maria Rosa is a common one for educators who have moved toward activity-based science and mathematics. As teachers, we are learning to become facilitators of learning-through-doing, rather than "tellers" or givers of abstract knowledge. Through GEMS and other excellent activity-based science and mathematics programs, we have moved away from emphasis on mechanical learning of facts to more meaningful construction of concepts, development of thinking skills, with a focus on large mathematical and scientific ideas and their interconnections. We encourage students to pursue questions and dig deeper, rather than memorize "answers." How can we assess the effectiveness of activity-based learning and communicate this clearly to students, parents, and colleagues? **As individuals and as a nation, we are faced with the challenge of finding ways to make assessment relevant to instruction.**

Terrarium Habitats

Pearl's Teaching Log

October

GOT A MATCH!

October 3

Maria Rosa came to school today, beaming. "I just may have found the solution to our assessment problem!" she exclaimed. I looked at her, quizzically. In her hands was the latest GEMS handbook, *Insights and Outcomes*. "Check out this book," she said. "It's filled with ideas about how to assess students in activity-based science and mathematics! It's just what we need! We've got a match!"

October 5

Today, we began to look through *Insights and Outcomes*. It's divided into three main sections and Maria Rosa and I can't agree about where to start! I like to start at the beginning; Maria Rosa prefers to skip ahead to the parts that grab her. She's delving right into the *Insights* section because she noticed that it contained an example of how to assess what students have learned in *Terrarium Habitats*. We both want to look at the *Outcomes* section. It has selected student learning outcomes for every GEMS teacher's guide plus many suggestions for assessment activities keyed to those outcomes. We're thinking that the *Outcomes* section could be used as a reference and resource for the entire staff, to help formulate school-wide goals for students and create a wider rationale for using GEMS units.

As Pearl and Maria are discovering, *Insights & Outcomes* is a handbook about assessment of GEMS activities and activity-based mathematics and science in general. Our intentions are to help teachers:

✓ validate the many ways that students learn, think and communicate.

✓ recognize and build on the strengths that each student brings to the classroom.

✓ gain insights into student knowledge, skills, and progress.

✓ evaluate student performance and give feedback to students and parents.

✓ evaluate the effectiveness of our teaching, and help determine the direction of our curriculum.

✓ reflect on specific student learning outcomes for each GEMS guide and on how well the activities succeed in helping students increase their understandings.

You can use *Insights & Outcomes* in a variety of ways. For example, for a practical overview of assessment issues, keep reading this section, Pearl's Journal. If you wish to explore a particular strategy for assessing your mathematics and science program, focus on the Insights section, which contains case studies that utilize these strategies with student work. Reading these classroom case studies is a good way to get a feel for the whole assessment process, including: choosing an assessment opportunity; evaluating the student work; and using the information gained to good advantage. If you're about to begin a GEMS unit, you may want to start with the Outcomes section for that particular guide, to identify possible goals for student learning and related assessment opportunities.

As you explore this assessment handbook, remember to validate your own experience, and to recognize the courage and commitment it takes to make math and science accessible and meaningful for all students through activity-based teaching. True to the spirit of discovery, we encourage you to use this handbook in creative and flexible ways, especially when these ways empower you and your students to take learning and assessment into your own hands! Recognize that it will take patience and perseverance to develop an assessment plan that truly reflects the range and diversity of learning styles and gifts that your students bring to the classroom. But also know that the rewards will be tremendous when you succeed!

Build It! Festival

Build It! Festival

Build It! Festival

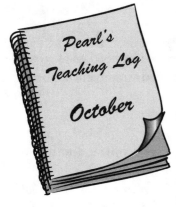

Pearl's Teaching Log October

MAKING THE GRADE: PART I

October 8

Today, Jamal asked if we were going to "have a test" on the terrarium unit. I told him I do want to find out what everyone is learning, but in a new way. Maria Rosa and I decided to take the plunge and try the Story-Writing strategy that is highlighted in the *Insights* section of the GEMS handbook. We'll conduct this assessment task in both classes tomorrow. The students will imagine they are isopods who live in the terrarium. They'll create journals describing their experiences on the first day, after one week, and after a year.

October 11

The students liked the imaginativeness of the assignment, although I could immediately observe a wide range in their abilities to make observations, write vivid descriptions, and predict changes in the terrarium over time. Some students wrote very little. Maria Rosa and I had agreed to encourage the students to use pictures and diagrams as they wrote their journals. Some of the quieter students surprised me with their elaborate pictures of the terrarium habitats! I encouraged them to label the pictures as I circulated around the room. Maria Rosa and I are going to look at the results on Friday. P.S. Jamal doesn't think that this was a REAL test!

October 13

After school, Maria Rosa and I gathered 65 Isopod's Journals and began to look at the students' responses. As we read the journals, the room was punctuated with laughter, delight, and an occasional, "Oh, no!" When our principal walked by the classroom, she remarked that we seemed to be having fun as we planned our curriculum. "We're not planning the curriculum," Maria Rosa said. "We're grading tests!" The principal responded with a quizzical look and wished us a good weekend.

We each read some of the journals. "This is fascinating," Maria Rosa said. "But how do we evaluate the results?" This time, I came to the rescue. We looked first at the student learning outcomes for *Terrarium Habitats* and then at the case study on the Isopod's Journal, which suggested a technique to use to assess the student work. This involved identifying four specific qualities or attributes that would be found in an exemplary response, then seeing which of these qualities were present in each journal. We listed the qualities on a checklist, photocopied it, and attached a copy to each journal. (Our luck held—the copier was working!) The checklist helped us sort the journals into two groups—those students who had accomplished the goals of the assessment and those who needed further support. Next week, we plan to share the checklist and the results with the students.

When students participate in GEMS activities, there are numerous opportunities throughout the school day to assess their understandings. We observe them as they work individually and in groups, interact with instructional materials, and participate in discussions. Different teachers evolve varying ways to observe, record, and track student progress from this vantage point and, throughout this handbook, there are more detailed suggestions about checklists and other observation techniques. Every teacher makes these observations regularly—they are a primary and crucial part of the assessment process.

At the same time, to more fully and accurately gauge and document our students' learning and achievement over time, and to evaluate their progress in light of the specific learning goals and big ideas in activity-based science and mathematics, we are also challenged to take advantage of, create, and implement new assessment opportunities, strategies, and tasks. This handbook is designed to help meet this challenge.

The Outcomes section lists selected (not exhaustive) student learning outcomes (sometimes called learning objectives) for every GEMS teacher's guide. For example, the first two outcomes listed for the GEMS guide *Mapping Fish Habitats* are:

1. Students can use a sampling system to map the movements of fish within an aquarium habitat.

2. Students are able to plan an experiment and make predictions about how fish behavior will change when the habitat is changed.

Also described in the Outcomes section, for each guide, are many opportunities to glimpse students' learnings and progress as they engage in GEMS activities. These assessment opportunities are keyed to the student learning outcomes. Some of these assessment opportunities are tasks/class activities built into the unit, and others are additional ideas that flow naturally from the activities in the unit. A logical first step is to select an assessment opportunity/task that addresses the particular student learning outcome(s) you have chosen for your course of study.

To assist you further with this process, the Insights section features 17 assessment case studies. Each case study highlights in much greater detail one of the assessment opportunities/tasks for a GEMS guide that is also summarized under that guide in the Outcomes section. The case study includes a range of actual student work that is evaluated, with discussion of how that information is useful in considering student needs, planning, and revising the curriculum, etc. If the specific learning outcome or outcomes you have chosen to emphasize are addressed by one or more of the case studies—that may be of special interest. In general, the Insights section is designed to catalyze your own creativity. It is filled with a variety of assessment approaches and methods that you can adapt to best meet your needs in coming up with your own assessment tasks.

Once an assessment task is selected, the challenge is to capture and perhaps quantify or otherwise evaluate students' learnings for the purpose of communication to students, parents, and administrators. This communication may be informal, as in a note or a checklist; or more formal as with report cards and grading systems; or creatively designed to fit the assessment task, as in the evaluation of a video portfolio over time. In this context it's important to emphasize that grading and numerical scoring are only one small component of a much larger aim—the overall goal of any assessment should be to provide concrete, accurate information on the progress of learning. Please refer to the case studies in the Insights section for more detail on a number of specific approaches that were used to evaluate student work. Following are three generic approaches for evaluating student responses to assessment tasks.

Checklists and Rating Forms

These describe behaviors, processes, skills, and ideas that can be expected to develop during the task and/or in the student work. For example, Maria Rosa and Pearl's checklist includes four qualities they decide will exemplify a high level response to the Isopod's Journal task. Another checklist could include behaviors that would be observable during cooperative learning, e.g., attentive listening, sharing of materials, and active participation. Of course there are many different and appropriate checklists, depending on your situation and the student outcomes

you value the most. Devise or select a checklist that best reflects your teaching objectives and the goals/values of the curriculum. **Checklists can be used during the task, as you observe behaviors and skills, or they can be applied to student work that is handed in when the task is completed.**

If necessary, teachers can assign numerical values to the checklists so they are expressed in a letter grade. For example, if a student's work contained three of the four qualities defined as an exemplary response to the Isopod's Journal, this could be the equivalent of a "B."

Some innovative schools have replaced report card grades with checklists that include skills, behaviors, and performance levels that pertain to a particular area of the curriculum. For example, in mathematics, a student can be assessed as to her knowledge of computation, problem solving, communication, or use of technology, as well as valuable qualities such as persistence, motivation, and creativity.

Rubrics

Rubrics describe a series of performance levels that are based on the most important expectations for a task. These standards are clearly articulated as the task is developed and scored. Student responses are evaluated in light of these expectations and students receive an overall score or rating (sometimes called an "holistic" score) that represents the degree to which the standards have been achieved. For example, on a 4-point rubric, scores can be classified as follows:

4—Fully accomplished the purpose of the task

3—Substantially accomplished the purpose of the task

2—Partially accomplished the purpose of the task

1—Minimally accomplished the purpose of the task

In several states, rubrics are used to score open-ended responses on standardized tests. Often, "anchor papers" are selected to represent a response that exemplifies each of the four points on the rubric. It is important to remember that **with rubrics, each stu-**

dent response is compared to a set of standards, rather than to the work of other students. When students are involved in creating the rubrics, they gain increased understanding of the evaluation process and their own learning.

Self/Peer-Evaluation

As students use standards to assess their own work and/or the work of their peers, they focus on the content of the learning and gain a clearer view of their own strengths, needs, and learning styles. You may find it effective to have students reflect on their own learning as well as the process they used to complete the task. They can also evaluate their attitude about the task and raise questions that they'd like to explore in the future. If cooperative learning is involved in the task, students can include an evaluation of their contributions to the group as well as the successes and difficulties that their group encountered. Peer evaluation is especially effective in situations where evaluation already occurs on an informal level, such as during class presentations, small group work, or during simulated conventions and debates.

Whichever techniques you use to assess student performance, be sure to inform students of your criteria for success, if appropriate, or develop criteria with them. Studies show students learn most from an activity when they have access to the standards for evaluation. In addition, if you provide students with opportunities to revise or further evolve their work after the evaluation, they will have positive opportunities to apply new insights they have gained from the evaluation process. These opportunities commonly occur in the world of work, where initial attempts (at measuring a pollutant, marketing a product, fixing a plumbing problem, or coming up with the cure for a disease) are often revised again and again until success is achieved.

If you want to learn more about the many issues and options involved, consider "Going Further" by pursuing some of the "Resources" listed on pages 271–272 for publications that include more extensive information on various assessment strategies and techniques.

Mapping Fish Habitats

Pearl's Teaching Log
October

MAKING THE GRADE: PART II

October 18

Maria Rosa and I returned the journals and checklists to the students and were surprised at the resistance we received. In both classes, students wanted to know the meaning of the checklists that were attached to their journals. In my class, several students immediately wanted to know their grade. Another group wanted to know the "right answer" to the assignment. I explained that there were certain kinds of thinking and ideas I was looking for in their journals, rather than "right answers." Jamal asked, "If there's not a right answer, how do we know how well we did?" It became clear to me that my students were accustomed to more traditional forms of assessment, which emphasize "right answers." Fortunately, the bell rang for lunch, so I could have some time to compare notes with Maria Rosa and come up with a response.

As we ate our sandwiches in the teacher's lunchroom, Maria Rosa said that her students had a similar response. "They think of assessment in terms of grades they get on tests and assignments rather than as a reflection of what was learned." We agreed that it would be both informative and empowering if our students had access to the standards of evaluation before the assessment. In turn, we hoped the standards would show the students what we, more generally, value in learning situations. We hustled to make overhead transparencies of three anonymous samples of student work, and additional copies of the checklist.

After lunch, I asked my students, "What do you think was important to learn in *Terrarium Habitats*?" We compiled a class list that was quite similar to the goals listed on our checklist and in the Outcomes section of the *Insights & Outcomes* GEMS handbook, but in fifth grade language. Their list included:

- KNOWING about the different animals and plants in the terrarium

- KNOWING about how the terrarium changes as things grow and die

- KNOWING that there is a life cycle about how things grow and die

- KNOWING that the different animals and plants depend on each other to live

I showed them the checklist that I had used and pointed out the similarities of our goals. I asked them if they could know, from looking at an Isopod's Journal, if the person who wrote it had learned these important things. Together, we reviewed the three student samples. There was plenty of great discussion. We used the checklist to score these three journals, with a maximum total of four points for the journal that had demonstrated full knowledge of the concepts.

At the end of the session, the students felt more comfortable with the assessment and understood how the checklist was used. Several asked if they could rewrite their journals, now that they had a better idea what was expected of them. I hesitated at first, but Jamal said, "Why not?" I couldn't think of a reason to deprive them of an opportunity to improve, and over half the class opted to redo their journals. I don't know who learned more today, the students or their teacher!

As we develop and implement assessment tasks for activity-based science and mathematics, we often encounter the reality that students, parents, and even a good number of our colleagues may be unfamiliar with these new strategies and techniques, as well as not understanding the goals and practice of activity-based science and mathematics learning experiences in general. **If we communicate and discuss our goals and techniques for both learning and assessment with all those affected by the curriculum, then the changes are likely to be received with greater understanding and support.**

Ideally, students should be aware of the expectations and the evaluation procedures for GEMS assessment tasks. This can also help them see how the assessment relates to important curricular goals and better understand the connection of what they are learning to their daily and future lives. When students assess their own work in light of clear evaluation standards, the assessment task becomes a learning experience in itself.

Pearl's Teaching Log
October

REFLECTIONS IN THE ASSESSMENT MIRROR

October 22

Maria Rosa and I are becoming the assessment trailblazers of the school! Today, we shared the Isopod's Journals with two other teachers who were about to begin the *Terrarium Habitats* guide. As we discussed the assessment, we suggested to our colleagues that they ask students to keep an Isopod's Journal as a regular part of the unit. Then, students can document changes and events in the terrarium as they occur. We realized, in retrospect, that creating a journal at the end of the unit was too difficult for our students, and they would be better able to demonstrate knowledge of essential concepts and skills if the assessment was conducted as part of the ongoing unit. In this way, students could get feedback about their progress as they proceeded. At the end of the unit, we could still ask students to predict what the terrarium would look like after a year had passed. After some discussion, we all agreed this was the best plan for the journals. While both of these teachers are looking forward to the unit, I can tell that one in particular is highly skeptical about all this talk of assessment. Oh well, you know the old saying: four teachers equals five opinions! For his benefit in particular I stressed that not only did this assessment task give us information about individual students' learning, it gave us information we could use to adjust our teaching of the unit to best meet the needs of our students!

Our colleagues had to laugh at our assessment zealotry! We gave them a list of the selected outcomes for students for *Terrarium Habitats*. We recommended that they review the outcomes, determine which ones were most important and appropriate for their students, and keep these goals in mind as they progressed through the unit. We explained how we discovered two unexpected student learning outcomes for *Terrarium Habitats*—students developed a curiosity about the small beings that live in and around the earth in our local environment and they also gained an awareness of and quite an appreciation for the interesting qualities of dirt . . . er, I mean soil!

I also confessed that if I'd read the outcomes in advance, I would have changed my emphasis during the unit and spent more time helping students notice the changes in the terrarium and determine when the changes are part of a larger cycle. This realization helped us decide to present *Earth, Moon, and Stars* to our students next. We had planned to present *Mapping Animal Movements*, but we agreed that the activities in *Earth, Moon, and Stars* would be a really powerful way to provide our students with more exposure to seeing individual changes as part of a larger cycle—something our assessment indicated was lacking in most of their understanding.

Student responses to assessment tasks can provide a mirror to reflect upon and evaluate the effectiveness of our own educational programs. In fact, ongoing assessment is a tool that can help us make and revise key instructional decisions. Pearl and Maria Rosa discovered this as they adjusted their plans for presenting future *Terrarium Habitats* units and as they adjusted their curriculum in response to students' needs.

Powerful assessment tasks also provide insight into the effectiveness of the activities and teaching materials themselves, information that is helpful for any conscientious teacher. If a large majority of students do not meet the standards of a particular task, this does not necessarily mean that the students have failed. It is possible, for example, that the task itself was inappropriate for that particular group of students, given their developmental levels and experience. Or, it is possible that the activity, as presented, did not provide students with sufficient information, or enough opportunities to practice skills or grapple with concepts, for them to successfully complete the assessment task.

Remember to notice and value your students' learning even when it is not related to the particular outcomes you selected for a unit. Many important scientific and mathematics discoveries have been made from unexpected findings. Just as Pearl and Maria Rosa discovered two unexpected student outcomes for *Terrarium Habitats*, so every teacher knows that the quick minds, intense curiosity, and brilliant creativity of their students constantly calls forth new and startlingly original ideas, concepts, theories. Validating *all* learning promotes strong student connection to the learning process *and* helps develop observant, creative, and independent-thinking, lifelong learners.

Curriculum, instruction, and assessment are intimately related. **Information gained from assessment tasks enables us to improve our curriculum and instruction, making it more responsive to our students' needs.**

USING THE ASSESSMENT HANDBOOK

November 1

Earth, Moon, and Stars is going really well, and I must admit that I'm surprised, given my lack of background in astronomy! So far, so good. Before we started, Maria Rosa and I read the selected student learning outcomes for the guide. We decided which of the outcomes would be our main focus—and we also added an outcome related to our goal of helping students see individual changes as part of larger cycles. Maria Rosa pointed out that it's a natural outcome for this set of activities, which involve students in making daytime observations of the moon and sun and discovering larger patterns and cycles. It's an interesting way to build from *Terrarium Habitats*—from the earth to the Earth!

So, we wanted to assess our students' progress in seeing individual changes as part of larger cycles, but there's no assessment task listed in the GEMS assessment handbook that specifically addresses this—it's an outcome we designed! That means we'll need to come up with an appropriate assessment task. I hesitated at first, but Maria Rosa says not to worry, she's been reading about various assessment strategies in the handbook and has a couple of ideas. We both decided to glance through the handbook and a few other resources for ideas and meet after school next week to talk about it. I'm sure we'll find a way!

We also like both of the built-in assessment activities that are listed in the Outcomes section for *Earth, Moon, and Stars*, and are planning to use the pre-post questionnaire about the Earth's shape and gravity. There also happens to be a case study of this same assessment task in the Insights section so we have a clearer idea of what to expect and a way to evaluate student responses.

I'm excited about using this strategy to assess
how students' understanding of these important
concepts in astronomy evolves. By assessing students' ideas before the lesson and then again
later, we really will be able to assess to what
degree students have adjusted their conceptions to
become more accurate. In the past, I always
graded student responses as correct or incorrect.
I never felt comfortable doing this, especially
when it came to complex concepts about which students' understanding is always changing. The best
part is that this assessment activity is already
an integral part of the GEMS unit, so doing it
won't be any extra effort or take additional class
time! I definitely like these built-in assessments.

Time—there's never enough, whether it be for planning, for teaching, or for assessing students' understanding! Using assessments designed for activity-
based math and science brings up the issue of time in
all of these areas.

Planning Time

To help save initial planning time, we made sure
to include, for every GEMS teacher's guide, a number of important **student learning outcomes** for that
unit, as well as multiple suggestions for **assessment
activities** keyed to those outcomes. These are listed
in the Outcomes section. These outcomes and assessments are designed to be used as is, and in most cases
have been trial tested with students so we know they
work well. Of course, there is nothing sacred about
these outcomes or assessment activities! You may want
to emphasize slightly different outcomes or to modify
certain assessment activities to reflect your emphasis
and/or your students' needs. **A goal of this handbook is to provide ready-made assessments for those
who want them, and to inspire and guide the creation of new outcomes and assessments for those
who need or want to do this.**

Teaching Time

Whenever possible, we have tried to highlight
those places, when teaching a GEMS unit, where a
natural, organic opportunity to assess students'
knowledge and understanding arises. We call these
Built-in Assessments—they are windows of opportunity embedded in the unit that enable us to glimpse
our students' thinking and abilities. Because they
are an integral part of the activities, no extra class time
is needed for the presentation of these built-in assessment activities (though additional time is needed for
evaluating student performance). The **Additional
Assessment Ideas** that are also suggested for each
GEMS unit are similar to the built-in assessments in
that they are seamless with the activities in the unit.
Unlike the built-in assessments, they do take some
extra time, but they fit nicely into the flow of the unit,
being natural spin-offs from the main activities and
Going Furthers. **Good assessment is indistinguishable from curriculum and serves as a learning activity in itself.** Thus, unlike the time away from teaching that occurs when students take traditional short
answer tests, students *are* learning as they participate
in these activity-based assessment tasks.

Time to Assess Students' Knowledge

There is no question that assessing students' work
does takes both time and careful thought. However,
in giving up the goal that students are to learn lots of
isolated facts and ideas, and instead moving toward
the goal of students learning fewer and larger concepts, ideas, and skills ("less is more"), we can also
become more efficient in our assessments. For in-

stance, in the five GEMS units that Pearl and Maria Rosa are presenting this year, there are similar outcomes related to identifying variables, designing experiments, and understanding about cycles of change. Assessments that are tied to these student learning outcomes can thus document student progress over the course of more than one unit. In addition, the kinds of assessment activities that are suggested in this handbook often address multiple student learning outcomes, in that they tend to focus on a variety of interconnected skills. Given real time constraints, there are also times when you will want to assess your students informally with a checklist or just by observation, and not take the time to provide written feedback to the students. This can be done as you are teaching. At other times you may want to be more formal in your approach. To save you time in these more formal situations, we include many different suggestions for ways to assess student work, as part of the case studies that appear in the Insights section. As with activity-based math and science itself, so it is with assessment—your first efforts are likely to take longer and/or seem more problematic than those you undertake after gaining some experience.

The fact that Pearl and Maria Rosa are able to work so well together clearly helps both of them when it comes to time factors, and in numerous other ways as well. Such cooperation may not always be possible, but it has incredible benefits. As the GEMS teaching staff discovered in devising this handbook, describing student learning outcomes clearly and coming up with realistic and motivating assessments is a demanding process that is immensely aided by back-and-forth group discussions and the multiple intelligences of many teachers.

Earth, Moon, and Stars

Earth, Moon, and Stars

Pearl's Teaching Log November

DESIGNING OUR OWN ASSESSMENT TASK

November 8

"Did you see the list of qualities of good assessment tasks in the GEMS assessment handbook?!" I asked Maria Rosa when we got together after school today. "I did, but what really made sense to me were the descriptions of various assessment strategies in the Insights section of the handbook," she replied. We both laughed—I'm always drawn to the general descriptions, and Maria Rosa prefers the specific examples. We talked about various ways to assess our students' understanding and after about fifteen minutes, developed the following task. Using the Story-Writing assessment strategy described in the Insights section of the handbook, we will tell the story of Henny Penny, but change it, so that it tells how, over the course of the month, Henny Penny runs from animal to animal exclaiming, "The moon is disappearing! The moon is disappearing!" We'll ask our students to complete the story of "Henny Penny and the Disappearing Moon," and explain why the moon disappears. After our Isopod's Journal experience, we realized that we need to be *very* clear in our instructions for students. So, we will specify that their stories must use what they learned in the *Earth, Moon, and Stars* unit to explain how the moon appears to change shape but really remains the same. Their stories should also shed light on their understanding of the moon's phases as part of a cycle. "I told you that designing our own task wouldn't be so hard," said Maria Rosa. I had to agree that reading a whole list of examples of how the story-writing strategy could be used for assessment in GEMS really did help us think of how to use this strategy to address our specific outcome for this unit.

The **assessment strategies** featured in the Insights section offer a variety of ways to assess units in the GEMS series, as well as other activity-based mathematics and science programs. It is our view that the use of a variety of assessment strategies during the year helps all students shine by giving them a chance to express their understandings in a variety of ways. Students with less developed language skills can express their understanding orally or through pictures. Those who are intimidated by tests can show their capabilities during daily class activities. Those who grasp additional concepts and skills that were not in the lesson plan have an opportunity to show what they've learned in open-ended situations. In brief, **use of a wide variety of assessment approaches validates the many ways that students learn, think, and communicate, and builds upon the strengths that each child brings to the classroom.**

The Insights section also features **additional assessment opportunities** in GEMS using each assessment strategy. This list is not complete, and is meant to inspire the reader as to the kinds of situations that are well-suited for use of that strategy. Reading through these lists, as Pearl and Maria Rosa did, is one way to begin getting ideas for and designing your own assessment activities.

Good assessment tasks for activity-based math and science embody a variety of attributes, as listed below. **While no one task will have all of these traits, a good assessment plan will include a variety of tasks which together will begin to reflect many of the qualities on this list.**

Qualities of Good Assessment Tasks for Activity-Based Science and Mathematics

➤ They focus on a variety of interconnected skills and relate directly to a significant instructional goal or goals.

➤ They emphasize application of concepts, rather than rote knowledge.

➤ They produce evidence of processes engaged in or products created.

➤ The process is often as important as the end product.

➤ They include clear and concrete criteria for evaluation.

➤ They produce a broad picture of students' abilities.

➤ They are relevant to the student and to the curriculum.

➤ They accommodate a variety of developmental levels and intelligences.

➤ They are often open-ended and encourage divergent thinking (the recognition that there are multiple solutions or approaches to a problem).

➤ They provide opportunities for students to incorporate their prior knowledge about the subject or the situation.

➤ Students construct their own responses, rather than produce the "correct" answer.

➤ Students have opportunities to work individually or in collaboration to complete tasks.

➤ Students are able to select their own best approach to the task as well as to the method of presentation.

➤ Students have an opportunity to revise their work after receiving feedback from teacher and/or classmates.

➤ Tasks are evaluated and refined/modified when necessary.

Terrarium Habitats

CONFERRING WITH PARENTS

November 15

We have parent conferences next week. I'm excited about sharing some of what I've discovered about my students' development of skills and concepts. I'm also more than a little nervous about possible reactions! Maria Rosa and I have kept a folder of student work from the assessment tasks we've used with our two GEMS units this year that we're going to discuss these with the parents. I guess we've created the beginnings of a portfolio!

November 24

Phew! Parent conferences are over. Like Henny Penny might, I can get pretty worried about parent conferences. These were challenging, to say the least, but, in some ways, I've never had such success before. By having student work there, and explaining the standards I used in assessing it, I was able to show parents more precisely how their child was doing. I even showed how students were able to revise their work to better address the standards. Some parents really appreciated seeing the standards I used in assessing the student work. Several wanted to know how the standards were developed and where they came from. The checklist of qualities pinpointed where each student excelled and needed additional work. From those checklists the parents could see what my objectives were. I am definitely going to put some work into creating more formal science portfolios, now that I know how useful they are.

There were a few parents who seemed uncomfortable that their children had taken no tests in science and were worried that they would not be prepared for middle school science next year. After all, this is not how *they* were assessed at this age! I really need to find a way to help parents evolve their understanding of the goals of our program and to see why multiple choice and short answer tests don't work very well to measure students' achievement. Next year I think I'll include some of this information at Back to School Night. Having some parents volunteer to help out during GEMS activities would be great too. I wonder if the *GEMS Parent's Handbook* would be helpful in getting parents used to the idea of activity-based math and science? Maybe I'll post the student outcomes I'm looking for in a particular unit next to displays of student work from that unit. I might also mention my goals for activities in the monthly newsletter I send home—just a few sentences after the description of what we're doing might be enough.

A teacher's work is never done—Do I earn my salary, or what? It's not hard to assess how exhausted I am, but it's a good exhaustion because I feel a real sense of achievement that our methods of assessing students are now more in line with our teaching goals. I can't wait to use these assessment strategies in other subject areas.

Discussions about a child's performance are often a teacher's main contact with parents. Thus it is understandable that changing the way we assess student performance is likely to be quickly noticed by parents, and potentially be very worrisome to them.

Parents naturally want the best for their children, but often need information to understand that their child's school experiences will be different from their own. Many parents, for example, are not aware of the overwhelming educational benefits of activity-based math and science.

It is therefore essential to educate parents about the proven effectiveness of the activity-based approach, explain the goals of science and math programs, and communicate information to them about appropriate methods for assessing student achievement of these goals. Such communication with parents may not be the job of the teacher alone, but the more we as teachers can do, the more beneficial our interactions with parents will be. All such communication will also contribute to a higher level of public understanding of the urgent need for educational change.

Sometimes parents, or others, question the subjectivity of assignments, or "tests," that are scored using holistic methods, or using other evaluation techniques in which there are not quickly determined right and wrong answers. There has been a great deal of discussion on this point in educational circles. It's important to note that several studies have shown a high degree of reliability among scores of holistically scored papers, in certain standardized testing situations. Providing specific examples of student work along with your standards for judgment to parents can also help them see that, when carefully defined, such standards/rubrics can provide an excellent and quite consistent measure of performance. In the case of the individual student in an individual classroom, it should be pointed out that **for the purpose of finding out what students know and can do, and how to better help students and improve teaching, a wide variety of activity-based assessment strategies is far more appropriate than, for example, reliance on multiple-choice "achievement" tests.**

A GREAT START

January 27

We've just finished the *Mapping Animal Movements* unit! *Terrarium Habitats*, *Earth, Moon, and Stars*, and *Mapping Animal Movements* are behind us; *Paper Towel Testing* and *Bubble-ology* still to come. Maria Rosa and I had a great chat after school today. We've made so much progress in developing an assessment plan for our program and we both feel much more fluent in how to use the GEMS handbook in helping us develop ways to assess our students. We were joking around about assessing ourselves on how well we've done. But when we started to list our achievements we quit joking! Check it out: We've chosen from the student outcomes that the handbook suggested and in one case made up our own outcome for a unit. We used the story-writing assessment strategy twice—once with the assessment activity featured in the case study, and once creating our own! We've also used pre-post testing and experiments as assessment strategies. We have used some of the built-in and additional assessments for each unit that are described in the Outcomes section. Reading the case studies in the Insights section has given both of us good ideas for how to analyze student work from the assessment tasks. We've assessed our students before, during, and after a unit. Sometimes we've assessed individual students; sometimes we've assessed the work of small groups.

I guess our most important realization is that there are many possible ways to gain insight into students' understanding. It's funny, but before we began doing this kind of assessment, it seemed very intimidating—like there was only one right way. Now I see that there are many effective assessment strategies which can become powerful tools in the hands of thinking teachers. Right now, we're feeling like we've made a great start in changing how we assess students, in a way that reflects the goals for their learning.

"Where do we start?" is a question often asked by teachers, principals, and school districts wanting to create meaningful assessments for activity-based science and mathematics programs. A good response is, "Just where Pearl and Maria Rosa started—with one appropriate assessment task for one GEMS unit you are teaching." Of course there are larger, more coordinated approaches that can be implemented, but the most important thing is to get started. Once teachers begin to actively use these assessment strategies based on student performance of tasks, they will begin to see that this kind of assessment is an attainable goal. It's fulfilling, useful for students and teachers, and sometimes even fun! Hopefully, the assessment tasks and strategies shared in this GEMS handbook will help you make a smooth transition to forms of assessment more fitting to an activity-based curriculum. Be patient, and view it as a transition, rather than an event! **Just as in constructing curriculum, it takes time to build a complete assessment plan, but you need not wait until the change is complete for you and your students to begin to reap the rewards.**

Mapping Animal Movements

Bubble-ology

THE BIG PICTURE

January 28

Maria Rosa and I are still feeling so good about the progress we've made so far this year that we didn't even let ourselves feel daunted by the list of things still to be accomplished that we generated at our grade level planning meeting today. That list includes:

1) Make stronger connections between the GEMS units in our program and our goals for students. Many skills and concepts build naturally from one GEMS unit to the next. After this year we'll both have taught each of the units once, so we'll be in a better position to come up with several student outcomes for the whole year in addition to the outcomes for each GEMS unit.

2) Involve other teachers at our school and our principal in dialogue about assessment. While we have been talking quite a bit with the other teachers at our grade level, we need to broaden the discussion. The principal needs to be kept informed as well. Already one of the parents in Maria Rosa's class spoke with the principal about "this ungraded approach" that Maria Rosa is using. Fortunately, we had already talked with our principal, and shared some of what we have done, so she was not surprised. She actually gave a great response—that there *are* tests being given (though they are not the conventional kind), and while students aren't receiving letter grades on these tests, they are being assessed in an even more demanding way. Our principal agreed with us that assessment would be a great topic for an upcoming inservice day. She even asked if Maria Rosa and I would present it! "We should be flattered!" I said to Maria Rosa. "She's just trying to save money," laughed Maria Rosa.

3) Finally, we want to use these active assessment techniques in our math program and extend them to other parts of our curriculum. This will

of course take time, but already we can see how some of the assessment strategies listed in the GEMS handbook could be useful in other subject areas as well.

Making connections is what the big picture is all about—connections between our goals for students and the instructional materials we select; between individual units within the curriculum; between assessment and curriculum; between the curricula at different grade levels; and between staff concerns and staff development. While full discussion of all these interacting aspects is beyond the scope of this GEMS handbook, it is important to acknowledge that assessment fits powerfully into a larger vision of education and educational reform, and relates directly to the many decisions that are made at a school or in a district.

Some teachers are in schools or districts where all aspects of the big picture are being addressed effectively and with input from all. Others are alone in their quest for strong connections between curriculum, instruction, and assessment. Most of us are somewhere in between! Wherever you are in this spectrum, remember that the process for educational reform has to begin somewhere—it might as well be in your classroom, at your school, in your school district. Sometimes the impetus for change at a school is inspired by the work of teachers like Pearl and Maria Rosa. They are the true "GEMS."

Moons of Jupiter

Moons of Jupiter

Moons of Jupiter

Moons of Jupiter

M IS FOR THE MATH IN GEMS...

February 14

Today, Andrea gave me the best valentine card I'd ever received in my entire teaching career. It said, "You are my favorite teacher because you made me realize that I want to be a scientist when I grow up. P.S. I'll send you some of the first million dollars I make when I invent a cure for cancer." Andrea's valentine reminded me that activity-based science often motivates students who have been intimidated by reading-intensive, "hands-off" science activities. I wish I could be this effective in mathematics!

February 15

Maria Rosa just returned from a GEMS workshop and brought a copy of *In All Probability*, a math guide that will fill a gap in the content of my mathematics program. The guide is featured in a case study in the Letter Writing section of *Insights & Outcomes*, but we didn't pay much attention to it until now. I'm going to wait until the spring to try it, but I already know I'll use the letter-writing strategy as part of my assessment plan because the student responses are delightful and also insightful!

Science and mathematics have traditionally been taught as separate curricular areas. No wonder teachers such as Pearl who develop expertise in one do not necessarily feel confident in the other. **However, there is a growing realization that our teaching and learning need to reflect the essential interconnection between math and science.** The engineer who helps design the next sensational computer breakthrough is constantly engaging in daily practice that combines math and science—in the real world, the distinction between the two is a false one. Nor can mathematics simply be relegated to being a tool of science, though it certainly is that as well. Whether seen in the old classical sense as the Queen of the Sciences, or as a driving force behind theoretical physics, astronomy, and the computer age, there can be no doubt that basic and diverse branches of math-

ematical learning and related skills are vitally important for the future career choices and life directions of our students. Skills such as estimating and doing mental arithmetic, construction-related and spatial visualization abilities, probability and statistics, and the whole area of modern technology all literally vibrate with mathematics—and interweave with logic, reasoning, scientific thought and methods. In the field of modern assessment, mathematics educators have been on the forefront—addressing important issues of equity and gender inclusiveness, while strongly advocating forms of assessment that relate to the real world, the development of logical and independent thinking skills, and innovative ways to involve students in their own growth of "mathematical power."

From its start, and increasingly in recent years, GEMS educators have recognized this essential integration of mathematics and science and the need to convey this to teachers and students. In order to strengthen the GEMS series in this regard, there are a growing number of GEMS guides that concentrate on mathematics—*Frog Math, Group Solutions, In All Probability, QUADICE, Build It! Festival* and upcoming guides such as *Math Around the World. Group Solutions*, with its central focus on cooperative logic, truly bridges both mathematical and scientific reasoning.

In many other GEMS guides, mathematics is strongly integrated into the activities, such as in *Bubble Festival, Paper Towel Testing, Investigating Artifacts, Discovering Density*, and *Fingerprinting*. Central to many GEMS guides is the application of math concepts, such as in *Height-O-Meters, Experimenting with Model Rockets, Moons of Jupiter,* and *Mapping Fish Habitats*. Important mathematical skills, such as estimating, graphing, sorting and classifying, as well as numerous optional opportunities for introducing and extending mathematical concepts, abound in the GEMS series. A GEMS handbook entitled *The Rainbow of Mathematics* is planned to explore these issues in greater depth.

You will notice that there are student outcomes related to science *and* mathematics for many GEMS units. Depending on your goals and your students' experience, you will want to emphasize or add certain outcomes. **Thus, even with GEMS guides that have an apparent science emphasis, the assessment tasks you select can also measure mathematical skills and concepts.** For example, in *Paper Towel Testing*, students design controlled experiments to test the absorbency and wet strength of various brands of paper towels. A comprehensive analysis of the paper towel test results involves a great deal of mathematical calculation, as Pearl and her students are about to discover! This application of mathematics skills and concepts provides an ideal opportunity to assess your students' mathematical abilities. Often, the "scientific" aspect of the activities, an experiment, for example, is a great motivator for students to get mathematically involved, leading to their own realization of the importance and usefulness of mathematics—the M in GEMS.

In All Probability

STUDENT-CENTERED ASSESSMENT

Pearl's Teaching Log April

April 21

Embarking on my last GEMS unit for the year, I had to laugh when Jamal asked: "So what are we expected to learn from this?" My students have not only accepted my new approach to assessment, some of them have begun to naturally reflect on their learning process without prompting by me. Taking Jamal's lead, I decided to really involve the students in an ongoing assessment of their own learning in this last unit. The next day I posted some learning goals on the classroom wall. When appropriate as part of an activity, we referred to the learning goals. At the end of each activity, I instructed students to reflect in their journals about what they had learned. Some days I gave writing prompts, focusing them on an area they thought needed improvement, or on a particular concept. Other days I let the writing be open-ended. Wow! I was unprepared for what I read. The self-awareness my students have is uncanny. Next week, I plan to write a note to each student in which I reflect on what they said in their journals about their learnings.

"What a great idea!" said Maria Rosa when I told her about the self-reflection I had my students do. "It was inspired by one of the case studies on reflection as an assessment strategy," I replied. "In the Insights section," we both said in unison. We laughed. We really do know the GEMS assessment handbook!

Assessment is not something we *do to* our students. Ideally, it becomes an organic part of the ongoing process of teaching and learning. It provides invaluable information to us about our students' progress in many areas and about the curriculum we present to them. For students, whose growth is after all the goal of our efforts, it provides information they need to have in order to know themselves, their strengths and abilities, their achievements and attitudes, and the areas where improvement in needed. Some students may not at first be forthcoming or articulate as they reflect about themselves, but this is a skill well worth developing. We are learners for life—we don't always have someone else to reflect upon and comment on our performance and achievements. **Involving students in assessing themselves is key to giving them full responsibility for their own learning.**

Pearl and Maria Rosa's efforts in this direction positively reflect the growing trend toward what has been termed "student-centered assessment." An upcoming GEMS guide, *Learning About Learning*, makes student consciousness of their own learning process an integral part of the entire unit. Students engage in activities to find out how people learn, investigate what helps and hinders learning, and connect learning to health and safety issues and the human brain. Guides such as *Acid Rain* and *Global Warming and the Greenhouse Effect* also bring this to the fore with their running lists of statements and questions of what students know and wonder.

As described in the Insights section under Teacher Observations as an Assessment Strategy (see page 195), many teachers have used student self-assessment techniques in connection with the GEMS cooperative logic activities in *Group Solutions*. In this case, students respond to a self-evaluation form that asks them to consider how well their group worked together, an overriding goal of the unit. Such an approach can be adapted to many other units and goals. The use of portfolios and other collections of student work lends itself well to ongoing student self-assessment, so students can perceive their own growing confidence and competence over time, gaining a sense of concepts grasped and skills honed. It's important to note, as the *Group Solutions* example demonstrates, that goals

for such student-centered assessment need not be narrowly limited to the "content" of the lessons. Other very important assessment issues can relate to, for example: social skills, such as cooperation; attitudes and feelings about science and math; student awareness of how their ideas about a concept or phenomena have changed over the course of a unit; student ideas about teaching a concept to others; and lots more!

It may be helpful to step back for a moment from the many specific issues raised by assessment and remember that the activity-based, guided-discovery approach to science and mathematics education above all seeks to empower the student, the learner. Its effectiveness in fact depends on that empowerment—it is **learning through doing** that enables students to experience, experiment, analyze, discuss, debate, and by doing so, revise old concepts and construct new ones. The teacher is a facilitator and encourager, seeking ways to motivate students to think independently, work together cooperatively, solve problems, and make decisions. Assessment tasks should reflect this same quest—at its best, assessment can be just as involving, motivating, and empowering. How best to involve students in reflecting on their own progress is up to you. It is our hope that this handbook provides a solid foundation for you to build upon.

Acid Rain

P IS FOR PORTFOLIOS

May 9

We have end-of-year parent conferences next week. In preparation, today my students and I began putting together their portfolios. It took all day. The students met in small groups to sort through their folders and create our first official science portfolio. We devised a list of items that would go into the folders. My bottom line was that each portfolio had to include at least two of the formal assessments from the GEMS units we did. Students voted to put in an example of their favorite work that resulted from a GEMS unit. I asked each student to stick a post-it to each piece of their work, saying why it is good work. The portfolios will also contain journal entries from before, during, and after doing a unit. Several students wanted to include photographs of their groups as they conducted the paper towel tests. Others selected the drawings that they made of their terrariums at different stages of development.

I decided to tell the students that there were some parents who needed to understand why we do **activities** as the main component of our science program. Lupe, usually a quiet child, said, "Let's write them a letter!" Her suggestion was well received. As a result, the students have now written a letter to their parents that will be the first page of their portfolios. The letters explain the contents of the portfolio and specify what the students like about the GEMS units as well as what they learned. Each student designed a personalized cover which highlighted their favorite GEMS activities.

I showed the portfolios to Maria Rosa and she decided to create them with her students. We recalled a section in the GEMS handbook that described portfolios. Maria Rosa says that I could have written that section myself!

A portfolio is a collection of assignments, projects, reports, and writings that demonstrate growth in a student's mathematical and/or scientific thinking over time. When used in conjunction with GEMS or other activity-based math/science units, portfolios provide insights into how students view themselves as mathematicians and/or scientists, and the many ways they engage in scientific inquiry and mathematical investigation. Teachers can gain information about students' problem-solving processes; students' abilities to refine concepts as new information is introduced; students' use of appropriate technological tools, as well as students' ability to work individually and in groups. Portfolios can be stored in file boxes, crates, or large scrapbooks that have been assembled throughout the school year. Some portfolios contain work from throughout the year; others may be showcase portfolios selected from the larger collection by students and teachers for parent conferences or year-end evaluations. Some schools have successfully implemented individual year-to-year video portfolios that provide a record of a student's presentations over time.

The contents of a portfolio will vary with each teacher. It is extremely effective to involve students in the portfolio development process. The development of a portfolio can be, in itself, a powerful learning experience.

Portfolios should contain a balance of work that can include:

- student-selected pieces
- teacher selected pieces
- responses to particular assignments
- photographs of the student engaged in activities
- a student's favorite work
- some formal assessments

Students can write or dictate a **cover letter** to explain the contents of the portfolio to a reader who may not necessarily be the teacher (i.e., parents, friends, students from other classes). The cover letters will vary according to the developmental level of the student. They can include the following:

- a brief description of the contents

- why each of the portfolio items was selected
- what the student learned during the unit
- unanswered questions or possibilities for further exploration
- students' attitudes about the activities

Portfolios can be evaluated with checklists or rubrics that contain significant instructional goals for a particular subject area. For example, all scientists must have the ability to communicate, observe, order, and categorize. Therefore, a significant instructional goal is to help students develop these essential processes. You can evaluate portfolios to see the degree to which students have developed these capabilities. Scientists also must know how to design and conduct controlled experiments. Portfolios can be assessed to determine how well students can demonstrate this important level of achievement.

In mathematics, significant instructional goals could be to help students become powerful problem-solvers; to develop and apply key concepts; and to effectively use the language of mathematics. Math portfolios can be evaluated for evidence of persistence; the use of multiple approaches in problem-solving; effective use of concepts in proper contexts; and clear communication through words, pictures, charts, and diagrams. Depending on your approach to the integration of science and mathematics, you may want to emphasize this by having both in the same portfolio, or by having students come up with their own ways to show the close relationship between the two.

Portfolios are often well received by parents because the contents provide information about the uniqueness of their particular child. A portfolio that includes student work on a variety of tasks, including art work, projects, and other creative opportunities, can display the many talents of a student and make the portfolio itself an attractive product. It can also be very effective to demonstrate to parents the breadth and depth of information that can be derived from analysis of an ongoing portfolio, as contrasted with the results of a textbook test in science or mathematics. In addition to all their other positive attributes, portfolios are a wonderful way to exemplify student growth and change over time, providing important insights to teachers, parents, and administrators, and most of all to the students themselves.

Pearl's Teaching Log
June

THE END, OR JUST THE BEGINNING...

June 20

The last student has left the room and there is a welcome but empty silence as they all leave for vacation, and eventually, sixth grade. During the last week of school, we cleaned up the classroom and made packets to send home with the students. I was pleased that almost all of the students took great pride in their portfolios. In fact, they were extremely disappointed when I told them I was planning to keep several assessment tasks to pass on to next year's teacher. Jamal asked insistently that I photocopy his Isopod's Journal because "it's the best thing I ever wrote this year."

In the few moments that I have before our final staff meeting, I must say that this has been an incredible year. My end-of-year conferences showed me that parents can change—one of the parents who was most concerned back in November is very enthusiastic now, after seeing the growth in his son. Maria Rosa and I have never before seen such a high degree of motivation and student involvement as we've experienced with GEMS activities, especially when we began involving students in active reflection on their own progress. With the help of *Insights and Outcomes*, we began to develop an assessment plan that is directly related to the goals of our program and reflects the beauty and the knowledge gained from activity-based units. Maria Rosa and I think we deserve hearty congratulations . . . and, of course, a vacation!

As you courageously set out on your assessment journey, we hope *Insights & Outcomes* will be a helpful tool to chart your course. **Our students can best prepare for the challenges that await them in the future through tasks that relate to real life.** A violinist is assessed by her concert; a baseball player by his ball-playing; scientists and mathematicians (and your students!) by their ability to conduct experiments, make observations, solve problems, and communicate. Change takes time; the roads are often bumpy, but persistence and collaboration will ease your journey. Luckily, you've got this intriguing book to read while you're travelling—*Insights & Outcomes*.

Good assessment
is indistinguishable from curriculum
and serves as a learning activity in itself.

◆

A goal of this handbook is to provide
ready-made assessments for those who want them,
and to inspire and guide the creation of new outcomes
and assessments for those who need or want to do this.

◆

The use of a wide variety of assessment approaches
validates the many ways that students learn, think, and
communicate, and builds upon the strengths
that each child brings to the classroom.

◆

Our students can best prepare
for the challenges that await them in the future
through tasks that relate to real life.

Insights

This section is designed to provide realistic insights into the assessment process by providing detailed and diverse classroom examples—case studies.

The following case studies analyze and evaluate student work on GEMS assessment activities to illustrate many different assessment strategies and methods that can be used in connection with activity-based science and mathematics.

In turn, flexible and creative use of these strategies can provide many insights into student progress, our own teaching, and the very nature of learning itself.

Convection: A Current Event

Story Writing as an Assessment Strategy

Stories have been invented and used throughout history as ways to explain the natural world. These stories, often personifying animals and/or inanimate objects, helped represent relationships between animals; humans and the Earth; and the Sun, Moon, and stars. Through stories, people of all cultures sought to make sense of their observations of the natural world. In this sense, these stories and legends represent some of the early roots of natural science. Stories are also told to pose fictional or symbolic accounts of real world situations that need solutions. Mathematical skills of logic and problem solving come into play as people come up with creative solutions to the problem or dilemma presented by the story.

Both teachers and students benefit when writing and reading of stories is integrated with science and mathematics. For teachers, stories are an engaging vehicle to present information and story writing is a great way to assess student knowledge. Story writing opens up unique, imaginative, and creative ways for students to incorporate knowledge and concepts gained from GEMS activities, and for teachers to see that knowledge. Imagination and creativity are mobilized through various forms of story writing as students communicate and make sense of their scientific observations, and as they connect mathematics concepts and skills to real world problem-solving situations. Students can:

- Write a story about animals and other living things they've explored through life science experiences.

- Describe a day in the life of a creature or its life cycle, from the creature's perspective.

- Describe a day in the life of the number zero (or any number), and include zero's importance in real-world situations.

- Describe and document changes that impact the environment, from the viewpoint of someone who lives in the environment.

- Create an imaginary conversation between inanimate objects, such as geological features, or between a square and two other shapes.

- Create a myth or legend to explain scientific phenomena.

- Devise a story that uses a counting strategy as a problem-solving tool.

- Write a play that demonstrates the relationships between living things or between chemicals that react and interact.

The most accomplished story writers are not necessarily the best test takers in math and science. Stories require students to merge communication skills and creativity to relate their knowledge to a new situation and reveal information about their observations and perceptions of their world. Stories can describe characteristics and features of people, animals, places and things; patterns of change; reactions and interactions; or changes and cycles in nature. Writing a story is a compelling and motivating context for students to tell what they know. Through story writing, we also address a broader spectrum of learning modalities so a larger group of students can be successful.

The more specific we can be with students about what elements their stories should contain, the more likely students are to produce stories that enable us as teachers to see what our students know. This is of course not intended to limit creativity. For instance, telling students to write a story about bees may or may not result in the kind of student work that would enable the teacher to know more about a student's knowledge of bees. More assessment information can be gained by saying, for example: "Imagine you are a bee. Write a story telling about your day: what you do, what you eat, what else is going on in your hive, who your enemies are, whether you've ever met the queen, etc." Some teachers like to tell their students that this story will tell her what they know about bees, so they should be sure to do their best and include a lot of the things they have learned so far about bees.

A case study using story writing as an assessment strategy in *Terrarium Habitats* begins on the next page. Opportunities for story-writing assessments in other GEMS units are listed on pages 42–43.

An Isopod's Journal from *Terrarium Habitats*

Students often write stories from a perspective other than their own. Through this process, they imagine what it would be like "in the shoes" of another living being, or even an inanimate object. Fourth grade students who complete activities from the *Terrarium Habitats* GEMS guide can be offered an opportunity to imagine themselves to be an isopod who lives in a terrarium over the course of a year.

An Isopod's Journal

Imagine that you are an isopod.
You have been put in a new terrarium ecosystem by a 4th grader.

1. Use pictures and words to describe what things you see as you walk around the terrarium on that **FIRST DAY.**

2. Use pictures and words to describe how things change over the course of **ONE WEEK.**

3. Write and draw what it might be like **A WHOLE YEAR** later.

Your finished product will be an isopod's journal.
As you create your journal, remember to:

- Be very detailed about what you see.

- Tell what changes you observe and what seems to stay the same.

- Describe a cycle that you see in the terrarium.

- Tell the whole story. For example, what happens to the plant after a snail munches on it? What happens to the snail?

REMEMBER:
USE YOUR OWN EXPERIENCES
WITH YOUR TERRARIUM IN YOUR STORY.

An optional pre-writing activity can help students develop a rich vocabulary so that they can better accomplish the assessment task. Students can look at their terrariums and name the different things they see. The teacher and/or students can record these words in a vocabulary bank that can be used as they write their journals. Teachers may also choose to assign the isopod's journal in three parts.

- Students can write a first entry on the day that the isopods are introduced to the terrarium.

- Students can write a second installment after the isopods have spent a week in the terrarium.

- The final entry can be written at the end of the unit, when students can project what will change and what will remain the same over the course of a year.

The teacher can provide ongoing feedback to students throughout the process to help them further understand the expectations of the task and to allow them time to improve their journals.

 ## What do I want to see?

Through this assessment activity, students demonstrate their observation skills and knowledge of a terrarium ecosystem. Their journals should address all of the following questions.

➤ What are the elements of the terrarium ecosystem?

➤ Which elements remain constant over time?

➤ Which changes occur in the terrarium and what is the impact of the changes?

An exemplary journal would:

➤ Include a detailed description/drawing of many different elements in the ecosystem.

➤ Describe soil, plants, and animals as the basic elements.

➤ Communicate some relationship between the elements in the ecosystem.

➤ Show how some elements change over time, while some remain the same.

➤ Describe a cycle that occurs in the terrarium, as illustrated in these examples.

- Animals eat plants and then excrete waste, which provides nutrients for other plants.

- Animals and plants complete a reproductive cycle.

- Earthworms and other terrarium animals play a unique role in the cycle of decomposition.

➤ Project a plausible one-year scenario.

How do I evaluate the student work?

Teachers have several options for evaluation of the students' work.

➤ Evaluate the journals, applying the standards for exemplary work that are mentioned above.

➤ Evaluate the journals for clues about the students' level of understanding of how the individual parts of a terrarium work together as a system of interacting parts, what stays the same, and what changes.

➤ Evaluate the journals for evidence of students' growing ability to make detailed observations over the course of the unit.

➤ Evaluate the language arts, writing, and communication abilities demonstrated by the journal entries.

The following fourth grade journals show a progression of responses from inadequate to competent, when considered relative to the standards for exemplary work that are described above.

This journal entry does not describe elements in the terrarium ecosystem, the relationships between those elements, or the notion of change. The writer endows the isopod with human characteristics and responds only to the apparent perception that life in a terrarium will eventually get claustrophobic! Although the journal is creative, the student has minimally addressed the expectations of the assessment.

I see some dead leaves, animals and twigs. I would also see some water and water puddles. The leaves would disappear into thin air. And there would be no more water and water puddles. There would be no more animals.

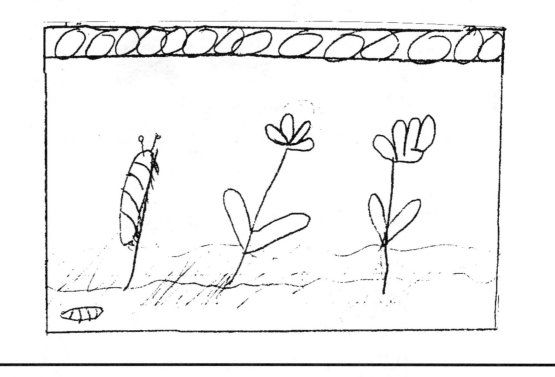

This journal entry's words and drawing provide more detail about the elements in the terrarium ecosystem. However, the story provides no information about the relationship between the elements. The writer predicts that "the leaves would disappear into thin air," clearly not yet grasping the process of decomposition and the role of decomposers.

1. I would see roots. I would see leafs, plants, weeds. It would have soil in it that I would see.

2. Things would change like the roots would grow, and it would get hotter.

3. It would be different. It might have longer roots. I would see a dead worm that was not there before.

This journal has a broader listing of elements of a terrarium than in the previous sample. The students cites evidence of the life cycle (growth, death) and temperature changes in the ecosystem over time. The one-year scenario is plausible but lacks detail about how the elements from Day # 1 will change at year's end.

An Isopod's Journal

Day 1

Today a classroom of children put snails, worms and some isopods like me in a terrarium. They put bird seed, grass seed, soil, leaves and, of course, us insects. They gave lettuce and green cabbage for the snails to eat. I've found a home for myself under a nice big leave in the back left corner. I've also made a couple of new isopod friends.

Week 1

This place is great! There are a couple of new baby snails squirming around and a few little baby isopods rolling around. My leaf is a little rotten, so I start taking little bites out of it. There are plenty of nice neighbors, except for a couple of old snails up in the front of the terrarium. But I still have lots of friends back around the rear of the terrarium.

Year 1

It's been a year and only a couple of snails are around, but lots of isopods. A lady gives the snails 3 pieces of lettuce and green cabbage every week. She sprays the terrarium every day. She also gives us isopods 1 dead leave every week. So everyone alive is doing pretty well. There's one thing that I miss about 1 year ago is all the nice worms but now they're all dead. A lot of the snails have died away. I sure miss all the others that died.

This journal entry creatively assumes the perspective of an isopod and is an example of a satisfactory response to the assignment. There is a detailed description of the elements of the habitat and their role in the terrarium life cycles. The journal continues with information about animal shelters, decomposition of leaves, growth and reproduction, and feeding behaviors. Maintenance of the terrarium is described and reference to time is clearly indicated. The student's writing ability, sentence structure, and active voice all enhance the journal entry.

Day 1. These fourth graders put me in a terrarium. Then, they put a plant in the middle of the terrarium and this big cone called organic matter. Then, they sprinkled some seeds in the terrarium. The fourth graders mixed the soil. They decided to put the terrarium in the sun. The left side of the terrarium was the bird seeds and the right side of the terrarium was the grass seed. Why did they do it like that?

This student's accompanying drawing showed soil, bird and grass seeds scattered on the soil; a large plant with various leaves; and an isopod ("me") walking on top of the soil.

Day 8. When I got out of the soil, I saw the seeds grew bigger and there were white things covering the seeds. I saw this one grass that grew about as tall as the plant. The soil is wet because the fourth graders sprayed water on the plants and soil. These two big seed plants were growing and they were called seed plants. I would see that the grasses' seeds are growing much taller than the bird seeds. The plant grew a little bit bigger.

This students' accompanying drawing showed mold on the soil; grasses of varying lengths; small sprouting growths (from bird seeds); a larger plant with leaves; and an isopod ("me") crawling out of a tunnel in the soil.

A Year Later. Some of the leaves are dried up. The leaves and the potatoes decomposed and made the soil rich. Almost all the grass is dead but some of the grass has grown very tall. The water in the terrarium made the soil moldy. Some of the other bugs have died and my babies aren't babies anymore. I have a dark area in the terrarium where I sleep.

This journal entries on this page are well-organized and provide a written and pictorial description of the procedure used to build the terrarium as well as the various elements in the ecosystem. The later entries contain a detailed description of the life cycle in plants, including the fact that they decompose. The student uses prior knowledge to establish a cause-and-effect relationship between mold and water. The journal could be improved with detailed descriptions of different terrarium elements, such as animals, and their relationship to other aspects of the habitat.

An Isopod's Journal

1. When I walked around the terrarium, I saw a worm's hole in the ground. I saw the worm eating the soil. When it was eating the soil, its body did this

    . I saw two snails munching on the lettuce in the terrarium.

I saw a big sow bug. It looked like this
It looked gross.

2. One week later, I saw grass growing. All the bugs gotten bigger. There were baby sow bugs hatching from its egg. The two snails got even bigger than before. The worms got fat and juicy.

3. A whole year later there would be thousands of isopods. The grass would be so big that they will come out of the holes. The flowers would be very big. Soon the worms and snails would die also the sow bugs. I saw egg cartoons, squiggly things, shells, rocks, carrots, lettuce and egg shells. I saw the baby isopods get so big I would hardly see them. The grass got so big they went out of the holes. The egg carton didn't change at all. The shell had lots of slimy stuff on it. When the snail munched on the plants, there were tiny holes. The snail had just have taken a rest after it ate.

This journal entry creatively assumes the perspective of an isopod and provides details about the terrarium elements. Multiple relationships between the elements are described when the isopod sees that a worm creates a home in the ground; observes that the worm's body changes when it eats; and watches the snails eat lettuce for food. The journal also notes that the elements change over time: grass grows; bugs get bigger; sow bugs hatch from eggs (inaccurate but plausible); the worms got fat and juicy. In the year-end entry, the student predicts a plausible scenario that includes specific references to the reproductive life cycle. This story could be further enhanced with a reference to decomposition and the nutrient cycle (organic material is cycled back into the soil for use by plants).

 What insights have I gained?

As we evaluated students' journals, we realized that students would be most successful if they were assigned the assessment in three sections during the terrarium activities. Each segment would immediately follow students' direct experience with the unit. The Day 1 journal could be assigned at the end of the first day, when students can view the terrariums and record their observations about its initial components. After one week, the Week 1 segment could be assigned, and students could note changes in the terrarium. After a month, students could note changes and make projections about how the cycle would continue a year ahead. Teachers can pose questions to help students with their predictions, such as: "What elements of the terrarium will change over time?" "Which of these changes are part of a cycle?"

It was difficult for some students to mobilize the necessary vocabulary to fully complete the assessment. In the future, in presenting this assessment, we would have the class create a word bank of important words that relate to the unit, and expand the list as the unit progresses. Students can refer to the bank to find words to help them express their thoughts.

Other Assessment Opportunities in GEMS Using Story Writing

Here are some other assessment opportunities in GEMS that use the assessment strategy of story writing. Use this list to find specific opportunities and to inspire you to create your own uses of this assessment strategy.

➢ *ACID RAIN*
In a Going Further activity at the end of this unit, students write their own plays about acid rain, or add an additional scene to the play in Session 6. These plays illustrate causes, effects, and solutions to acid rain.

➢ *ANIMAL DEFENSES*
During Session 1, students can write or dictate stories about their defended animal and then perform these stories for classmates and families.

➢ *BUZZING A HIVE*
Ask students to draw a picture and tell about "The Day the Honeybee Hive Was Raided."

➢ *CHEMICAL REACTIONS*
Challenge students to design a comic strip that depicts, step-by-step, what occurred in the ziplock bag experiment and what they discovered. Explain that this comic strip will be used to teach other students about chemical reactions, reactants, and products.

➢ *FROG MATH*
Use the Frog and Toad characters to create a story in which Frog spots a beautiful bird in his yard and wants to identify it. He needs to observe all of its attributes and asks for Toad's help in classifying it.

➢ *GROUP SOLUTIONS*
Students can draw or construct a fictitious animal and list its attributes. Then, they can write a story about the animal. In the Maps section students could make up an adventure story that uses a map they make to find buried treasure.

➢ *IN ALL PROBABILITY*
Write a story about two Pomo Indian women who create a new version of Game Sticks, or a new game involving equivalent probabilities.

➢ *INVESTIGATING ARTIFACTS*
Use the classroom and its related "artifacts" as an excavation site unearthed at an imagined time several thousand years in the future and have students write their own version of the book *Motel of the Mysteries* by David Macauley (Houghton Mifflin, Boston, 1979). Ask students to include at least two incorrect inferences about actual artifacts that could possibly be thought to be true if little else were known.

➤ *INVOLVING DISSOLVING*

In a Going Further activity for Homemade Gel-O, students create stories about a Mystery Solid that is dissolved in a Mystery Liquid. The stories explain what happens to the solid as it is dissolved and what it does to the liquid.

➤ *LADYBUGS*

Send students home with the ladybug projects they made in class and a piece of paper. Ask families to help the student write a story that describes an aspect of ladybug life.

➤ *LIQUID EXPLORATIONS*

Have students pretend they are blue drops of coloring. Create a story about their experiences when dropped in the Great Salt Lake. What would happen to them? Where might they end up?

➤ *MYSTERY FESTIVAL*

In Session 5, students can write the story of what they think happened to Felix or Mr. Bear.

➤ *RIVER CUTTERS*

Have students write an imaginary conversation between a young river and an old river. As the two rivers talk to each other, they can compare their features. Students can also write an imaginary legend or story that explains why the Earth's surface is shaped as it is. The story can have whatever characters and events the students decide, but it must include a character who represents the power of water.

➤ *TREE HOMES*

Have students write or dictate stories about their owl's, raccoon's, or toy bear's life in a tree.

Liquid Explorations

Liquid Explorations

Letter Writing as an Assessment Strategy

At the beginning of World War II, Einstein's letter to the President of the United States, describing the feasibility of an atomic weapon, changed the course of the war and helped to shape the modern world as we know it. While Einstein's letter is one of the best known examples of how letters have influenced both science and society, there are many others. For example, Pascal's letter to his brother-in-law in 1648 is the first description of a controlled experiment intended to test a scientific theory—the theory that we live at the bottom of a "sea" of air.

Much mathematical correspondence has focused on energetic exchange of opinions on whether or not a new proof might be acceptable as the solution to a famous unsolved problem.

Letters and persuasive writing have always been central to the process of science and mathematics, and to the relationship between science and society. Now that electronic mail is becoming commonplace, scientists and mathematicians rely even more heavily on personal communication in their work.

In the classroom, letter writing can also be an important force to advance science and mathematics education. Letter writing offers students opportunities to demonstrate their abilities to apply and communicate concepts they have learned through GEMS units. Students can write letters to a variety of real or imaginary audiences such as:

- Siblings, parents, or other involved adults.
- A class member or students from another class.
- The school principal, secretary, or maintenance person.
- Prominent community members.
- Famous movie stars, athletes, scientists.
- Fictitious characters from comic books, novels, or television.

Through letter writing, students can demonstrate, among other skills, their ability to:

- Articulate the steps taken to solve a problem.
- Explain a strategy they used to win a game.
- Outline important information about a subject.
- Describe what they learned during a particular activity.
- Raise issues or convince someone of their opinion about a controversial issue.

Letter writing has many benefits for both students and teachers. Students become deeply and personally involved in the assignment as they write to a person or character from their world. They are encouraged to communicate clearly because they write to someone who has not shared their experience with the GEMS unit. In addition, students who are unsure of themselves may feel less threatened or afraid of failure when they write to someone other than the teacher who they may think of as knowing the "right" answer.

Through letter writing, teachers gain detailed information about what each child has synthesized from a GEMS lesson or unit. In contrast to short-answer questions and multiple-choice tests, students' letters demonstrate the range of learning styles in a classroom and each student's mode of expression.

A case study using letter writing as an assessment strategy in *In All Probability* begins on the next page. Opportunities for letter-writing assessments in other GEMS units are listed on pages 51–52.

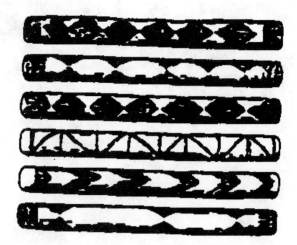

Game Sticks from In All Probability

Letter to a Jockey from *In All Probability*

Letter writing is a particularly effective way to assess students' ability to interpret data and explain basic probability as a follow up to the Horse Race session of *In All Probability*. In that session, twelve horses race to the finish line, propelled by the roll of two dice. Pairs of students play the game several times and post their results on a class data chart.

Class results are then discussed and students are asked to formulate hypotheses as to why Horse #7 wins most often, with Horses #6 and #8 close behind.

Through analysis of the data and use of a two-dice outcome chart, students learn the basic probability concept that all numbers are not as equally likely to result from the roll of two dice. They also see the difference between *estimated probability*, which results from a mathematical experiment, and *theoretical probability*, which can be shown on an outcome chart.

To assess students' understanding of the session, we presented the following situation to a class of fourth grade students.

At the Roll 'Em Race Track, the horses move one space each time their number comes up when two giant dice are rolled. Before each race, the jockeys can choose which horses they will ride. Of course, they want to ride a horse that wins!

Write a letter to a jockey and suggest which horses should be their first and second choices to ride. Be sure to explain why you've made your recommendation. Drawings and diagrams in your letter will help the jockey understand.

 ## What do I want to see?

As you plan this assessment activity, it is necessary to define the specific goals you have for lesson. Ideas for these might come from the objectives of the unit or session, but may be different depending on your own specific curricular goals and the emphasis of your teaching. In the letters that follow the Horse Race activity, students should be able to make a first-choice and second-choice recommendation to the jockey and demonstrate an understanding of the following probability concepts.

> ➤ If two standard dice are rolled, some numbers (6, 7, 8) will come up more often because there are more ways to create these sums on the dice. Numbers such as 2 and 12 are less likely to result from the roll of two dice.

> ➤ Seven is the most likely result because there are six combinations that add up to seven (out of 36 possible combinations). This point can be effectively illustrated with an analysis of class data and a list or outcome chart that describes the likelihood that each sum will result.

 ## How do I evaluate the student work?

Keep these concepts in mind as you read students' letters. We were able to divide the letters into four levels. Each level demonstrated a greater degree of understanding than the previous level, as illustrated in the following pages.

Level One

Students selected particular horses. They based their recommendation on extraneous factors or the results from the few games they played in pairs. They did not support their conclusion with class data or probability concepts.

Steve

Dear Jocky

I think you should ride number 7 first then 6. I picked thous horses becase number 7 has a good pastern and a good loins and a hock and a good shank and a good fetlock.

Dear Jocky,

I think you should pick seven and if you don't get number seven, I would pic number six. I think you should pick seven because seven is my lucky number and I'm rooting for you. And, if you don't get seven, get six because six is an awesome number.
Sincerely, D.J.

Level Two

Students selected particular horses. They based their recommendation solely on an analysis of class data. They did not include an application of probability concepts.

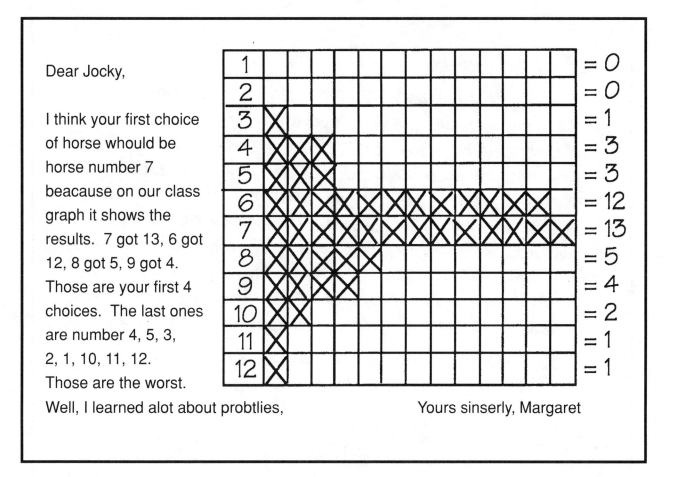

Dear Jocky,

I think your first choice of horse whould be horse number 7 beacause on our class graph it shows the results. 7 got 13, 6 got 12, 8 got 5, 9 got 4. Those are your first 4 choices. The last ones are number 4, 5, 3, 2, 1, 10, 11, 12. Those are the worst.

Well, I learned alot about probtlies,

Yours sinserly, Margaret

1													= 0
2													= 0
3	X												= 1
4	X X X										= 3
5	X X X									= 3
6	X X X		X X X X X X X X	= 12
7	X X X X X X X X X X X X X	= 13
8	X X X X X						= 5
9	X X X X					= 4
10	X X					= 2
11	X				= 1
12	X				= 1

Dear jockey,

If I where you, my first choice would be # 7 Because # 7 has the most wins. If you can't be #7, then be #6 because it has the second most wins. I hope you win.

— Robert S.

Level Three

Students selected particular horses and supported their conclusion with an analysis of class data and a limited application of probability concepts.

Dear Jockeys,
 I think you should pick number seven for your first choice. The reson why I think you should is because if you count all the ways how to make seven you'll get 6 of them and more often you'll get seven. A nother reson is for it is in the middle of all numbers on the horse race. Now for your second choice I would pick 6. For instance it has five ways to make to make it is only one number less than seven.
Hope you pick a good horse.

From
Kira

Dear Jockey,

I think you should ride on horse number seven first because it has six chances to win and that's more than the eleven other horses. The next horse you should ride on is number six or eight because it has five chances to win and that's more than the nine other horses.
In the all the races, horse number seven still has more chances.
That is why you should ride on those horses.

Sincerely,
Jack L.

Level Four

Students selected particular horses and supported their conclusion with an analysis of class data and an extensive application of probability concepts.

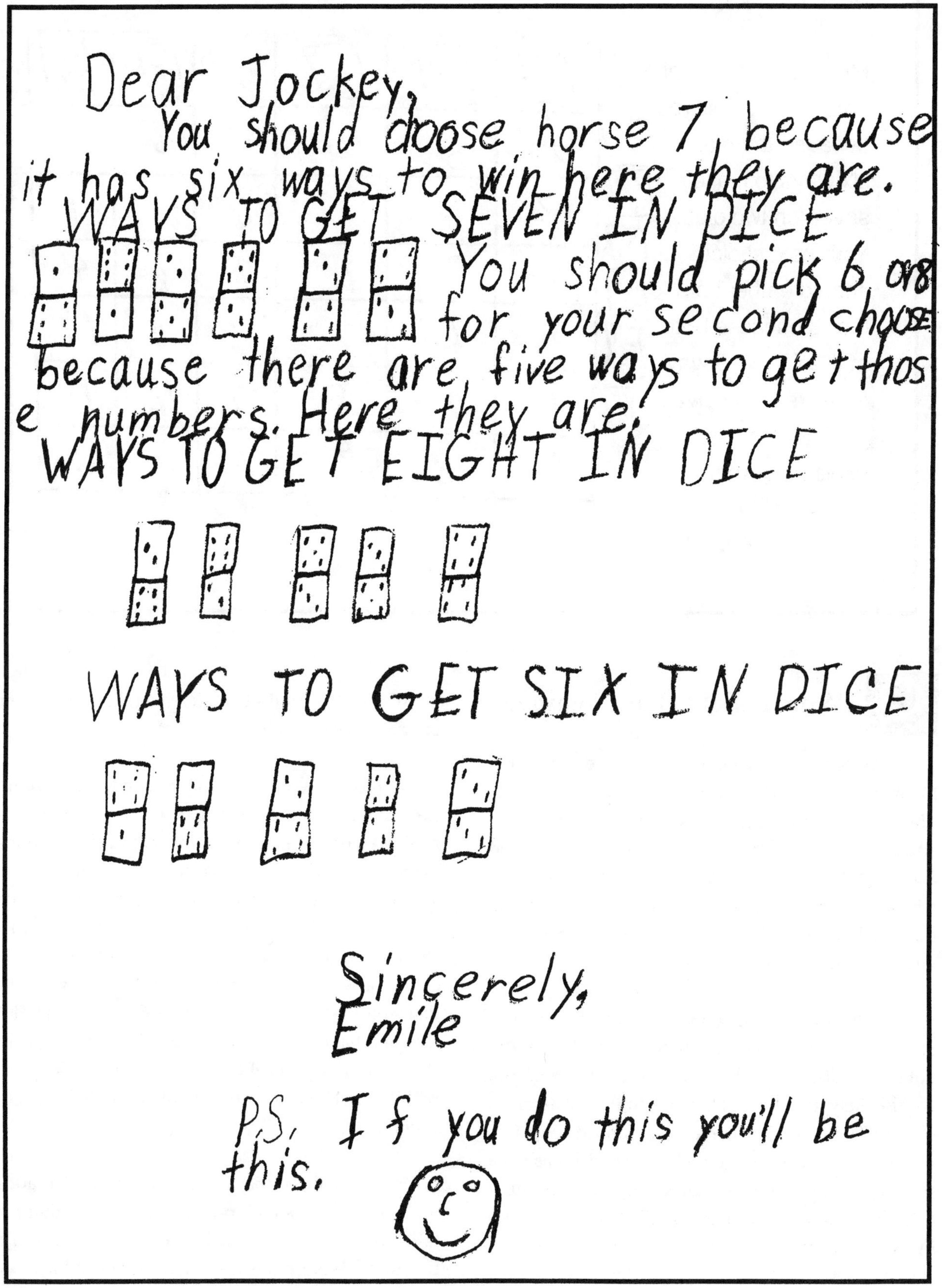

Dear Jockey,
    You should choose horse 7, because it has six ways to win here they are.
WAYS TO GET SEVEN IN DICE

You should pick 6 on for your second choose because there are five ways to get those numbers. Here they are:

WAYS TO GET EIGHT IN DICE

WAYS TO GET SIX IN DICE

Sincerely,
Emile

P.S. If you do this you'll be this.

Dear Jockey,

I think you should pick horse number seven because there are six ways to make seven on two dice. Your next choice should eather be a 6 or 8 because both of them have 5 ways to make themselves. Look at this chart explaining what I just told you.

--- Robert E.

	⚀	⚁	⚂	⚃	⚄	⚅
⚀	2	3	4	5	6	7
⚁	3	4	5	6	7	8
⚂	4	5	6	7	8	9
⚃	5	6	7	8	9	10
⚄	6	7	8	9	10	11
⚅	7	8	9	10	11	12

Q What insights have I gained?

As we sorted the students' letters, we found that the majority were classified as Level Two and Level Three, with a small number of papers at Levels One and Four. All students recommended horses 6, 7, and 8 to the jockeys. This meant to us that the entire class was able to predict a likely winner at the Roll 'Em race track, though they supported their conclusions with varying degrees of success.

We also gained insight about particular students. Steve, whose letter was featured at Level One, did not relate his conclusion to the Horse Race game, but would likely have been at Level Four if we'd assessed students' knowledge of horses. Margaret at Level Two was able to analyze class data but we had a sense that she knew more about "probtlies" than she communicated in her letter. In fact, our students varied greatly in their ability to communicate their conclusions clearly.

We used the results to make several curricular and instructional decisions.

We recognized that students needed additional experiences to help them articulate their thinking. We realized we needed to be clearer in our expectations. In the future, we will discuss the assignment in greater length with students before we have them work individually. In addition, we will provide more time for students to write their letters. We could also make copies of several exemplary letters to share with students on the overhead, discuss the merits of the letters, and have students work in pairs to revise them. We plan to pair Level One and Level Two students with Level Three and Level Four students for the revisions.

We also realized that some students needed additional experiences with probability to grasp that certain numbers are more likely to result from the roll of two dice. Because the interest in the Horse Race was high, we set up a Math Center where students could play the game and add the results to the class data chart. Each week, we revisited the data and offered explanations for the results.

Perhaps most importantly, it was a joy to see our students' response to this assignment. They truly enjoyed writing the letters and even the more reluctant writers had words of advice to the jockeys. And, we must admit that reading the students' letters was a lot more enjoyable and rewarding than correcting a stack of math problems. In all probability, we'll do this again soon!

Other Assessment Opportunities in GEMS Using Letter Writing

Here are some other assessment opportunities in GEMS that use the assessment strategy of letter writing. Use this list to find specific opportunities and to inspire you to create your own uses of this assessment strategy.

➤ *BUBBLE FESTIVAL*
Students can write a letter to a parent and explain at least two things they learned as they explored bubbles.

➤ *BUBBLE-OLOGY*
Students can write a letter to someone who is about to try the Predict-a-Pop activity. The letter should include what they observe just before a bubble will pop.

➤ *BUILD IT! FESTIVAL*
Write a letter to the developers of a Dowel City. Give them advice on how to construct the sturdiest building.

➤ *CHEMICAL REACTIONS*
Students can write a letter to the principal to explain what caused the heat reaction in the ziplock bag.

Crime Lab Chemistry

> *CRIME LAB CHEMISTRY*
Students can write a letter to a police investigator and explain where the colors in the chromatography test come from and why chromatograms from different pens have different colors.

> *EARTH, MOON, AND STARS*
Students can write a letter to a younger child, explaining why the Earth *looks* flat, but is really round.

> *EARTHWORMS*
In Worm County, USA, many residents have worms as pets. Students can write a letter to the new veterinarian to help her understand more about earthworms, their bodies, and how they work.

> *EXPERIMENTING WITH MODEL ROCKETS*
Students can write a letter to the aeronautical engineers at NASA to explain how they could make rockets that fly higher.

> *FROG MATH*
Students can write to a younger student and explain their plan or strategy about how to win the Frog Pond Game.

> *GLOBAL WARMING*
  AND THE GREENHOUSE EFFECT
Students can write a letter to the President of the United States to explain why global warming is a problem and what they think should be done about it.

> *GROUP SOLUTIONS*
Each student can write a letter to her group pointing out what worked well in their cooperation and suggest changes to help the group cooperate even better!

> *HEIGHT-O-METERS*
Write a letter to a group of Girl Scouts or Boy Scouts who are going on a tree investigation, explaining how they can measure the height of trees.

> *INVESTIGATING ARTIFACTS*
Students can write a letter to the curator of your local museum to telling about the midden that you've just excavated. Have them describe the midden and the objects they found, explain what they concluded about the people whose artifacts were buried in the midden, and then ask the curator a question that they still have about the midden.

> *INVOLVING DISSOLVING*
Students can explain to Big Bird or another familiar children's television star where sugar goes after it is mixed with water.

> *LIQUID EXPLORATIONS*
Students can write to a person in charge of cleaning up an oil spill and describe how oil behaves when it spills.

> *MYSTERY FESTIVAL*
Students can tell a friend their thoughts about who committed the crime in the mystery that their class investigated (the theft of Mr. Bear or the disappearance of Felix Navidad). They must be sure to include the reasons why they think they are right.

> *PAPER TOWEL TESTING*
Students can write a letter to the manufacturer of one brand of paper towels they tested. The letter should explain what their group discovered about the paper towels when they tested them for strength and absorbency.

> *QUADICE*
Write a persuasive letter to highlight the benefits of the cooperative version of the game, or vice versa.

> *TREE HOMES*
Students can dictate letters to a real estate developer or logging company explaining why owls and other animals need trees.

> *VITAMIN C TESTING*
Students can write a letter to explain the results of their vitamin C testing to the person or people who do the shopping in their family.

Advertisements as an Assessment Strategy

We rarely think of advertising and marketing as having anything to do with science or mathematics. However, science and math are social activities, and the ability to communicate and convince others is very important. If a scientist or mathematician cannot convince others that their claim is correct, the value of his or her work to the entire field is greatly reduced, or at best delayed.

Advertisements marshal facts and ideas to communicate one point of view. Consequently, there is great value both in creating advertisements and in critically examining them.

Students are bombarded with advertisements through exposure to newspapers, magazines, radio and television. Often statistics or purported experimental results are used in advertising, sometimes skewed in favor of the product being advertised. Most students are aware of the power of advertisements as a marketing tool. Because students have direct experience with the media, they often are intrigued, challenged, and enthusiastic when asked to create their own brochure, commercial, poster, or videotape as part of a GEMS unit. These projects can be used to:

- Present important information about a product, service, or place.

- Convince consumers to buy a product or service.

- Evaluate or compare products.

- Persuade people to agree with a point of view.

Students' written, oral and visual presentations provide valuable insight about their ability to:

- Use data and results from math and science investigations as evidence to support a conclusion.

- Use persuasive writing to present information and data.

- Design visual aids to illustrate a particular aspect of science or math.

- Create graphs and charts.

- Organize and communicate information that they know, visually, orally, or in writing.

A case study using advertisements as an assessment strategy begins for *River Cutters* on the next page for *Paper Towel Testing* on page 61. Opportunities for using the advertisement assessment strategy for other GEMS units are listed on page 70.

River Cutters

Design a Travel Brochure from *River Cutters*

Advertisements can be created as promotional tools during the *River Cutters* unit. To assess students' ability to demonstrate their knowledge of river systems, students were asked to design a travel brochure which advertises a river area. The following instructions were presented to several classes of middle school students immediately after they completed *River Cutters*.

RIVER CUTTERS: DESIGN A TRAVEL BROCHURE

You would like people to visit your river area. Design a travel brochure that describes and includes the following information about the natural beauties and tourist attractions of your river area.

- Descriptions of important river-related and geological features.

- Environmental conditions, recreational facilities or other attractions that would appeal to visitors.

- Evidence of human impact on your river area.

- Maps, drawings, or diagrams about the area's physical features should be used to make your brochure clearer and more attractive.

Remember, your brochure will be an advertisement for the river area.

As students write and design the brochure, they demonstrate their ability to use river terminology and river-related geological features and the degree to which they understand that rivers are dynamic, changing systems. In addition, the brochures offer students an opportunity to integrate their artistic, creative writing, language arts, and organizational skills.

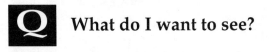 **What do I want to see?**

The goals for this assessment are listed in the assignment for students. Elements of a successful brochure would demonstrate students' ability to:

➤ Use appropriate river-related terminology.

➤ Provide descriptive detail about geological features, environmental conditions and recreational facilities.

➤ Articulate their knowledge about river systems and human impact on them.

➤ Organize and present information so that it is clear and attractive.

Q How do I evaluate the student work?

Students were told ahead of time that their advertisements would be evaluated in the six categories listed below. Evidence in four categories would include mention of some of the following river-related vocabulary.

Geological Features

Canyon, rapid, cave, terrace, gorge, waterfall, oxbow lake, channel, valley with flood plain, gully, delta, ocean, bay, alluvial fan, old versus new rivers, meandering rivers, the source, tributaries, mouth, riverbank, and riverbed

Environmental Conditions

Erosion (sediment and load), rain and flooding, drought, drainage patterns, depth and length of river, mountains, forests, glaciers, native animals and plants

Recreational Facilities

Camping, naturalist programs, hiking, swimming, fishing, boating, and rafting

Human Impact

Dams, hydroelectric power, erosion, toxic waste, logging, structures, bridges, trails, roads, and highways

Two categories focus on the visual appeal of the advertisement.

Maps/Drawings

Accurate details of features, facilities, and attractions

Format

Legible writing or typing, clear communication (punctuation, spelling), effective layout, and promotional features (e.g., quotes from visitors, headlines)

The advertisements can be evaluated with a point system using the above categories as a checklist. We used a scale of 4 (complete) to 1 (not at all) to assess each of the six categories with a possible total of 24 points for an exemplary advertisement.

Teachers may opt to assign different point values to each category or use a "+" for good, a "√" for satisfactory or a "−" for needs improvement.

River Cutters

4	Geological Features	4	Environmental Conditions	2	Recreational Facilities
2	Human Impact	4	Maps/ Drawings	4	Clear/Attractive Format

José's attractive, well-planned brochure includes extensive description of the river itself, a detailed map, and humorous promotional quotes (not shown) from celebrities such as Bill Clinton, Will Clark, and Johnny Carson. He used a computer word processing program to communicate a clear message to potential river travelers.

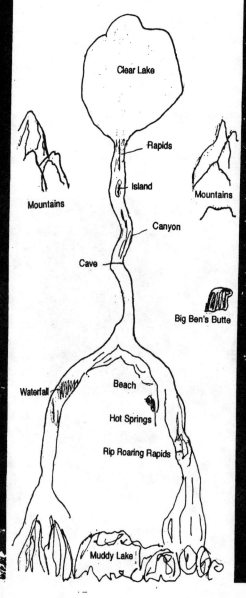

The Roaring River

On our river rafting trip we will start on the shore of Clear Lake. As we go down the river we will go through some rapids and then arrive at an island on which you can see the high mountains which surround the river. You will also see the glaciers that are high up on the mountains. After we eat lunch there we will continue down the river. Next we will go through a very deep canyon. We will spend the night in a large cave area where we will have dinner.

We will stay in the cave to eat breakfast, we can also play games. If you want, you can also look at the anticline in the rocks. After an hour or so of playing and exploring, we will continue down the river. When we stop for lunch on Pebble Beach, you are welcome to go and enjoy the near by hot springs.

As we will continue down the river. The river will split into two, at this point we will go to the right, instead of going down the dreadful waterfall that lays just around the corner. While we are on the move you can look at the fantastic arches that were created by erosion over thousands of years.

Then comes the suprise part, THE RIP ROARING RAPIDS. So you better hang on because it is NOT a smooth ride; but it is very fun, unless you get sick when you go up and down and sometimes upside down.

We will camp out on the shore and eat our dinner.

For lunch on both days you can have a choice of either a ham or turkey sandwich. On the first night you can choose from hamburgers or spaghetti. For breakfast, we will have pancakes and syrup. For our last dinner we will have a surprise, and believe me it will be a good meal!

There are lots of wildlife in and on the river, including deer, rainbow trout, mountain goats, and cod. And please do not feed the animals because human food is not good for them.

There is a lot of beautiful scenery such as Big Ben's Butte which can be seen from outside the canyon. If you are more interested in anticlines and synclines, you may view them around the river.

As our trip comes to an end, all the water will be peaceful, just wildlife and the wind. No rapids just slow flowing water. At the end we will come out into another lake, Muddy lake.

The Roaring River

Rip Roaring Rapids Co.
45 Main St. New York City
New York, 82433

2	Geological Features	*2*	Environmental Conditions	*4*	Recreational Facilities
2	Human Impact	*3*	Maps/ Drawings	*3*	Clear/Attractive Format

Davida's advertisement is close to José's in total points but has strengths that are quite different. In contrast to José, she describes in great detail the recreational features and human impact (highways, bridges, buildings) on Slowimpy River.   However, she includes few details about geological features and environment, a strength of José's brochure.

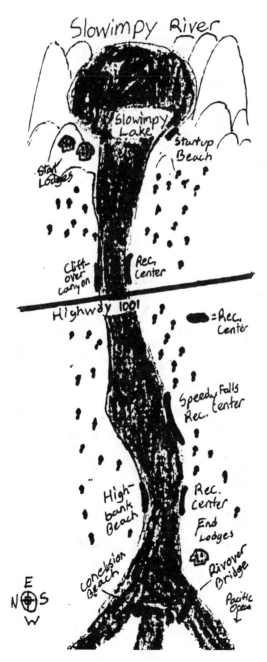

Slowimpy River Information

Have you ever been to Slowimpy River? What's that you say? No!!! Well, if you are the slow and unadventerous type, then this vacation is perfect for you.

You start on top of Small'nlow Peak using three perfectly safe rubber rafts per group; then start at a beach called Startup Beach and push off into Slowimpy Lake, at the top of the river, around noon. Then you will start at a nice slow pace you can all handle, even Grandma.

Next, you will travel all afternoon until around 5:00 when you will reach Cliffover Canyon.

There you will stay overnight and eat dinner from a choice of fresh trout with bread, or a huge Ceaser Salad bursting with fresh vegetables, with your choice of dressing.

The next mourning at 7:00, reveille will sound, and you will have hot creal and choice of toast or bagel, and some O.J. to wash it down with.

Continued from right flap.

The next day of the slow but fun journey has begun. You will pass the neck of Wide Pass and the Highbank Beach. This part is the most fun. You will go through the toughest of the trip, Speedy Falls. This is where all the water sucked up in the overhanging cliffs is dumped into the river again. If you're lucky you may exeed five M.P.H.

There, where there is plenty of crayfish, we will catch lunch.

Lastly we will coast into the last beach where the river joins into the ocean. This beach is called Conclusion Beach. There you will be shuttled home by Whistle Stop Wheels.

There, you just rafted three whole miles in two days and one night.

Sample 3   **MARK**   TOTAL: 13 points

3	Geological Features	*3*	Environmental Conditions	*2*	Recreational Facilities
1	Human Impact	*1*	Maps/ Drawings	*3*	Clear/Attractive Format

Mark's advertisement includes sufficient information about geological and environmental conditions and could be improved with additional details about the human impact on the area. His map minimally describes his river and lacks river-related terminology.

RIVER RAFTING RAPIDS

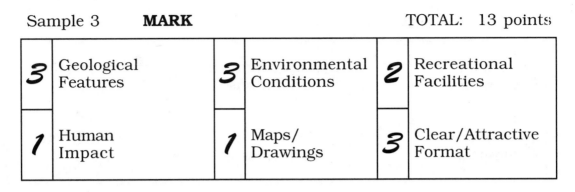

WACKY WATER RIVER

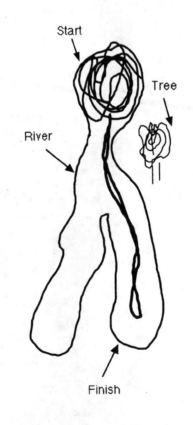

Come and see the exiting new River Rafting Rapids. The river is a nice and quite rafting area located in Larkspur and is about one hundred meters long. Near the river sight, you will see some: deer, Badger, and maybe even a few bears. Just around the river you will see some interesting rocks. This river is very deep. The water in the river is extremely cold. It can reach down to a freezing 22 degrees. You might spot some fish or some deadly barracudas. The water is very white when it is a windy day. Once in a while, the undertow is tremendously strong. Come to Alex's River Rafting at your own risk.

Some of the highlights of the river are that there is a giant waterfall right in the middle of the river. When you are about 500 meters or so across the river. Also, there is one part of the river where it is not so deep, so your raft might hit the rock underwater.

The company will prepare some great food for you. Especially, if you like spaghetti, this is the place for you!

The scenery that will be seen is: Rocks, trees, flowers, mountains, and of coarse, water.

TESTIMONIALS:

1. FUN
2. CRAZY
3. SCARY
4. LOW PRICES

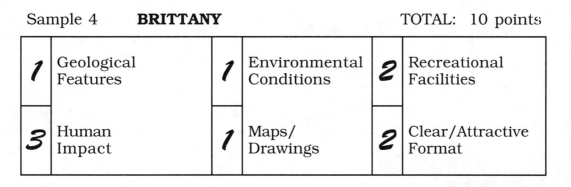

1	Geological Features	1	Environmental Conditions	2	Recreational Facilities
3	Human Impact	1	Maps/ Drawings	2	Clear/Attractive Format

Brittany's advertisement includes limited description of most river features. A minimal map and several spelling errors appear to be the result of hasty completion of the assignment. However, Brittany's brochure is unique in that it is the only one that discusses the history of the human impact on the river.

White Water Cavern

Have you ever been to White Water Cavern before? Well, you should go! If you go you will be spending five adventurous days on a fast-moving roller coaster ride. The White Water Cavern starts at the heart of Mt. St. Helen and ventures all the way to Marin County. If you were wondering about the food, then you will be glad to know that we have a chef that comes with us on the trip.

The owner of White Water Cavern started this company in 1845 right in the middle of the Gold Rush. He thought if he had a rafting company that he would become rich because so many people wanted to come to the Gold Rush. Well, his dream came true. After he died, Ben Bell gave his company to his grandson Frank Bell. Frank changed the company name to White Water Cavern.

Frank made so much money that he started rafting companies al over the western part of the USA. The most popular of all is White Water Cavern.

They call it White Water Cavern because the water moves so fast and rafters call moving water white water. The cavern part comes from the deep cavern on the right side of the river. Afater yho to agout half way down the river, you see it. Scientists say that it is over a 500 foot drop.

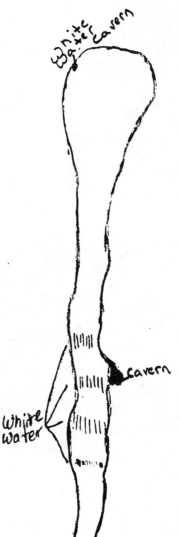

Old Man Rivers age 87
"I will never forget the day I went down the White Water Cavern."

Sally Smith age 24
"I loved the trip it was the best honeymoon ever."

Mike Moor age 26
"Soon as I got on the raft my drenilan started pumping so hard it almost exploded!"

John Smith age 35
"This was the best experince of my life."

Tony Larrso age 36
"I wish I could go another round on this super river!"

This assignment requires students to combine their knowledge of rivers with the information that they have about effective advertising and attractive visual art. It validates a wide range of learning styles and provides a forum for students to utilize a variety of skills and talents that are often undervalued in science and mathematics classes.

You may find that students who do not score well on traditional tests will excel when asked to represent their knowledge in a visual format. Other students, who are accustomed to conventional assessment forms, may have difficulty when asked to represent their knowledge through other vehicles.

Teachers will need to determine what elements of the brochures are most important to assess. This philosophy must be clearly stated in the presentation of the assignment as well as the assessment. For example, a teacher who wishes to focus only on the "scientific" aspects of rivers may decide to ask students to emphasize geological and environmental features in the brochure. A teacher who uses a more integrated approach may decide to emphasize language arts, visual arts, and science in the assignment.

To strengthen the students' ability for self-assessment and to improve their assignments, provide opportunities to display, share, and evaluate brochures with classmates, other teachers, and/or parents.

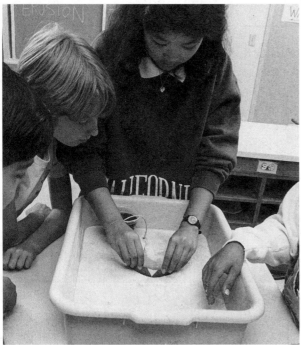

River Cutters

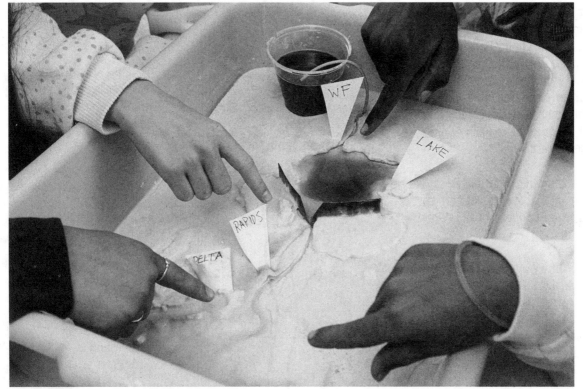

River Cutters

CASE STUDY USING ADVERTISEMENTS

Create an Advertisement from *Paper Towel Testing*

Students can be asked to create an advertisement as a marketing tool at the end of the *Paper Towel Testing* unit. During the unit, students design controlled experiments to test absorbency and wet strength of four brands of paper towels. In addition, they compute the cost per sheet for each brand. The results are discussed and students determine which brand of paper towel they think is best.

To assess students' ability to analyze results from their experiments and draw conclusions based on objective data, the following assessment was presented.

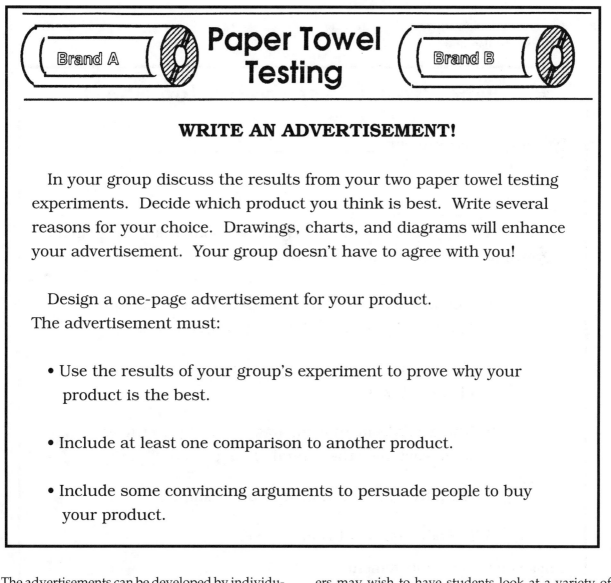

Paper Towel Testing

Brand A   Brand B

WRITE AN ADVERTISEMENT!

In your group discuss the results from your two paper towel testing experiments. Decide which product you think is best. Write several reasons for your choice. Drawings, charts, and diagrams will enhance your advertisement. Your group doesn't have to agree with you!

Design a one-page advertisement for your product.
The advertisement must:

- Use the results of your group's experiment to prove why your product is the best.

- Include at least one comparison to another product.

- Include some convincing arguments to persuade people to buy your product.

The advertisements can be developed by individuals or pairs of students. If students work in pairs, have them attach a sheet of paper which describes each student's role to create the final product. Teachers may wish to have students look at a variety of magazine and newspaper advertisements first to identify what are elements of a successful written marketing tool.

What do I want to see?

The goals for this assessment are listed in the assignment for students. Elements of a successful advertisement would include:

➤ An appealing visual presentation.

➤ A clear recommendation for one brand of paper towel.

➤ Appropriate use of statistics from the experimental results to support the recommendation.

➤ Use of experiment results to compare the chosen brand to at least one other product.

➤ Clear communication supported by drawings, charts, and/or diagrams.

 ## How do I evaluate the student work?

There are several methods to evaluate the results.

Peer Evaluation

Develop and discuss the elements of a successful advertisement with your students. Have them share their advertisements with classmates who are asked to list the strengths and make suggestions for improvement. Students can have the option to modify their advertisement after the peer consultation. Teachers may wish to devise a checklist to help students evaluate a partner's work, as illustrated below.

Paper Towel Test Evaluation Sheet

Writer of Advertisement: _____

Reviewer: _____

Date: _____

Label each statement with a ☆ (yes), ✔ (somewhat), or ✕ (no) to evaluate your classmate's advertisement.

___1. The writer uses information from the experiments to state why the brand of paper towel was best.

___2. The advertisement clearly recommends one brand of paper towel.

___3. The advertisement compares the best paper towel to at least one other brand of paper towel.

___4. The advertisement is easy to understand.

___5. The advertisement is attractive.

Suggestions for improvement:

Teacher Evaluation

Evaluate student work to determine which elements of a successful advertisement are included and how well they are presented. You may wish to use the peer evaluation sheet and develop a point scale to assess each element (e.g., 5 elements, 20 points).

The Paper Towel Test Evaluation Sheet was used as a guideline to identify strengths and areas for improvement in the following sixth grade advertisements.

Bounty is the best brand because it has more strength in absorbency!

This student clearly recommends one brand of paper towel and states one reason for the recommendation. However, the meaning of "strength in absorbency" is unclear, and there are no specific references to the paper towel tests nor are there comparisons to other brands. The advertisement appears to be hastily done.

BRAWNY

It's you, it's me, it's totally fat free. It's the best bargain paper towel, it's

Brawny!

It's second in absorbency and wet strength but it costs less than all leading brands.

This student has created a clever rhyme about Brawny that points out that it is not only healthy ("fat free") but also inexpensive! The writer apparently believes that cost is more important than wet strength and absorbency. The advertisement could be strengthened with specific data from the paper towel tests. Charts or drawings could be added to make the work more attractive.

In the results of our consumer test lab Bounty outranked Scott brand—which was ranked last in both wet strength and absorbency. Bounty also has more sheets then Brawny and Sparkle, and is the best buy. Buy Bounty, it's the best and beyond the rest

This student makes a strong case for consumers to buy Bounty towels (wet strength, absorbency, and number of sheets). The advertisement would be strengthened with further description of the two experiments and specific results.

Paper Towel Testing

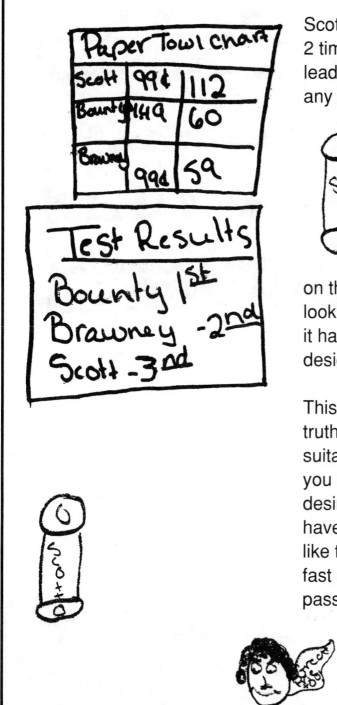

Scott is the best buy because it has 2 times more paper towels then the leading Bounty. It is cheaper than any other brand. In our experi

ments it was about the same wet strength and absorbency as one of the leading brands. It extends longer than other brands. It has beautiful scenery on the paper towel; it is kind of like looking through a kaleidoscope, but it has no color and it only has one design.

This is not rubbish -- all this is the truth. I think that this is the most suitable paper towel for you. Once you buy this paper towel, you will desire no other than Scott. You will have no chance of finding a deal like this. If I were you, I would act fast and not let this opportunity pass by.

This advertisement is attractive and contains vivid descriptions about Scott's appearance ("like looking through a kaleidoscope") as well as its strength and absorbency features, and the length of the roll. A chart is included to compare three brands of paper towels, but could be improved with labels ("cost per roll" and "number of sheets") to clarify the numbers listed. The test results are also unclear because the reader does not know the test conditions. In addition, the advertisement recommends Scott towels although the test results rank Scott as third. The student has used persuasive language effectively, but needs to clarify experimental details and elaborate on the reasons for the conclusion that Scott towels are best.

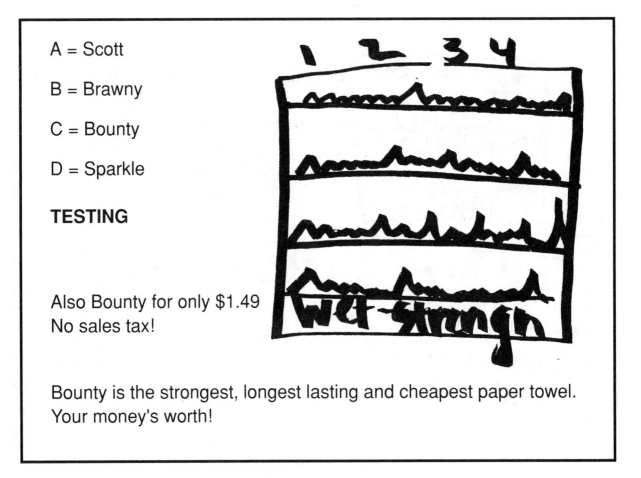

A = Scott

B = Brawny

C = Bounty

D = Sparkle

TESTING

Also Bounty for only $1.49
No sales tax!

Bounty is the strongest, longest lasting and cheapest paper towel.
Your money's worth!

This advertisement appeals to the consumer's sense of value ("money's worth") and even repealed the government's sales tax! A graph is included to describe the wet strength test results, but the findings are unclear because the unit of measurement is not listed on the x-axis. It appears that Bounty surpassed the others in wet strength, but we do not know how this feature was tested. Although Bounty is described as the "cheapest," there is no information about the price of the other brands of paper towels, which, in fact, were less expensive than Bounty. Perhaps a synthesis of experimental results, cost per roll, and number of sheets per roll could have better justified the conclusion that Bounty is the best buy.

Paper Towel Testing

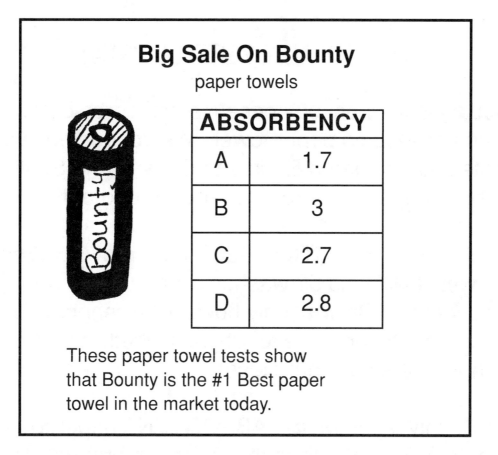

Big Sale On Bounty

paper towels

ABSORBENCY	
A	1.7
B	3
C	2.7
D	2.8

These paper towel tests show that Bounty is the #1 Best paper towel in the market today.

This attractive advertisement includes details about the absorbency test. However, the student does not indicate whether Bounty is Brand A, B, C, or D, and does not explain what the absorbency ratings mean. The advertisement would be more convincing if other factors (i.e., wet strength, cost) were noted.

Paper Towel Testing

BUY BOUNTY PAPER TOWELS

Bounty is the best buy because it absorbs better than any leading paper towel. We conducted two tests that compared Bounty to Brawny and Scott paper towels and here is what we found out!

→ Bounty is the STRONGEST paper towel. When it's wet, it will hold 52 washers. Scott holds 30 washers and Brawny only holds 27 washers. You'll need Bounty for those tough jobs whether you work at home or somewhere else!

→ Bounty is the MOST ABSORBENT paper towel. It held more water than the other two brands. That means Bounty will be better whether you have a big or small mess to clean up. You could probably dry an entire car with just a few Bounty towels!

→ Bounty costs just .4 cents a sheet more than Brawny and Scott, but you'll get your money's worth! It's better to spend a little more on the best paper towel.

As President Clinton says, "If I had the time, I'd use Bounty to clean the whole White House!"

This student acknowledges that Bounty costs more than the other brands and effectively uses test results to present the case that Bounty's slightly higher price is more than justified by the paper towel's strength and absorbency. The advertisement provides clear comparisons to the other two brands of paper towels and is enhanced by the endorsement from the U.S. president. Charts and illustrations are unnecessary, but could enhance the advertisement's appeal.

What insights have I gained?

These advertisements represent the range of student responses we reviewed from the paper towel testing assessments. In analyzing the students' work, the following observations can be made.

Paper Towel Testing

➤ The majority of students need additional support to incorporate the results from the paper towel testing experiments into their advertisements. These students may need more experience with data interpretation, and how to represent data in graphs, charts, and tables.

➤ Many students need to develop further awareness about what elements are essential to effective advertising. To facilitate this awareness, teachers can ask students to select "good" and "bad" advertisements from newspapers and magazines and develop a list of techniques that persuade consumers to purchase a product (attractiveness of layout, use of convincing statistics, and comparisons to other brands).

➤ To assure that all students understand the expectations of the task, teachers may wish to ask small groups of students to discuss the assignment and develop questions for clarification. If appropriate, teachers may wish to create a model of an advertisement for an imaginary brand of paper towel (e.g., "Wipe-it!") to illustrate how to incorporate experimental results and other effective techniques.

➤ Teachers may need to provide additional time for students to evaluate and improve their advertisements, after feedback from peers and adults.

Paper Towel Testing

Other Assessment Opportunities in GEMS Using Advertisements

Following is a list of some other assessment opportunities in GEMS that use the assessment strategy of advertisements. Use this list to find specific opportunities and to inspire you to create your own uses of this assessment strategy.

➤ *BUBBLE-OLOGY*

Students write, design, narrate, and produce a short commercial to advertise their originally designed bubble makers. Commercials should explain to the viewer why their bubble maker makes the kinds of bubbles it does. Videotape the commercials if possible.

➤ *BUILD IT! FESTIVAL*

Students create original tessellation designs for an advertisement on exquisite tiling for the bathroom. They can include a comparison of their product to tiles from other "companies."

Experimenting With Model Rockets

➤ *EXPERIMENTING WITH MODEL ROCKETS*

The Ace Rocket Company is selling a rocket to companies who wish to launch their own space satellites. Students create advertisements to convince customers that their rocket will fly higher than conventional rockets, and report on the laboratory work that supports their conclusions.

➤ *HOT WATER AND WARM HOMES FROM SUNLIGHT*

Students create a poster to advertise a house that makes efficient use of the sun. What are the advantages of this house? What special features does it have? How do you know that these features will be better than the standard features?

➤ *LIQUID EXPLORATIONS*

Students create a commercial for the secret salad dressing that they develop.

➤ *MOONS OF JUPITER*

Students imagine they work for the Interplanetary Travel Agency and are trying to interest space tourists in a jaunt to several of the most interesting moons of Jupiter. Students create a radio or television advertisement emphasizing the wonders, mysteries, and special features of the moons they choose. Students can make posters or other visual aids to highlight the attractions of the moons.

➤ *MORE THAN MAGNIFIERS*

Students can write, produce, or present an advertisement for any one of the optical instruments made in the unit. Explain how the device works, how the lenses are placed, and what it might help a person do. Or, they can invent their own optical instrument and write an advertisement for it.

➤ *VITAMIN C TESTING*

Students write, produce, or present an advertisement for their favorite fruit juice. The ad should emphasize the ingredients in the juice, particularly the vitamin C content, and how it compares to other juices.

Reflections as an Assessment Strategy

Oral and written reflections provide teachers with valuable insight into a student's thoughts and thought processes. When students are asked to think about or analyze a situation, topic or problem, they are likely to find new ways to articulate thoughts and ideas. As teachers, we often refine our knowledge as we share it with our students. We are constantly learning as we discover new ways to approach a topic and to organize our thoughts so they are clear and comprehensible. Students, too, have the opportunity to organize and articulate their thoughts as they respond to a specific challenge.

Traditional science and mathematics textbook assessments rarely require students to reflect on their own knowledge. Mathematics textbooks often give several examples then present a large quantity of very similar problems for the student to solve. Science textbooks often ask students to read a passage and answer a list of questions that ask them to recall the content of the material. Some textbooks require students to draw conclusions from information that has been presented, but far too often, the knowledge of a learner is overlooked or inaccurately assessed because textbook questions and expectations are limited and narrow. Students are seldom asked to apply their knowledge in new situations or to write an open-ended response about what they know and wonder. When teachers ask students to reflect about a topic, we broaden the view of what is important and empower them in the process.

Strong science and mathematics programs provide numerous opportunities for reflection. Oral reflections are evident in individual and group questioning, discussions, and student presentations. Written reflections are often recorded in journal entries, persuasive writing, articles for school publications or reports to present at class meetings or conferences on a particular topic.

When students make reflections, they mobilize many of the processes used by professional scientists and mathematicians. They communicate their thoughts and results as they observe, compare, order, categorize, relate, and infer. They use creative, independent thinking to draw their own conclusions based on what they've discovered and learned over the course of a GEMS unit. The GEMS series offers students opportunities to reflect about:

- Evidence gained during a laboratory test or investigation.

- Interpretation of data.

- The validity of conclusions based on evidence.

- Explanations of physical phenomena.

- Interactions among elements of a system.

- What they liked or disliked about the activity or unit.

Through reflective writing, students demonstrate their ability to:

- Identify the concepts and skills they can use effectively and those on which they need more practice.

- Make accurate observations and generalizations.

- Apply knowledge to new situations.

- Use various science and mathematics process skills.

- Think creatively.

- Present a strong case for a conclusion and use evidence to support inferences and conclusions.

- Recognize there are different viewpoints and different sides to an issue, and that scientists may sometimes disagree.

- Understand that conclusions are rarely final— further thought and reflection may help to find faulty reasoning, or new ideas which might overturn earlier ideas.

- Communicate effectively in a variety of ways.

A case study using reflection as an assessment strategy in *Mystery Festival* is on the next page. Opportunities for reflections assessments in other GEMS units are on pages 80–82.

Newspaper Report from *Mystery Festival*

Reflective writing can be used to assess whether students can determine if a conclusion is based on a fair or unfair inference. In *Mystery Festival*, students attempt to solve a mystery as they analyze evidence at many crime lab science stations.

The mystery for older students is especially complex and open to many interpretations. They investigate evidence and make conclusions based on their findings. As they share their results, students learn that it is possible for several groups to interpret the same evidence in very different ways. They are asked to evaluate the plausibility of their hypotheses.

Throughout the *Mystery Festival*, teachers emphasize the difference between evidence (fact) and infer-

ence (a conclusion that is based on evidence). For example, students recognize that a chromatography test may or may not contain enough evidence to implicate a criminal. They learn if a conclusion is not supported by valid evidence, an unfair inference has been made.

To assess students' understanding of fair versus unfair inferences, the following scenario was presented to a class of fifth grade students. The scenario is read to the students several times, and, if necessary, acted out in a skit. All students receive a copy of the scenario on the next page as well as the newspaper article with the editor's instructions on page 74. The instructions are reviewed orally.

Mystery Festival

THE SCENARIO

Imagine that you are a news reporter! You're assigned to write an article about a grass fire in a nearby town. You go to the burning field where fire fighters are trying to put out the fire. There are huge flames, but the fire chief tells you that the fire is under control. This is lucky because the field is next to an oil refinery. As you ask more questions, you learn that there is some evidence that the fire was started on purpose (arson).

You go to the police department's crime lab to talk to the criminalist who is assigned to the case. You learn that a note was found nailed to a telephone pole next to the field. The note says, *"The price of gas is too high. I'll make this company pay!"* Through chromatography tests, it was found that the note was written with a black NIKKO—a common brand of pen.

While at the police station, you find out that the police have questioned three suspects. One is a high school student who works at a local gas station owned by the company whose field was set on fire. Another is a man who used to work for the oil company but lost his job. The third suspect is the mayor herself!

All three of these people were seen near the field in the hour before the fire began. The mayor had a black NIKKO brand pen with her when she was questioned. The other two suspects did not have black pens in their pockets at the time they were questioned. No arrests have been made in the case.

When you return to your office, you find that another reporter has already written an article about the fire, but it is not totally accurate. Your editor gives you the following assignment.

Mayor Is Arrested For Arson!

A fire is burning out of control in a grassy field. Fire fighters are worried that a neighboring oil refinery may burn down. The mayor was seen nailing something to a telephone pole near the grassy field. A note found on the telephone pole was written with the mayor's pen. According to the police, there are two other suspects, but they probably didn't light the fire.

EDITOR'S INSTRUCTIONS

1. Read the other reporter's article.

2. Underline the places where the reporter stated an inaccurate fact or made an unfair inference.

3. Rewrite the article so that it is true. Change any parts that are not based on fact or evidence. You may need to add details to make the article more accurate.

 What do I want to see?

As you plan this assessment activity, it is necessary to define the specific goals of the lesson. In this case, a student who has fully accomplished the purposes of this reflective writing task will be able to complete the following.

➤ Read and comprehend the scenario and resulting news story.

➤ Underline the six aspects of the story that are misstatements of fact or unfair inferences.

➤ Rewrite the story to clearly correct the aspects of the story that are misstatements of fact or unfair inferences.

Students who fully accomplish the task would identify and correct the errors in the story.

Mayor Is <u>Arrested</u>[1] For Arson!

A fire is burning <u>out of control</u>[2] in a grassy field. Fire fighters <u>are worried that a neighboring oil refinery may burn down.</u>[3] The mayor <u>was seen nailing something to a telephone pole</u>[4] near the grassy field. A note found on the telephone pole was written <u>with the mayor's pen.</u>[5] According to the police, there are two other suspects, <u>but they probably didn't light the fire.</u>[6]

[1] The mayor was not arrested. She was only questioned by the police.

[2] The fire chief says that the fire seems to be under control.

[3] Because the fire is under control, the oil refinery will not burn down.

[4] All three suspects were seen in the field before the fire began, but no one saw the person who nailed the note to the telephone pole.

[5] The note was written with a black NIKKO. The mayor was the only suspect who had a NIKKO with her, but it is a common brand of pen. We do not have enough evidence to make the inference that the mayor's pen was used to write the note on the telephone pole. This could be a coincidence.

[6] No arrests have been made. There is no evidence to suggest that the other suspects did NOT light the fire.

 ## How do I evaluate the student work?

Read each paper and compare it with the exemplary response. If you wish, you can create a checklist with the following information to help delineate the degree to which each student accomplished the purposes of the task.

Student's Name	# of Errors Underlined	Specific Errors Corrected					
		1	2	3	4	5	6

In our class of fifth graders, we found that the large majority of students were able to underline at least four inaccurate parts of the newspaper article. However, students varied considerably in their ability to correct misstatements and unfair inferences as they rewrote the article.

Samples 1 and 2

Full Accomplishment of the Task

FIRE IN A GRASSY FIELD!

A fire started in a grassy field near a oil refinery, but firemen say it's under control. Experts say that this fire was started by arson, but no one knows yet. We found a note stuck to a telephone pole. In the note, it tells us that someone wanted to actually try to burn the oil refinery. We have 3 suspects—one a high school kid working for a gas station, the other a person who worked for the oil refinery but lost his job. The other, the Mayor, she has the same kind of pen that wrote the note but it's a common brand. No arrests have been made.

Mayor is 1 of 3 ARSON Suspects!

A fire is burning in a grassy field. The fire is in control and luckily the fire fighters say that the oil refinery nearby is safe. The police say that they found a note nailed to a telephone pole near by. It was written with a NIKKO pen. All 3 suspects were found near the seen of the crime. The police found a NIKKO pen in our beloved mayor's pocket. The police have no hard evidence because a NIKKO is a pen that many people have, so it could be anybody.

Samples 1 and 2 are two of few that **fully accomplish** the purpose of the task. Students corrected all misstatements and unfair inferences and provided details that the chromatography test did not provide enough evidence to reach a valid conclusion.

Samples 3 and 4

Substantial Accomplishment of the Task

Fire!

A fire is burning but they have it under control. Next door is a oil refinery. On a telephone pole near the grassy field, a note was found the note was written with a pen like the Mayor's. The mayor and two other suspects were seen near the field before the fire started.

Mayor Suspected for Arson!

A fire is burning in a grassy field next door to an oil refinery. Though the flames are large, the fire chief says it is under control. The police's three suspects were seen by the field an hour before the fire. A note was posted on a nearby telephone pole. It was written with the same type of pen the mayor uses—a black NIKKO.

These samples **substantially accomplish** the purpose of the task. All facts in the stories are accurately presented. However, the students did not mention why the NIKKO pen was not enough evidence to implicate the mayor.

Samples 5 and 6

Partial Accomplishment of the Task

Mayor is Suspected For Arson!

A fire is being put out in a grassy field. Fire fighters are worried that an oil refinery might burn down. But they have the fire under control. They say the mayor was nailing something to a telephone pole near the grassy field. A note was found on the telephone pole. According to the police, there are two other suspects.

> ## Three Suspects For Fire
>
> A fire was burning in a grassy field. But fire fighters kept it in control. It has been suggested that either 3 suspects has been reported. People believe the mayor had done it since there has been a piece of paper nailed to a pole with a NIKKO pen. Later, she was using a NIKKO.

These students **partially accomplish** the purpose of the task. They successfully correct some of the errors in the original story. Other errors remain uncorrected and several of the misstatements and unfair inferences are validated.

Samples 7 and 8

Little or No Progress Toward Accomplishment of the Task

> ## The Mayor is Arrested!
>
> A fire is burning out of control. A neighboring oil refinery may burn down. Someone was seen nailing something to a pole. There was a note on the pole written in the mayor's pen. There are two other suspects, but they probably didn't do it.

> ## MAYOR IS ARRESTED FOR ARSON!
>
> A fire downtown is burning uncontrollably in a grassy field. The people are worried about a neighboring oil refinery may blow up. FACT 1: The Mayor was seen earlier nailing a note to a pole. There are 3 suspects. A note was found on the pole later. They say the note was writing in a pen—the Mayor carried the same pen, the other 2 suspects did not have a pen with them that day. We still don't know who done it!

Samples 7 and 8 indicate that these students made **little or no progress** toward accomplishment of the task because their information is largely false. Their versions repeat many of the inaccuracies in the original story and misrepresent unfair inferences as fact. Ironically, the author of sample 8 reaches the accurate conclusion that no one knows "who done it!"!

Q What insights have I gained?

These samples represent a typical range of the hundreds of student responses we reviewed from this reflective writing assessment. The assessment operates at two levels—identification of errors in the original story, and correction of those errors. In analyzing the students' work, we made the following observations.

➤ All students appeared able to identify the errors in the story.

However, many of their stories indicated that they had only partially grasped the concept of fair versus unfair inference. This raises several issues.

Because the story was largely false, it is possible that some students may have merely underlined the main ideas without evaluating whether the key points were accurate. Or, they may have randomly underlined sections of the story.

If we were to evaluate the students on the first task of the assignment, we would not have an accurate picture. Therefore, it is essential to look at the second level of the task.

➤ The story revisions provide more detailed information about individual levels of understanding. In addition, we can assess each student's ability to write a coherent and accurate story.

Teachers will need to determine whether students were lacking in scientific reasoning skills (in this case, the ability to construct fair inferences from evidence) or in language arts skills (the ability to communicate their reasoning skills). This determination can be made through a class discussion of the assessment and results, and/or in individual student conferences.

➤ There is also the possibility that the assessment tool did not match the preferred communication mode of the students who wrote less than satisfactory stories.

Some students may have preferred to create an accurate radio/TV news report, rather than to write a story. Others may have had more success if they acted out the revised version of the story.

Information from this assessment can impact instructional decisions.

➤ You may wish to further emphasize the concept of fair versus unfair inference when you next teach *Mystery Festival* in the future.

➤ You can use newspaper articles, mysteries, or crime shows to discuss whether the evidence presented is sufficient to reach a fair inference.

➤ Students can design their own stories or scenarios to illustrate the concept.

➤ You can revisit the concept of fair versus unfair inference through other GEMS activities. This concept is emphasized in *Mystery Festival, Animals in Action,* and *Investigating Artifacts* and is also a common theme in language arts and social studies.

➤ Students may need further practice to develop sound journalism skills in order to fully succeed on this assessment task.

Animals In Action

Other Assessment Opportunities in GEMS Using Reflections

Here are some other assessment opportunities in GEMS that use the assessment strategy of reflections. Use this list to find specific opportunities and to inspire you to create your own uses of this assessment strategy.

➤ *ACID RAIN*
In a Going Further activity at the end of this unit, students write a story about a fictional region called Lake County. The teacher supplies students with a map that includes lakes and their pH's. Students' stories must explain why each lake has a certain pH. While students are encouraged to be creative, their stories must take into account the system of variables which determines lake pH.

In Session 8, students pretend they are the president and share their personal solution to the problem of acid rain. After their plans have been presented and discussed, students have an opportunity to critically assess the solutions and decide which they would choose. Students can also write about the solution they feel is best, explain their reasoning, and describe how they would modify that plan in response to other ideas.

➤ *BUBBLE FESTIVAL*
In the Closure: Sharing Discoveries and Writing and Bubbles activities of the guide, students tell, draw, and/or write what they discovered and what new questions they have after they explore a bubble station. The guide suggests that the teacher ask activity-specific questions to allow students to share specific findings from each station in the festival. As students write or tell about their discoveries and questions at various points during the festival, the teacher can observe any increased detail in students' observations.

➤ *BUILD IT! FESTIVAL*
The Architect/Builder activity requires students build a structure with pattern blocks. Then, they write directions for their partner to recreate the structure. The teacher can learn the extent of stu-

dents' ability to use geometric and spatial terms to describe structures clearly.

➤ *BUZZING A HIVE*
Use drawings in the guide and student drawings as the basis for student writing and/or dictation about honeybee life and natural history.

➤ *COLOR ANALYZERS*
The suggested questions in Session 4 are designed to help your students "reflect" on what they've learned so far, and discover how people perceive color. By listening to their responses, the teacher can determine how well the students have understood that all colors originally come from light sources, and that the reason an apple appears red is because it reflects only red, and absorbs all other colors.

➤ *CRIME LAB CHEMISTRY*
Show students a chromatogram made from black ink. Ask them to explain how it was made, where the colors come from, what the colors are, and what the colors tell us. Show a second chromatogram made from the same substance that looks similar but has differences. Explain that this is a chromatogram of the same ink, but made by a different person. Ask students to explain how two chromatograms of the same ink could have different appearances.

➤ *FINGERPRINTING*
In the Going Further activity for Session 3, students are invited to write newspaper articles about the crime, draw pictures, and create stories about each of the suspects. Teachers can ask half of the students to write their stories based on evidence, where any inference made is qualified. The other half of the class can be asked to write their stories for a tabloid newspaper, where evidence is secondary and wild inferences are welcome. Selected articles can then be read aloud, and the class can determine whether the article is based mostly on evi-

dence or mostly on unfair inference. Individual papers and class discussion provide the "evidence" on which the teacher can assess students' ability to distinguish factual evidence from unfair inference.

➤ *FROG MATH*
In the Going Further activity after the Hop to the Pond game, students write their thoughts about which frog is most likely to win the race. This activity can be used to assess students' understanding of probability and to observe how they apply their knowledge of probability to formulate a winning strategy.

Present students with the rules to a simple game, such as Tic-Tac-Toe. Ask them to write about whether they would want to go first, or second, and why.

➤ *GLOBAL WARMING*
AND THE GREENHOUSE EFFECT
As a class project, have your students create a newsletter that discusses what is known and what is controversial about global warming, and what all citizens need to know about this important topic.

In the first activity, the students list the information they know and the questions they have about the greenhouse effect. Their lists provide insight into the prior knowledge that students bring into the classroom. At the end of the unit, review the list with the students and have them comment on what ideas have changed, or what questions they have answered.

➤ *GROUP SOLUTIONS*
As a pre-assessment in the Bear Line-Up section, students place themselves in a line according to specific directions. The teacher can use this activity to assess students' understanding of directional and spatial vocabulary.

➤ *IN ALL PROBABILITY*
After the Penny Flip activity, students are asked to predict what they think would happen if a penny were flipped 100 times. Students articulate their predictions and reason in writing. The teacher gains insight into the students' ability to generalize from previous information.

At the conclusion of the Native American Game Sticks activity, students write about the game results in the context of what they know about probability. They are encouraged to extend the results of the two-stick and four-stick game to analyze the six-stick game. The teacher will notice the level of sophistication in the students' thinking about the patterns of probability as they relate to this game.

➤ *INVESTIGATING ARTIFACTS*
Have students select two of their favorite stories, legends or myths. In a brief essay, students should state at least two inferences about the culture of the people who originated each story. Students can also discuss ways the stories are similar and different.

In All Probability

➤ *MAPPING ANIMAL MOVEMENTS*
Students can view videos of animal research, such as the movie, "Never Cry Wolf," or the 1987 National Geographic Special, "The Grizzlies." Discuss how their own investigations compare with the research methods used in the videos.

➤ *MAPPING FISH HABITATS*
At the end of Sessions 3 and 4, teams are asked to analyze their maps and to relate to the physical structures that have evolved in fish to adapt them to their habitat. For example, catfish have feelers and are flat on the bottom. These structures enable them to gather food from the bottom of the tank. The teacher should listen for other evidence that the students understand how fish are adapted to their environment.

➤ *MYSTERY FESTIVAL*
Session 5, Solving the Mystery, offers the teacher three options to have students evaluate their findings and attempt to solve the mystery. To assess students' abilities to think logically and distinguish evidence from inference, listen carefully to the reasons they use to support their conclusions. If no written work is involved, teachers may need to interview students to discern the reasons why they believe a particular suspect is guilty.

➤ *OF CABBAGES AND CHEMISTRY*
Ask students to reflect on and then write about the least powerful acid and the most powerful acid they know. Have them explain why that particular acid is most powerful (or not) and the ways each acid can be useful.

➤ *PAPER TOWEL TESTING*
Students evaluate the advertising claims from magazine or television ads. They suggest experiments that should be done to test those claims. This activity provides the teacher with another opportunity to observe students' abilities to identify unfair tests and design fair tests.

➤ *QUADICE*
After the students have had ample chance to play the game, ask them to write about their strategies. You may want to give the whole class the same set of simulated dice rolls, and ask individuals to discuss what they might do to combine the numbers to win, depending on whether they were the adder, subtracter, or divider. Ask students to share their strategies with one another.

➤ *RIVER CUTTERS*
Have students write a paragraph about a river area they have visited. Students should be able to mobilize vocabulary used throughout the unit to describe river and geologic features. After they have finished their descriptions, students can compare their own river model with the real river area.

Mapping Fish Habitats

Game Playing as an Assessment Strategy

Some books and articles about science and mathematics have referred to the these entire enterprises as games. From a certain point of view, this is a very insightful way of thinking about what scientists and mathematicians do. First, professional scientists and mathematicians have a fervor for what they do. They are as involved and intent on what they are doing as a chess master in the middle of a tournament, or children playing in a playground. Just as in game playing, in science and mathematics there is a quest, whether it be to find a cure, detect a pollutant, formulate a proof, or decode a system. Second, scientists and mathematicians form teams that sometimes compete with each other in being the first to make new discoveries, or to test each others' results. And third, scientists and mathematicians "play" according to a certain set of rules, such as the need for conclusions to be based on evidence, and for experiments/findings to be repeatable by others.

If we can involve our students in playing science and math games, we will be able to tap into that level of total involvement and interest that we see in professional scientists, and that we see in our students during recess and lunch break. If students are having a great time applying concepts and methods in math and science, they will be quicker at grasping new ideas and merging what they learn in science and math classes with everyday life.

Game playing is also excellent as an assessment strategy because skills and knowledge are vividly revealed when students participate in mathematics and science games. For most students, games are less intimidating and more engaging than formal tests or oral and written presentations. Students can:

- Play a game based on GEMS activities.

- Formulate, articulate, and revise strategies for winning a game.

- Evaluate a game and explore the impact of rule and design modifications.

- Participate in a simulation that replicates a mathematical or scientific concept or phenomenon.

- Create a game that incorporates information gained from a math or science unit.

Students use a variety of mathematical and scientific processes when they play games. Games from GEMS guides require students to:

- Sort and classify.

- Create models to explain a concept.

- Use mathematical and scientific knowledge to make predictions and solve problems.

- Predict the likelihood that certain results will occur.

- Demonstrate techniques to collect evidence.

- Evaluate evidence and make conclusions.

- Develop and describe specific logical steps or strategies to successfully reach the goals for the game.

- Synthesize information to develop extensions for games.

A case study using game playing as an assessment strategy in *Frog Math* begins on the next page. Opportunities for game-playing assessments in other GEMS units are on page 90.

Frog Math

Button Treasure Hunt from *Frog Math*

During the first three sessions of *Frog Math*, students describe, sort, and classify buttons as well as other objects. In Session 3 of the guide, students create "designer buttons" from a template with a variety of shapes. They select a shape and decorate their buttons. Then, they punch one to four holes in the button and write their names on the back of their creations.

To assess students' ability to use attributes to describe their buttons, your class can embark on a Button Treasure Hunt. To play the game, provide students with index cards or lined paper and ask them to write words or sentences to describe their buttons. Then, collect the buttons and place them in a central area of the classroom or post them on a bulletin board.

Collect the index cards and redistribute them to the students. Challenge them to find the button described on the card. When students think they have found a particular button that matches the description, they can check with the classmate whose name appears on the back of the button. If the description for the button is unclear, the designer and the searcher can meet together to think of words they could add to the card.

Frog Math

Q What do I want to see?

The Button Treasure Hunt provides students with an opportunity to demonstrate their ability to accomplish the following.

➤ Follow a series of directions.

➤ Design a button with one, two, three, or four holes.

➤ Use multiple attributes (shape, color, size, number of holes, decorative pattern) to create an accurate written description of their button.

➤ Match a written description with visual information to identify a particular button.

➤ If necessary, work with a partner to identify additional information that would improve the description of a button.

Q How do I evaluate the student work?

The following second grade samples represent a typical range of the many student responses we reviewed from the Button Treasure Hunt game. Students enjoyed the game, and varied greatly in their ability to produce a written description of their buttons. Also, students used different techniques to describe their buttons.

To evaluate the samples, we created a simple checklist with a list of attributes that students could use to describe their button. If an attribute was mentioned, the box was checked. The most vivid descriptions included a variety of attributes. Not coincidentally, a button was most easily located when multiple attributes were included in the student's written description.

My button has 4 holes.
It has red on it.
It is triangle.
My button has blue.
It has a littile bit of pink.

| SHAPE ■ | COLOR ■ | PATTERN ☐ | HOLES ■ | SIZE ☐ |

This student's button is easily identifiable because of the variety of colors that are mentioned.

My Speshol Button

I bib had wrc
I crib had as I cud
to mec It bifrit.

"I did hard work. I tried as hard as I could to make it different."

| SHAPE ☐ | COLOR ☐ | PATTERN ☐ | HOLES ☐ | SIZE ☐ |

This student's poignant writing ("I did hard work. I tried as hard as I could to make it different.") shows that she needs additional support to develop and use attribute vocabulary to describe her button.

My Button is cobrful.
It is Nice, I like
it it is good!

SHAPE ☐   COLOR ☒   PATTERN ☐   HOLES ☐   SIZE ☐

This student describes his positive feelings about his button but only includes one detail about its physical features.

My botten has
① thriteen holes.
② Looks Like the world
③ is a circle
④ yellow, blue, green, pink.
ornage, Light blue.

SHAPE ☒   COLOR ☒   PATTERN ☒   HOLES ☒   SIZE ☐

This student describes her button with great detail in an organized list. Her button is readily identifiable in part because she was one of few students who did not comply with the limit of four punched holes!

MY _____ button.

my _____ **is** _____ **a** _____ **triagle**

my _____ **button** _____ **has** _____ **stripeds.**

my _____ **button** _____ **dots.**

My _____ **buton** _____ **has** _____ **to** _____ **holes.**

SHAPE ■ COLOR ☐ PATTERN ■ HOLES ■ SIZE ☐

This student includes a variety of details in her description. Although she did not include information about the color of her button, it was easy to find because of its unique shape and its stripes.

iT isq ▢

iT hoes 4 ∞

iT'S Big

This IS WhaT

iT Kookslike

SHAPE ■ COLOR ☐ PATTERN ■ HOLES ■ SIZE ■

In the above sample and in the following two samples, pictorial clues were essential to the students' descriptions of their buttons. The first two samples include a variety of details and the last description is simple, yet complete.

SHAPE ☐ COLOR ■ PATTERN ■ HOLES ■ SIZE ☐

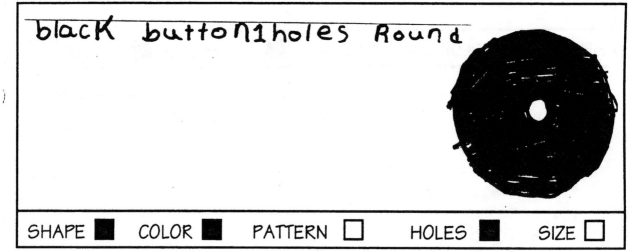

SHAPE ■ COLOR ■ PATTERN ☐ HOLES ■ SIZE ☐

Q What insights have I gained?

The game provided us with valuable evidence about what the students learned in the first three sessions of *Frog Math*. The button descriptions led us to the following conclusions.

➤ Many students were unable to fully describe their button so it could be identified by someone else. These students need additional support to develop and use attribute vocabulary.

➤ Some students did not recognize that they were writing for an intended audience (their classmates). Therefore, their descriptions were highly personal and did not include clues to help someone find their button.

➤ The samples revealed spelling and grammatical errors that may need further attention. However, these errors are common in Grade 2 and,

in most cases, did not interfere with the basic elements of the message.

The above evidence might lead to the following instructional decisions.

➤ It would be helpful to model the game with the entire class before they work individually. The game could be played first with a small group of buttons. Students could provide oral descriptions that lead to the identification of a particular button.

➤ An Attribute Word Bank can be developed and continued through Sessions 1, 2, and 3 of the guide. On butcher paper or sentence strips in a pocket chart, teachers and students can list words that describe buttons. The word bank might look like the chart on the top of the next page.

WORDS TO DESCRIBE BUTTONS

round	big	one	orange	red	stripes
square	small	two	yellow	blue	hearts
triangle	hole	three	black	green	stars
oval	holes	four	pink	purple	

➤ To assure all students feel successful during the game, teachers can have students work in pairs to trade their button descriptions. Partners can exchange feedback as to whether the buttons are accurately described and make suggestions for revisions. Students can then revise their writing with their partner's comments in mind.

Frog Math

Other Assessment Opportunities in GEMS Using Game Playing

Here are some other assessment opportunities in GEMS that use the assessment strategy of game playing. Use this list to find specific opportunities and to inspire you to create your own uses of this assessment strategy.

➤ *ACID RAIN*

Students can write a response to one or more of the questions that arise from the Startling Statements game.

➤ *BUILD-IT FESTIVAL*

In Cooking with Pattern Blocks, students can write a "recipe" for pattern block "delicacies," and challenge a classmates to recreate the shape from the recipe.

Students reach into the Feel-y Box, touch a shape, and guess what shape it is.

➤ *BUBBLE-OLOGY*

Play Predict-A-Pop, where students invent a method for counting down, to the second, when their bubbles will pop.

➤ *FINGERPRINTING*

Play Guess Whose Thumb! game. The teacher secretly makes a copy of a student's thumb and then invites the class to ask "yes" or "no" questions to see if the thumb print is theirs.

➤ *FROG MATH*

Students can play Guess the Sort game in which they sort buttons or natural materials and record their method of classification. They then observe other groups and guess how their classmates sorted their buttons.

➤ *GROUP SOLUTIONS*

Play Stand Up! Sit Down! in which students stand up and sit down according to attributes named by their classmates.

To accompany the activities from the Maps section, each group hides a treasure in the classroom and makes a map of the room with clues to the location of the treasure. Classmates from other groups use the map to find the treasure.

➤ *IN ALL PROBABILITY*

This GEMS unit is filled with games, along with opportunities and suggestions to modify the rules to make a game more or less fair.

➤ *INVESTIGATING ARTIFACTS*

Students can play Guess the Sort game in which they sort buttons or natural materials and record their method of classification. They then observe other groups and guess how their classmates sorted their buttons.

➤ *LADYBUGS*

Students can go on a Symmetry Hunt to find symmetrical objects in the classroom or at home.

➤ *OF CABBAGES AND CHEMISTRY*

In Session 2, students play a game called Presto Change-O in which they attempt to change all the chemicals in their reaction trays to green and then to pink.

Following Sessions 1 and 2, students can play the Acid and Aliens from Outer Space game in which they apply their knowledge of acids, bases, and neutralization to save a friend—an invisible alien from outer space.

➤ *QUADICE*

Students can extend the game to add new rules; or, they can create their own mystery puzzles.

Pre–Post Testing as an Assessment Strategy

When students are tested at the end of a unit, teachers find out who understands the concepts and who doesn't. However, a final test does not provide information about what students have learned over the course of the unit. A student who did very well on the culminating test may have understood the concepts before the unit began, and thus did not actually learn anything new. On the other hand, a student who performed less well may have started out with misconceptions that were substantially changed during the unit.

If students are assessed in a similar manner before *and* after the unit, teachers can measure what the students learned, not just what they know at a fixed point in time. This information can be very useful in curriculum planning. The results of pre-post testing can help teachers determine what to emphasize during the unit, or what methods of teaching are most effective.

For example, many students directly associate global warming with the "hole" in the ozone layer. If a pretest indicates that many of your students had labored under this false impression, then you would want to emphasize distinguishing these separate phenomena when you present the activities. The post-test would indicate how fully students integrated the new knowledge and reevaluated their previous misconception.

It is tremendously valuable to start a new unit by finding out what your students know or have heard, and what they wonder about a topic. At the end of a unit, students can modify and expand these initial lists and develop questions for future exploration. Together, these two activities create an effective pre-post testing assessment. The students' assumptions and questions helps us as teachers plan the implementation of the unit. The students' initial statements and questions can be compared to their later views to map the evolution of their knowledge and curiosity.

Pre-post testing can be used with many activity-based math or science units. This tool helps students participate more consciously in the process of con-structing their own knowledge as they expand, correct, and modify preconceptions. It also provides an insightful measurement of what was learned in a unit.

There are a variety of techniques for pre-post testing assessment.

- Ask students to write down what they know about a given topic before the unit begins, and to list what they'd like to find out. At the end of the unit, ask them to respond to the same questions. When you compare the two assignments, you will see evidence of growth in your students' knowledge about the subject. Students who have difficulty with written expression can dictate their thoughts to an adult or more fluent classmate.

- Students can record their predictions, and then evaluate their hypotheses after the experiment is completed. They can compare their earlier thoughts with what they now know as a result of the experiment.

- A questionnaire can be designed to assess key concepts that are emphasized during the unit. The questions you choose can be focused or open-ended. Administer the survey before and after the unit to determine changes in students' perceptions about the topic.

Case studies using two of the above techniques for pre-post testing assessment are on the following pages. A case study of having students write down what they know of a topic before and after the *Acid Rain* unit begins on the next page. A case study using a questionnaire in *Earth, Moon, and Stars* begins on page 102. Opportunities for pre-post testing assessments in other GEMS units are on pages 110–111.

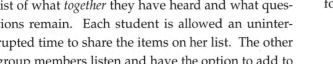

CASE STUDY USING PRE–POST TESTING
Pick Your Brain from *Acid Rain*

Students write individual lists of what they've heard about acid rain and what they wonder about the topic. Next, they participate in a Mind Swap, activity where they work in small groups to compile a list of what *together* they have heard and what questions remain. Each student is allowed an uninterrupted time to share the items on her list. The other group members listen and have the option to add to their lists as they gain new information. After all group members have shared, they discuss the information. Additional questions are also posed and recorded.

A class list is compiled in a round robin manner, as groups take turns to report one "fact" that their group has heard about acid rain. The information is listed on a large sheet of paper. Students are asked to find and discuss contradictory information or information that is controversial. Lastly, a class list of questions about what they wonder about acid rain is compiled.

In subsequent sessions, these lists are revisited and modified to accurately reflect the new information students have gained. In the last session, Everything You've Always Wanted to Know About Acid Rain, the lists are revised as students have a last opportunity to add to and modify the lists of class knowledge and questions. Teachers may choose to have students reflect individually about acid rain at this time and/ or at other points in the unit.

Throughout the process, teachers emphasize that this method is how scientists actually begin an investigation. Scientists must find out what is already known in order to figure out what to investigate next, and how to do it. Scientists' knowledge changes and evolves as they learn more about the world—sometimes something they once thought to be true is discovered to be false. Scientists have many questions, too. It is their job to wonder, reflect, and reevaluate!

Q What do I want to see?

Through this activity, you will gain important information about:

➤ Students' prior knowledge about acid rain.

➤ Students' curiosity about acid rain, and the aspects of the topic they would like to explore.

➤ Students' concerns about acid rain, and the level of emotional response that may be clouding their understanding.

➤ Students' ability to deal with controversy and disagreement in science.

➤ Students' ability to revise and expand their knowledge as they gain new information that may contradict their initial assumptions about a subject.

Q How do I evaluate the student work?

The following responses from seventh grade students created a pre-post test that demonstrates how they expanded and modified their knowledge about acid rain over the course of the unit. On the first session of the unit (May 11) and the last session (May 25), students recorded information about what they had heard about acid rain and what they wondered about the topic.

The students' pre-knowledge ("What We've Heard") and questions ("What We Wonder") have been sorted in two general categories.

➤ How acid rain forms, what it is composed of, and where it occurs.

➤ The effects of acid rain.

Of course, there are other ways to classify students' statements. Some teachers opt to have students organize the lists themselves.

What We've Heard About How Acid Rain Forms, What It's Composed Of, and Where It Occurs

MAY 11

→ Acid rain is not regular rain.

→ It comes from the sky.

→ It is usually just rain with acid in it.

→ I've heard that acid rain is green.

→ I heard it was brown.

→ Acid rain is full of pollution and is poisonous.

→ Acid rain has water vapor in it.

→ Acid rain is a mixture of water and CO_2.

→ Acid rain forms from pollution.

→ Smog creates it.

→ A mixture of vapor and pollution.

→ It comes from chemicaled pollution.

→ Acid rain is a polluted chemical evaporating into cloud.

→ Acid rain is collected in the clouds.

→ Acid rain is a dangerous chemical.

→ Acid rain occurs often on Venus.

What We've Heard About How Acid Rain Forms, What It's Composed Of, and Where It Occurs

MAY 25

→ Normal rain is a little bit acid.

→ A little acid in rain is good.

→ Normal rain and acid rain look the same.

→ They call rain "acid" if it is more acid than normal rain—has a pH below 5.6.

→ Not all acid rain has the same amount of acid in it.

→ Sometimes rain is really acid, esp. in smoggy places like L.A.

→ Even in L.A., sometimes rain has a lot of acid in it and sometimes not.

→ There is acid fog and acid snow, too.

→ Acid rain forms from a chemical reaction when air pollution reacts with moisture and sunlight.

→ Acid rain is made high in the atmosphere in the clouds where air pollution collects.

→ The air pollution that makes acid rain comes from car exhaust and from factories and power plants.

→ Not all air pollution makes acid rain—it's mostly from chemicals called SOx and NOx.

→ Air pollution made in Ohio can blow over the border to Canada and become acid rain there.

→ Acid rain is not new—it was made in prehistoric times by volcanoes.

→ These days there is way more acid rain than in the old days.

→ If we made less air pollution, there would be less acid rain.

What We've Heard About How Acid Rain Forms; What It's Composed Of, and Where It Occurs

MAY 11

Students' initial comments reveal much about their preconceptions about the nature of acid rain and how it forms. For example, there is a very general and vague understanding that acid rain is not normal; that it is somehow connected to pollution; and that it affects the water cycle. The details of how acid rain is formed, what it is, and where it occurs are not understood. There is the common misconception that acid rain happens by proximity—where acid pollution just mixes with rain or clouds and that makes the rain become acid. In fact, acid rain forms through a chemical reaction.

Students' early responses include references to the process of evaporation; they appear to imply that liquid chemicals are responsible for creating acid rain. This is a misconception. The major chemical contribution to acid rain is gaseous.

The students' statements about acid rain reveal the misunderstanding that acid rain contains water vapor. Their lists also contain several references about the harmful effects of acid rain. There is the very common misunderstanding that acid rain is colored, and an interesting (correct!) note that it occurs on Venus.

MAY 25

By the end of the unit, several major misunderstandings are corrected. Students now realize that normal rain is somewhat acid, and that this slight acidity is beneficial to the environment. They know acid rain is rain with a pH below 5.6. However, their description that acid rain is "rain with acid in it" shows a limited understanding of acids and pH as something that can be added to a substance, rather than as a property of liquids.

Students now recognize that acid rain is formed by a chemical reaction and that this process occurs in the clouds, clarifying where acid rain enters the water cycle. They have also gained the knowledge that acid rain comes from some gaseous pollution, specifically oxides of sulfur and nitrogen, and thus can be transported by the wind. They know that acid rain has always occurred (as it has natural causes as well as human-made causes) but that it is more common recently. This general trend is reflected in the statement that it happens more now "than in the old days." To further explore this assumption, it might be useful to point out that during some periods of "the old days" (such as coal burning times in certain isolated urban areas, such as Pittsburgh or London), there was a great deal of acid rain. Becoming aware that these kinds of extreme deviations can take place, even within larger trends, can be an important breakthrough for students, helping them gain greater understanding of complex situations. Also, in this particular case, it provides students with some hope that changes in what humans do—such as not burning soft coal—can improve the situation.

Acid Rain

What We Wonder About How Acid Rain Forms, What It's Composed Of, and Where It Occurs

MAY 11

→ What is acid rain?

→ Why can't rain be without acid?

→ Why does smog create it?

→ How does smog get into acid rain?

→ Does it cause a chemical reaction in a cloud?

→ How long has it been around?

→ How did it evolve?

→ How far can it travel?

→ Who discovered it?

→ When was it first discovered?

→ When did acid rain first start to rain on Earth?

→ What is acid rain composed of?

→ What chemicals are in acid rain?

→ Is it really green?

→ Is it always green?

→ Where on Earth is the most acid rain?

MAY 25

→ Could acid rain be prevented by seeding the clouds with a base?

→ Would it be possible to blow the air pollution out of the atmosphere, into space, so that it would not cause acid rain on our planet?

→ How do they measure how strong acid rain and acid fog is?

→ How was it found out that acid rain forms in clouds? Did scientists go up in planes to observe and measure what happens there?

What We Wonder About How Acid Rain Forms, What It's Composed Of, and Where It Occurs

May 11

Students' questions such as "How does smog get into acid rain?" and "Does it cause a chemical reaction in a cloud?" reveal clear attempts to understand how smog causes acid rain. These initial responses indicate that students are ready and motivated to understand the connection. Their inquiries also reflect some awareness that everything they have heard may not be true, as indicated by the questions such as "Is it really green?"

May 25

Students' later inquiries reveal a new level of sophistication that clearly connects to knowledge they've gained throughout the unit. For example, when they wonder whether a base could be added to the clouds to neutralize acid rain before it falls to earth, students demonstrated a newly acquired understanding about the relationship between acid rain and the water cycle as well as the fact that bases neutralize acids. These questions also highlight possible areas for further exploration of the topic.

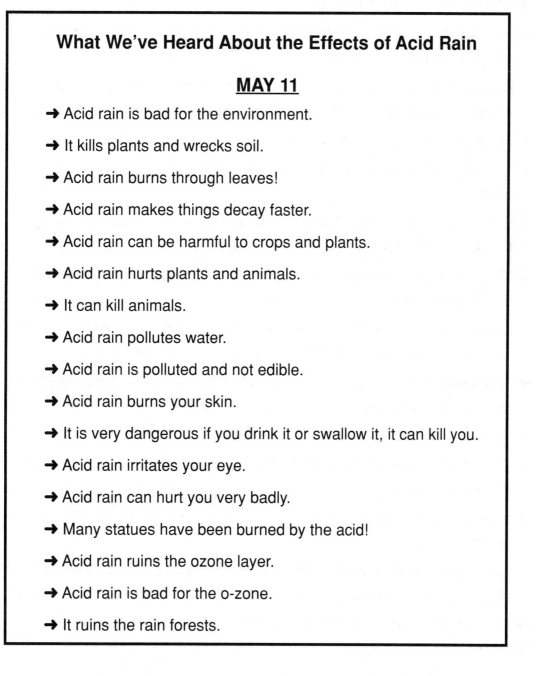

What We've Heard About the Effects of Acid Rain

MAY 11

→ Acid rain is bad for the environment.

→ It kills plants and wrecks soil.

→ Acid rain burns through leaves!

→ Acid rain makes things decay faster.

→ Acid rain can be harmful to crops and plants.

→ Acid rain hurts plants and animals.

→ It can kill animals.

→ Acid rain pollutes water.

→ Acid rain is polluted and not edible.

→ Acid rain burns your skin.

→ It is very dangerous if you drink it or swallow it, it can kill you.

→ Acid rain irritates your eye.

→ Acid rain can hurt you very badly.

→ Many statues have been burned by the acid!

→ Acid rain ruins the ozone layer.

→ Acid rain is bad for the o-zone.

→ It ruins the rain forests.

What We've Heard About the Effects of Acid Rain

MAY 25

→ Acid rain probably does not hurt humans directly but it affects our lives by the effects it has on plants and animals.

→ Acid rain can keep some seeds from sprouting.

→ Acid rain can damage new growth on some plants.

→ Plants that grow in mountains that often have fog can be the worst affected if the fog is acid because the fog touches the leaves for such long periods.

→ Acid rain can cause acid lakes.

→ In a lake that is acid, there can be some parts that are more acid and some parts that are less acid.

→ Animals that live in the water are most affected by acid rain, because they are in constant contact with the acid (if their lake is acid.)

→ Some aquatic animals can survive in more acid than others.

→ Sometimes aquatic animals can survive in acid lakes but they can't reproduce.

→ Some animals die in acid lakes, not because of the acid directly, but because the food they eat has died from the acid.

→ There are some lakes that are considered dead because they have so much acid in them.

→ Some dead lakes have been revived by dumping in buffer but this process is expensive and probably the lakes aren't like they used to be.

→ Lakes surrounded by granite soil become acid the fastest because granite soil has no natural buffer.

→ Acid rain has damaged many statues and dissolves certain kinds of rocks.

→ Certain laws have made cleaner air in some areas which has decreased the amount of acid rain.

→ More cars and more driving has increased the amount of acid rain in some areas.

→ There are a lot of different solutions to the problem of acid rain but not everyone likes the same solutions and most of the solutions cost money.

→ There might be some effects of acid rain that we don't know about yet.

What We've Heard About the Effects of Acid Rain

May 11

The students' initial statements indicate that they have a general understanding that acid rain is harmful. Their responses include a large number of exaggerated and inaccurate statements, which include the statement that acid rain can cause death in humans. There is no indication that the group understands that sometimes rain is "normal," and sometimes acid, or that acid rain can have a whole range of acidity. Students are also unaware that safe or harmful conditions are relative to specific circumstances or organisms—safe for fish? safe for one-cell organisms? safe for humans? In addition, students raise the very common misconception that acid rain connects closely to other environmental problems, from depletion of the rain forests to the thinning of the ozone layer.

May 25

At the end of the unit, much of the information from May 11 has been refined as students now recognize that the effects of acid rain are specific to particular situations. They also have gained an understanding of primary (direct) and secondary (indirect) effects. Their focus has broadened to include the impact of acid rain on aquatic animals and lakes, most likely as a result of the Fake Lakes and Acid Rain Play activities in the unit. The May 25 statements also reflect a much more accurate view of the direct personal risk of acid rain. They express only a few of their initial concerns about the unknown direct effects of acid rain on humans.

By the end of the unit, a new pattern has emerged as students begin to explore solutions to what they see as the problem of acid rain. They have become more aware of differing points of view. Students' lists and subsequent questions show an awareness that the issues may be both scientific and societal, and there are various special interest groups, each with a particular concern and position.

The responses from May 25 pinpoint several areas for further exploration. For example, student responses also indicate a rudimentary understanding that solutions are costly. However, they have minimal awareness that the cost can be levied on one group —those who drive gas-powered vehicles—and yet would ultimately affect everybody in the system—everyone who buys products that were transported by trucks. Students also do not demonstrate an understanding that individual conservation, such as driving less or buying fewer of certain products, would lessen the amount of acid rain. It is possible that this was overlooked or that students did not look extensively at how they could personally help to alleviate the problem.

In addition, students made a few mentions of the effect of acid rain on plants but rarely discussed the impact on soil. This omission poses a logical next step for focus, as the secondary effects on soil can be significant, although perhaps not as captivating as the thoughts of an ailing salamander!

Acid Rain

What We Wonder About the Effects of Acid Rain

MAY 11

→ Does acid rain pollute our environment?

→ Does acid rain go through the water cycle?

→ Does it contaminate the water cycle, like radiation contaminates the food cycle?

→ Does it hurt all plants?

→ What other things, besides plants, does it harm?

→ Does acid rain kill people and animals?

→ Does it hurt animals?

→ Is it bad for concrete?

→ Is it bad for the paint job on cars?

→ How does acid rain harm our earth?

→ What are its long term effects?

→ Could acid rain cause things to mutate?

→ Does acid rain really affect the ozone layer?

→ Can acid rain happen in the rain forests?

→ Has there been acid rain in our city?

→ Can we ever get rid of it?

→ If acid rain burns up statues, why won't it burn us?

→ Will it kill you?

→ I know acid rain wouldn't kill adults, but could it cause death in small children?

→ Could acid rain extinct the human race?

→ If you sit in acid rain would you get sick?

→ Are there any birth defects caused by acid rain?

→ Has it hurt me, but I just haven't known that it has?

→ If the place you live doesn't have acid rain, could you still be affected by other places that do have acid rain?

→ Why isn't the government solving the problem?

→ Why does the government say it is just a theory, if it has been proven in experiments many times?

What We Wonder About the Effects of Acid Rain

MAY 25

→ What are the long term effects of acid rain?

→ How are we sure that it doesn't affect humans directly?

→ Why doesn't our government hurry up and make laws to solve the problem?

→ Even when some laws are made why does it take countries so long to make changes?

→ Shouldn't factories have to tell people that buy the things they make how much acid-rain-making pollution they create?

→ Who should have to pay the cost of solving the problem?

→ Why don't we make the people who cause the pollution pay to clean it up?

→ Why don't we make the people who buy the things that are made by the polluting factories and people who drive cars pay to clean it up?

→ Aren't there some solutions that don't cost so much?

What We Wonder About the Effects of Acid Rain

May 11

Students' initial questions about the effects of acid rain reflect significant concern about the harmful effects of acid rain. Their responses also express some doubts about things they have heard, as reflected by the question: "I know acid rain wouldn't kill adults, but could it cause death in small children?"

In a number of instances, students wonder about how acid rain directly impacts their lives and their environment as well as concern that the problem continues to exist. Given the misunderstandings that students have about acid rain, there is justifiably a great deal of emotional reaction to the problem.

Some of the general questions about the effects of acid rain show sophisticated thought. For instance, students wonder, "Does it contaminate the water cycle, like mercury contaminates the food cycle?" This cues the teacher about a potential misconception—these two situations are not the same—and sets the

scene for a relevant teaching opportunity of contrasting the two situations.

May 25

By the end of the unit, students' questions relate specifically to information they've gained over the course of two weeks. Although a few questions remain about the long term effects of acid rain, many of their prior misconceptions do not appear in their questions.

The May 25 questions reveal that students have made a transition from a misinformed focus on the problem of acid rain to a realistic understanding of the impact of acid rain in different environments and under a variety of conditions. This transformation has enabled students to pose questions about cost effective solutions and who should be responsible to pay the price to clean up the environment. At the end of the unit, the students' responses appear to be less emotionally charged because they are based on fact rather than fear. However, their questions continue to reflect an impatience about the situation, an insistence that the government "hurry up and make laws" so that the problem of acid rain can be solved.

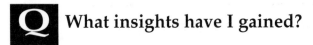

Q What insights have I gained?

Pre-post testing can be a helpful tool to shape student-centered instruction. As teachers gain insight into students' preconceptions and questions about acid rain at the beginning of the unit, we are able to improve and hone our instruction to address their misconceptions and gaps in knowledge. We also find out what students would like to learn about a particular topic, and thus, are able to focus the unit on their information, interests, and concerns. We can adjust our plans as we pay close attention to what students know at various points during the unit.

For example, students' preconceptions about acid rain indicate a great deal of fear that the condition will personally harm them. While the problem of acid rain is indeed serious, one of the major goals of the unit is to assist students to understand that there are possible solutions, and in general, to empower them as they evaluate environmental issues. As we recog-

nize and address emotional and highly personal issues, it is also extremely important to help students work through these fears to improved understanding.

At the end of a unit, students can formally update their information and questions. Through this process, students become aware that their views will change as they construct new knowledge about a topic. They recognize that learning is a lifelong process. To support this crucial understanding, teachers can ask students to reflect on their misconceptions, pinpoint the modifications they made, and highlight what new information they've acquired.

Finally, students' questions can inform future instruction and ideas for student-conducted investigations. For instance, students might choose to investigate: the effect of acid rain on the painted surface of a car; whether wood smoke from fireplaces contributes to acid rain; or to inquire about the extent of gas emissions from several local industries.

CASE STUDY USING PRE-POST TESTING

What Are Your Ideas About the Earth? from *Earth, Moon, and Stars*

A pre-post test can be particularly useful in conjunction with the *Earth, Moon, and Stars* GEMS guide. Several research studies have shown that students typically have many misconceptions about the Earth's shape and gravity. When asked what shape the Earth is, most students say "the Earth is round." However, further questioning reveals that most students in upper elementary school state something quite different from what the teacher assumes they are thinking.

Some students believe the Earth is round like a plate or record, so it looks round when they look down on it, but it looks like a disk when seen from the side. Other students think the round Earth is up in the sky, where astronauts travel. They maintain that we live on the flat Earth. Some say that the ball-shaped Earth consists of two parts: the bottom part of the ball, made of dirt and rocks; and the top part of the ball, which is the sky. These students believe we live on the flat part in the middle. Some students, whose ideas are

closer to the modern scientific view, understand that the Earth is shaped like a ball, but they assume that people live just on top of the ball because people on the bottom would fall off.

The questionnaire on the next page is a central component of Activity 2 in the *Earth, Moon, and Stars* GEMS guide. The guide suggests that students first complete the questionnaire individually. They then discuss the questions in small groups before they convene as a whole class. To use the questionnaire as a pre-post assessment device, collect the students' papers after they have written their answers individually; then proceed with the activities in the entire guide. Finally, distribute the questionnaire after the unit is completed. To determine how much their ideas change over time, you can give them the post-test questionnaire a month or more after they have finished the unit rather than immediately following it.

WHAT ARE YOUR IDEAS ABOUT THE EARTH?

QUESTION 1: Why is the Earth flat in picture #1 and round in picture #2?
(Circle the letter in front of the best answer.)

A. They are different Earths.

B. The Earth is round like a ball, but people live on the flat part in the middle.

C. The Earth is round like a ball, but it has flat spots on it.

D. The Earth is round like a ball but looks flat because we see only a small part of the ball.

E. The Earth is round like a plate or record, so it seems round when you're over it and flat when you're on it.

QUESTION 2: Pretend that the Earth is glass and you can look through it. **Which way would you look, in a straight line, to see people in far-off countries like China or India?**

A. Westward? **B.** Eastward? **C.** Upward? **D.** Downward?

QUESTION 3: This drawing shows some enlarged people dropping rocks at various places around the Earth. **Show what happens to each rock by drawing a line showing the complete path of the rock, from the person's hand to where it finally stops.**

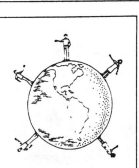

Why will the rock fall that way?

QUESTION 4: Pretend that a tunnel was dug all the way through the Earth, from pole to pole. Imagine that a person holds a rock above the opening at the North Pole, and drops it. **Draw a line from the person's hand showing the entire path of the rock.**

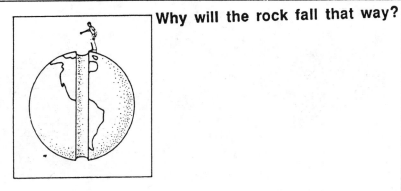

Why will the rock fall that way?

What do I want to see?

In *Earth, Moon, and Stars*, students find patterns in the sky, and then construct models to explain the patterns that they see. They observe the daily movement of the sun, phases of the moon, and the regular motions of the constellations. To explain their observations, students construct concrete models with objects such as Styrofoam balls, lamps, and their own bodies. They are encouraged to argue and debate the merits of one model over another, and to change their minds when evidence and logical arguments convince them that another model is more accurate. Through this process, students develop critical-thinking skills that are essential for all scientists.

The pre-post questionnaire asks students to select an answer and then to explain their reasoning. The assessment illuminates students' perceptions about the earth and the information they use to support their beliefs, both before and after the unit.

When students work as a community of scientists, most eventually come to adopt the modern view of the Earth's spherical shape, with an attractive force of gravity acting towards the center of the Earth. What is more important, however, is that students become aware of what they believe and are better able to justify their conclusions.

How do I evaluate the student work?

On the next page, you will find the sheet Levels of Understanding About the Earth's Shape and Gravity. These levels are based on how students' ideas gradually change from early elementary school through high school and adulthood, although not all adults reach the highest levels. As illustrated in the examples on the following pages, this sheet helps you to characterize your students' levels of understanding of the Earth's shape and gravity.

These seventh grade pretests illustrate a typical range of perceptions that you may find with middle school students, both before and after the unit. Two patterns consistently emerged from the student work. First, many students were able to circle or draw the correct result, but their written explanations revealed a wide range of different ideas about these concepts and a range of communications skills. Second, while most students develop an understanding of the Earth's shape first, and gravity second, a few students appear able to grasp the meaning of gravity before they fully understand we live on a large ball in space.

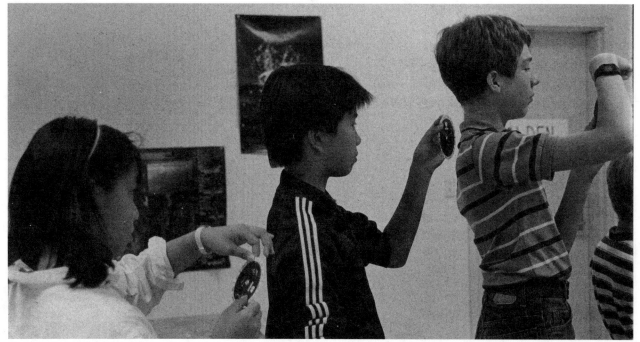

Earth, Moon, and Stars

Levels of Understanding About the Earth's Shape and Gravity

EARTH'S SHAPE		Definition of each level	How to classify answers	Number of students
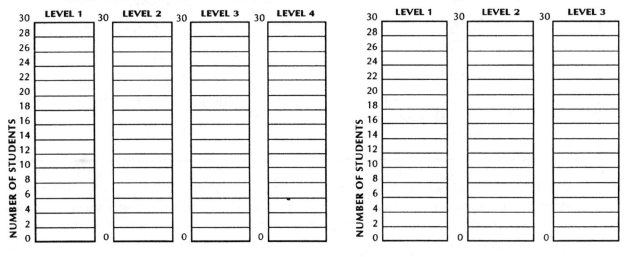	SHAPE LEVEL 4	The Earth is shaped like a ball, and people live all around the ball.	**QUESTION 1:** Answer D and **QUESTION 2:** Answer D.	
	SHAPE LEVEL 3	The Earth is shaped like a ball, but people live just on top of the ball.	**QUESTION 1:** Answer D and **QUESTION 2:** Answers A, B, or C.	
	SHAPE LEVEL 2	The Earth is shaped like a ball, but people live on the flat parts of it (or inside the ball).	**QUESTION 1:** Either answer B or C.	
	SHAPE LEVEL 1	The Earth is flat.	**QUESTION 1:** Either Answer A or E, or no answer at all.	

GRAVITY		Definition of each level	How to classify answers	Number of students
	GRAVITY LEVEL 3	Objects fall toward the *center* of the Earth.	**QUESTION 3:** Rocks are shown falling straight down to the surface of the Earth, near each figure's feet, and **QUESTION 4:** The rock is shown falling toward the Earth's center, where it either falls through and bobs up and down, or stops in the center.	
	GRAVITY LEVEL 2	Objects fall toward the *surface* of the Earth.	**QUESTION 3:** Rocks are shown falling straight down to the surface of the Earth, near each figure's feet, and **QUESTION 4:** The rocks do not end up in the Earth's center. (They may be shown passing all the way through the earth, sticking to the Earth's surface, or taking some other path.)	
	GRAVITY LEVEL 1	Objects fall *down* in space.	**QUESTION 3:** Rocks are *not* shown falling straight down to the surface of the Earth. (They may be falling down to the bottom of the page or shooting at some other angle around the planet.)	

CLASS PROFILE—EARTH'S SHAPE

LEVEL 1 LEVEL 2 LEVEL 3 LEVEL 4

GRAVITY

LEVEL 1 LEVEL 2 LEVEL 3

NUMBER OF STUDENTS

NUMBER OF STUDENTS

JASMINE

➤ **Shape Level 4**
   *The Earth is shaped like a ball and
   people live all around the ball.*

➤ **Gravity Level 3**
   Objects fall toward the center of the Earth.

Jasmine was one of few students who scored at the highest levels on the Earth's shape and gravity scales and is also able to clearly articulate her reasoning. She selected answer **D** for the first question, indicating her belief that "the Earth is round like a ball but looks flat because we see only a small part of the ball." Her correct answer of **D** on Question #2 shows her premise that if the Earth were made of glass, one would look "downward" to see people in far-off countries like China or India.

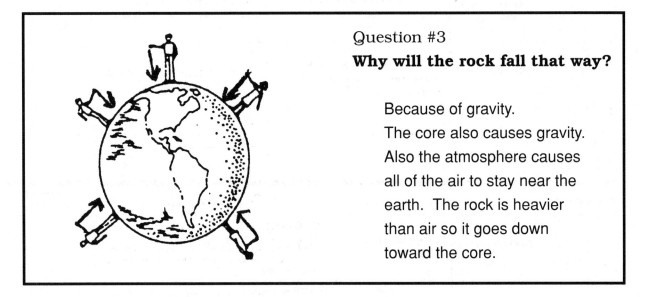

Question #3
Why will the rock fall that way?

Because of gravity.
The core also causes gravity.
Also the atmosphere causes
all of the air to stay near the
earth. The rock is heavier
than air so it goes down
toward the core.

For the third question, she correctly drew rocks that would fall to people's feet all around the world.

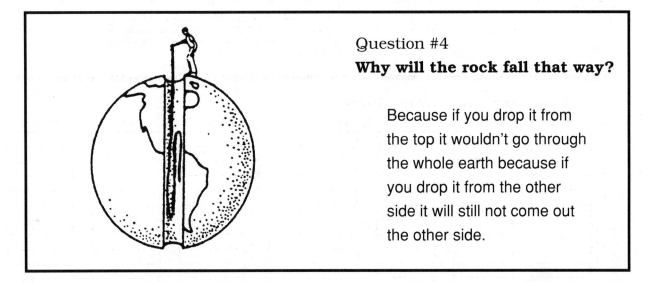

Question #4
Why will the rock fall that way?

Because if you drop it from
the top it wouldn't go through
the whole earth because if
you drop it from the other
side it will still not come out
the other side.

Jasmine offered a sophisticated answer to the last question. Her drawing shows that the rock passes the center of the Earth, then falls back and forth, eventually settling in the middle. Her written explanation is somewhat confusing, but she does indicate she understands that the rocks would fall to the center of the earth, regardless of where they were dropped.

TYRONE

➤ **Shape Level 3**
*The Earth is shaped like a ball but
people live just on top of the ball.*

➤ **Gravity Level 2**
Objects fall toward the surface of the Earth.

This student also selected answer **D** for the first
question, but circled **B** for the second question. He
understood that we live on a ball, but along with many
other children at and beyond the middle school level,
he did not understand where we live with respect to
people in distant countries. It is very difficult to con-
ceptualize that people actually live "down there, under our feet!"

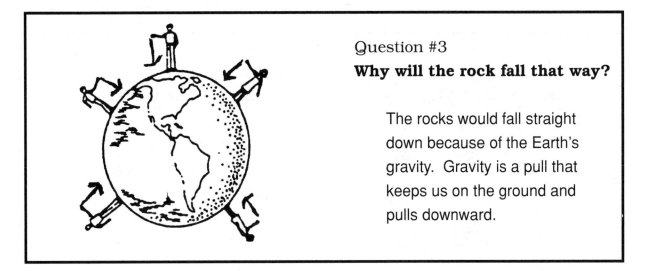

Question #3

Why will the rock fall that way?

The rocks would fall straight
down because of the Earth's
gravity. Gravity is a pull that
keeps us on the ground and
pulls downward.

The student's drawing for question #3 correctly shows rocks falling to each person's feet. His rationale indicates that he thinks of gravity as a pull that keeps us "on the ground." This view of gravity is acceptable, if it relates only to the surface of the Earth. However, the concept is limited because it does not consider that gravity pulls all objects toward the center of the Earth.

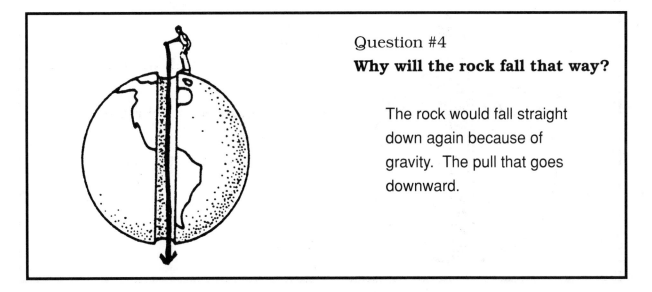

Question #4

Why will the rock fall that way?

The rock would fall straight
down again because of
gravity. The pull that goes
downward.

For the last question, this student returned to his earlier view that gravity is something that pulls "down," regardless of the Earth's shape. Since he does not believe that people live on the other side of the world, there is no conflict between his understanding of the Earth's shape and gravity at this time.

ERIC

➤ **Shape Level 1**
   The Earth is flat.

➤ **Gravity Level 1**
   Objects fall down in space.

This student, and one other in the class, selected answer **E** for the first question: "The Earth is round like a plate or record, so it seems round when you're over it and flat when you're on it." From his point of view the Earth's shape is just as it appears—flat. Like a pancake, the Earth is both round *and* flat. For question #2, the student circled both "Upward" and "Downward" indicating considerable confusion about where he sees himself with respect to other countries on this flat, pancake-shaped Earth.

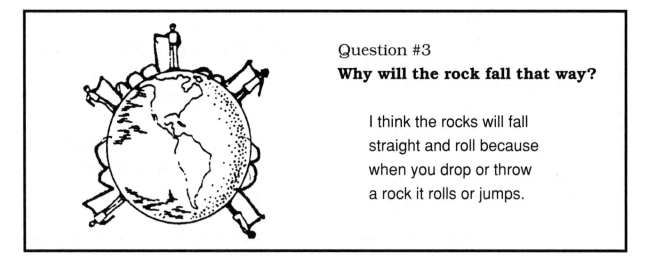

Question #3
Why will the rock fall that way?

I think the rocks will fall
straight and roll because
when you drop or throw
a rock it rolls or jumps.

This student was unable to imagine that the rock would fall to the person's feet and stop. In his unique drawing, the rocks appear to bounce around on the surface of the earth.

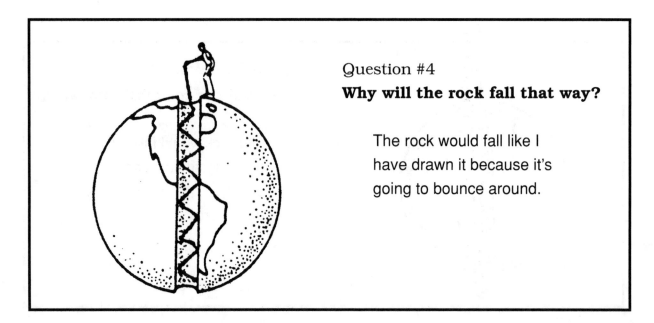

Question #4
Why will the rock fall that way?

The rock would fall like I
have drawn it because it's
going to bounce around.

In the student's writing and drawing for question # 4, he does not take the action of gravity into account inside the Earth, as well as on the surface. The rocks will bounce and roll around, similar to how balls move on Earth.

Q What insights have I gained?

Since it is always administered before instruction begins, the pretest is a valuable tool to help you assess the knowledge that students bring to a particular learning experience. For example, if nearly all of your students have well-developed, correct responses to the pre-assessment, you might want to accelerate the unit, omit selected activities or have students formulate investigations to extend their knowledge.

However, if most of your students have misconceptions or developing perceptions about the Earth's shape and gravity, you will need to provide enough time for them to fully discuss their personal ideas during the class. This will allow them to compare, contrast, and debate different points of view about the four questions, as suggested in *Earth, Moon, and Stars*.

Analysis of the questionnaires can also help you decide in advance where to focus your instruction, in the unit and as it relates to the assessment. If most students have correctly answered questions #1 and #2, you might want to spend more time on the concepts that relate to the drawings in questions #3 and #4. You might find that students can respond to the questions with scientific accuracy but are unable to articulate their rationale. In this instance, you might want to have a debate about whether or not the rock will pass through the center of the Earth as it falls. This will help students clarify and explain their perceptions.

Once the unit is completed, present the same questionnaire again, and compare the results to the pretest. You can analyze the changes in one or more individual student's understanding, or you can create a profile of the entire class, before and after the unit. This will help you understand the instructional strengths of your program, as well as areas where students need further experiences. Here are the results of a fifth grade class with 30 students, before and after the *Earth, Moon, and Stars* unit.

	PRE-TEST	**POST-TEST**
Shape Level 4	10 students	19 students
Shape Level 3	12 students	11 students
Shape Level 2	6 students	0 students
Shape Level 1	2 students	0 students
	PRE-TEST	**POST-TEST**
Gravity Level 3	4 students	24 students
Gravity Level 2	13 students	4 students
Gravity Level 1	13 students	2 students

It is unrealistic to expect that all students will attain the highest levels of understanding. Consider yourself successful if, as in the above classroom, many of the students have changed their ideas, and all are better able to justify their current beliefs. If this is so, the class as a whole will have moved beyond their initial ideas towards higher levels of understanding.

Other Assessment Opportunities in GEMS Using Pre-Post Testing

Here are other assessment opportunities in GEMS that use the assessment strategy of pre-post testing. Use this list to find specific opportunities and to inspire you to create your own uses of this assessment strategy.

➤ *BUILD IT! FESTIVAL*

You could begin the polygon/polyhedra sections in the guide by having students write down all they know about "shapes," including real world examples of shapes. After completing the unit students could come back to their lists and modify them, using the geometric knowledge and terminology they have learned.

➤ *BUZZING A HIVE*

To begin the unit, have students write or dictate a list of what they know about bees and their habitats. At the end of the unit, conduct the same activity with students. The two sets of results will provide evidence of knowledge gained during the unit.

➤ *CHEMICAL REACTIONS*

Before the first session, ask students to carefully describe something. This could be a lemon, a piece of chalk, a pile of flour, Epsom salts, or a substance or object which has many characteristics. Challenge them to use as many senses as they can to create a detailed list of the item's attributes. Assessment can be done before and/or after students have participated in the activities from this guide. Evaluate the detail and quality of students' observations to determine whether students improved their ability to discern and describe properties.

➤ *FINGERPRINTING*

Have students make a print of their own thumbs and write about the patterns they see both before and after doing the unit. Observe how the students' descriptions change and whether they've used new vocabulary.

➤ *FROG MATH*

In Session 6, students tell or write what they know about dice before they play the Hop to the Pond game. From this activity, the teacher can gain a sense of students' knowledge and misconceptions about dice. The teacher can use this information to adjust the lesson so that it is appropriate to the students' developmental level.

➤ *GLOBAL WARMING AND THE GREENHOUSE EFFECT*

This unit begins and ends with students brainstorming what they've heard and what they wonder about the topic.

➤ *GROUP SOLUTIONS*

As a pre-assessment in the Secret Number section, students work with 50's and 100's charts to find, record, and describe number patterns. The teacher can gain information about students' familiarity with patterns and properties of numbers, and their readiness level for the ensuing activities. The teacher could use this activity again at the end of the section to measure students' growth of knowledge as a result of working with the problems in the section.

➤ *HOT WATER AND WARM HOMES FROM SUNLIGHT*

The unit begins with a hypothetical experiment to illustrate how plants grow with different amounts of fertilizer. Questions are posed to reveal students' understanding of controlled experiments. Teachers can ask the same questions after the unit to determine how much students have learned about the characteristics of controlled experiments.

➤ *IN ALL PROBABILITY*

In the Horse Race game, students are asked to predict results of the game, which uses two dice. If students are also asked to provide a rationale for their prediction, the teacher will glean some insight into students' early thinking about this two-dice probability, particularly in light of the preceding section of the book, in which students have used a die. After the activity, have students write a prediction and an explanation for which horses are likely to win the next game. The letter to the jockey—see Letter Writing as an assessment strategy on page 45—can be used as a post-test for this unit.

➤ *INVOLVING DISSOLVING*

During each activity in the unit, students make predictions about what they think will happen when a solid is dissolved in a liquid, and where they think the solid has gone after it disappears. The teacher can observe students' willingness to make predictions/guesses, and whether they become more confident over the course of the unit.

➤ *LADYBUGS*

Before beginning the unit, have children draw a picture of a ladybug. Save their drawings and compare them to a ladybug they make at end of unit.

➤ *LIQUID EXPLORATIONS*

In Activity 1, students play a Guess My Rule classification game. If the activity is repeated at the end of the unit or later in the school year, teachers can look for improvements in students' ability to observe, compare, and classify liquid attributes.

➤ *MYSTERY FESTIVAL*

In an introductory section, A Note About Pre-Teaching, several activities are noted to encourage your students to be active observers and notice small changes. If used as pre- and post-unit assessments, these activities will offer teachers concrete evidence of students' developing observation skills.

➤ *TREE HOMES*

Open the unit by asking children what they know about trees. Record their responses on chart paper. Put it aside until the end of the unit. Then ask children what they know about trees and compare the new list to the old one, or modify the original list based on new knowledge.

Buzzing A Hive

Model Making as an Assessment Strategy

Realizing that the Earth beneath our feet must be supported by something very sturdy, the thinkers of ancient India envisioned the land under our feet was supported on the back of a huge elephant, which in turn was supported on the back of a strong turtle, swimming in a cosmic sea. At a different time and place, thinkers in ancient Greece imagined a different model, in which the land of our experience is a tiny area on a vast sphere.

In one sense, these alternative images of the Earth are very simple. They are ways of thinking about a very complex world in terms of a concrete model that we can imagine holding in our hands. In another sense, they are profound ideas that allow us to imagine what it would be like to see the entire Earth from outside. Although the idea of actually seeing the Earth from space is not unusual today, it must have been an amazing stretch of the intellect for people who lived thousands of years before the dawn of the space age.

Models are simplified representations of the world that enable us to think about it in new ways, to make predictions, and to test our ideas. They allow us to go beyond the world of our everyday experience, and try to grasp the underlying reality. Model making is at the core of the scientific and mathematical world view that originated with the ancient Greeks and flowered in the Renaissance—that numbers and equations, geometric shapes and angles, can help us understand the vast complexity of our everyday experience.

Although the models that students work with in GEMS activities may be simpler and more concrete than those used by professional mathematicians and scientists, they likewise provide students with a way to visualize the world in a deeper way than just looking at it. For example, in the case study which follows, the students create defensive structures on a defenseless animal. As their physical models of the animal take on added dimensions, so does their understanding of the concept of defensive structures.

There are many different kinds of models. A model can help us better understand a phenomenon, system, or process.

Models can be:

- devices
- plans
- drawings
- dioramas and other 3–D presentations
- equations
- computer programs
- mental images
- dramatizations

Models illustrate how things work or might work. Whether they are physical, conceptual, mathematical, or computer-based, models serve invaluable functions to enhance human scientific understanding. Models are essential components of scientific and mathematical inquiry and communication. Math and science practitioners and researchers regularly create models to explain their thinking, illustrate a concept or principle, and visualize solutions or approaches to a problem. However, models can also be misleading and can suggest characteristics, mechanisms, or analogies that do not exist or are inaccurate. Therefore, it is important to realize the limitations of models.

In the GEMS series, students create models to demonstrate their knowledge about how things work or might work; simulate relationships in nature; and describe or illustrate scientific principles, hypotheses, or conclusions. Students' models provide information about their ability to concretely represent their thinking and knowledge. Models provide a picture of the scientific world from the child's perspective. Teachers can evaluate how well students can communicate what they know and what they wonder. Models give students opportunities to organize their thinking as they create the models and use them to communicate ideas.

A case study using model making as an assessment strategy in *Animal Defenses* begins on the next page; another case study of model-making assessment in *Build It! Festival* begins on page 119. Opportunities for model-making assessments in other GEMS units are on page 127.

Make a Defended Animal from *Animal Defenses*

Most young children love to design imaginary animals and use them in dramatic play. The models they create, and the accompanying dramas, provide much information that teachers can use to assess students' understanding. The models often reveal thinking and knowledge that young children are unable to express in writing. The dramas motivate students to express their thoughts within an engaging and nonthreatening context.

In the *Animal Defenses* GEMS guide, children are introduced to a story about an animal that needs to defend itself from *Tyrannosaurus rex*. The class thinks of structures and behaviors that would assist the animal in a face-to-face confrontation with the giant dinosaur!

the defenseless animal

Each child is given a paper animal, paper scraps, scissors, and glue. Students design a "defended" animal as they add horns, claws, teeth, wings, and other features. Each animal then engages in a confrontation with a large *Tyrannosaurus rex* that is featured on an overhead projector. Students show how their animal attempts to protect itself with its new defenses. Children enjoy the storytelling and drama, and explain the uses of each defense verbally and through movement of their model animal.

What do I want to see?

The models and subsequent dramatizations will provide information about the students' ability to do the following.

➤ Apply their knowledge of defensive structures to create a model of a defended animal.

➤ Demonstrate their knowledge and understanding of defensive behaviors through dramatic play.

How do I evaluate the student work?

To evaluate the model and dramatic play, teachers directly observe the children's efforts and ask questions during the process to elicit further description of the structure and functions of the animals' defenses. For example, a teacher might ask, "What's on the back of your animal?" and receive the response, "These are big spines to poke T. rex with!" Listen for descriptive terms as well as an explanation of how the structures will be used. A one-on-one interview may uncover a whole plan for defense: "First he's going to scratch him with the claws, then whip him with the tail, and then fly away!" During the drama, listen for defensive behaviors such as running or flying away, climbing a tree, or staying very still. Again, don't miss those informal opportunities during free play to observe the children using their models in spontaneous storytelling and play acting. Parents, too, are good sources for feedback. Children love taking their creations home to share dramas with family members and friends.

Teachers can write anecdotal notes about each child's model and its role in dramatic play during the unit. The newly defended animals or copies with the teachers' comments can be included in the child's science portfolio. Students can also design multiple creations over the course of a year to serve as indicators of growth and understanding.

The following samples represent a typical range of the many kindergarten and first grade student responses we reviewed for this guide. Animal defenses could include claws, spikes, spines, shields, horns, sharp teeth, or other defensive structures. An analysis of the students' work revealed the following information.

➤ All students were able to create a model of an animal with at least one defensive structure. Some students added multiple defensive struc-

tures to their animals and thought of defensive behaviors as well.

➤ Several students invented defenses that were not discussed during the unit, incorporating defenses from our modern world such as "a little ping-pong thing . . . to shoot out and bonk the other dinosaur that tries to eat it."

➤ All students were able to verbalize that defenses are used to protect the animal, although students explained the defenses with varying degrees of detail.

Individual student's models, as well as their dictated explanations, are on the next few pages.

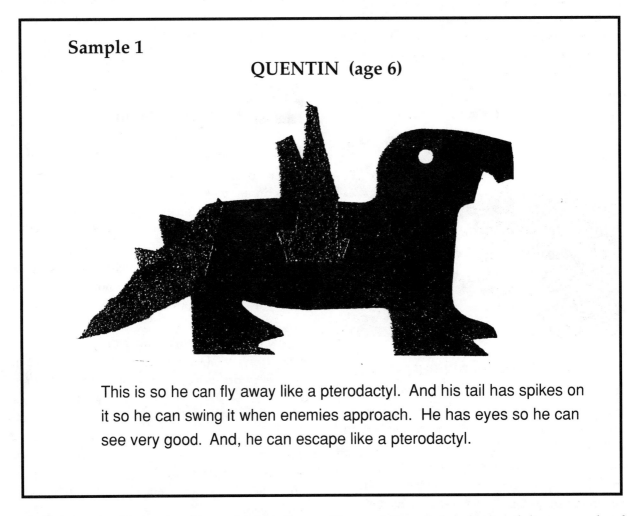

Sample 1

QUENTIN (age 6)

This is so he can fly away like a pterodactyl. And his tail has spikes on it so he can swing it when enemies approach. He has eyes so he can see very good. And, he can escape like a pterodactyl.

Quentin's animal is protected by multiple defenses. He reveals knowledge about real dinosaurs when he adds an actual pterodactyl's defense (wings) to his model. He assumes that if an animal has eyes, it "can see very good." Although Quentin altered the shape of the original animal's head, he did not say why he made the decision to do so.

Sample 2

MAX (age 6)

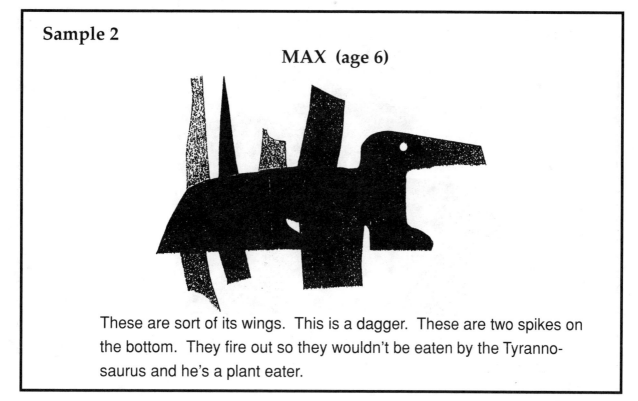

These are sort of its wings. This is a dagger. These are two spikes on the bottom. They fire out so they wouldn't be eaten by the Tyranno-saurus and he's a plant eater.

Max adds an assortment of features to his animal, including a "dagger," which changes the shape of the head. Max's animal has defenses on both top and bottom and he has created spikes that "fire out" at the *Tyrannosaurus rex*. He only discusses the protective purpose of the spikes.

SAMPLE 3

NANA (age 6)

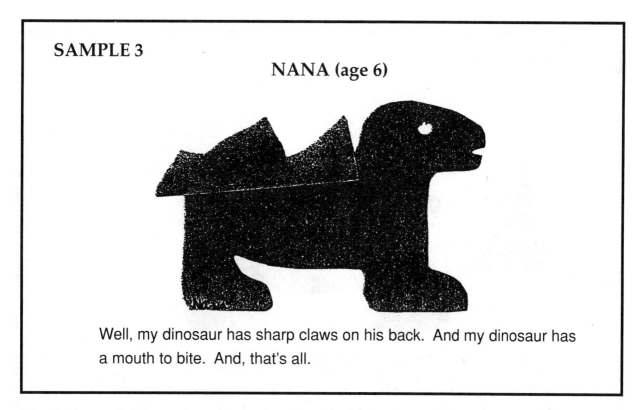

Well, my dinosaur has sharp claws on his back. And my dinosaur has a mouth to bite. And, that's all.

Nana adds two defenses to her animal—sharp claws and a mouth "to bite." Her animal and explanation have few details, but she has met the requirements of the assignment to create a defended creature.

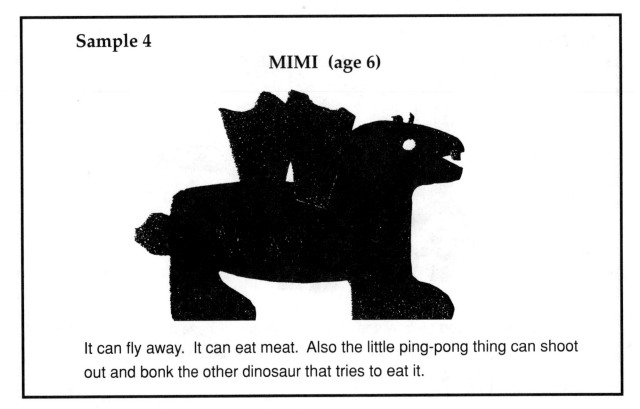

Sample 4

MIMI (age 6)

It can fly away. It can eat meat. Also the little ping-pong thing can shoot out and bonk the other dinosaur that tries to eat it.

Mimi adds wings ("to fly away"), a tail (to shoot out "ping-pong" things), teeth (to "eat meat"?) and head spikes (no explanation) to her animal. Her response indicates that she knows her animal will be prey to a carnivore who will try to eat it.

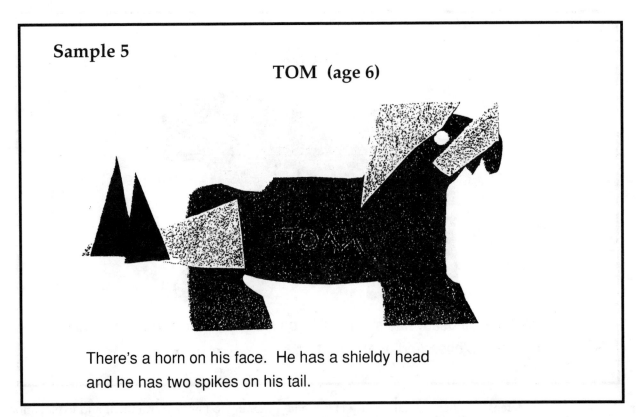

Sample 5

TOM (age 6)

There's a horn on his face. He has a shieldy head and he has two spikes on his tail.

Tom adds a variety of defenses to his animal—a horn, a shield, and two tail spikes. His oral response does not explain the purpose of these defenses or any defensive behaviors his animal might have.

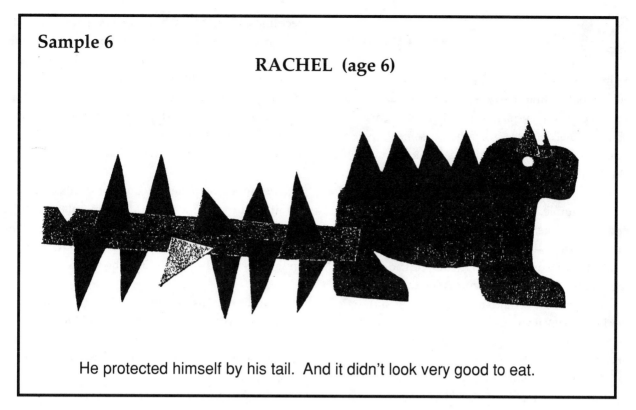

Sample 6

RACHEL (age 6)

He protected himself by his tail. And it didn't look very good to eat.

Rachel adds an elaborate tail and spikes to her animal. Her response implies that the spikes may make her animal an unappealing meal for its predator.

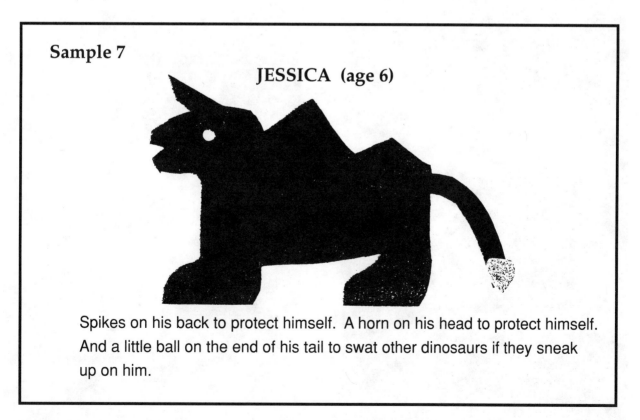

Sample 7

JESSICA (age 6)

Spikes on his back to protect himself. A horn on his head to protect himself. And a little ball on the end of his tail to swat other dinosaurs if they sneak up on him.

Jessica adds multiple defenses to her animal and elaborates on the protective purpose of the "ball on the end of his tail."

What insights have I gained?

Information from this assessment can impact instructional techniques. We recognized that we did not have a complete picture of what the students knew about animal defenses. After the assessment, we identified areas that we could pursue when interviewing children about their animals.

For example, Max tells us that his animal is a plant eater, which may be a reason that the creature does not have sharp teeth. To determine the function of the teeth, we could ask, "Why did you add teeth to the animal?" or "How do you know that the animal is a meat eater?" Nana may have revealed more of her knowledge if we'd asked, "How do the claws protect your animal?" We would have found out more about the origin of Mimi's "ping-pong" defense if we'd inquired where she'd gotten the idea! Jessica mentions twice that her animal has features "to pro-tect himself" and may have spoken more about the predator-prey relationship if we pursued her comment about dinosaurs who might "sneak up on him." Next time, we might ask students to first explain the **defensive structures** their animal has—things on its body that help to defend it. We might ask then what **defensive behaviors** their animal can use—ways it can behave to help defend itself.

The models help identify those students who need additional experience with dramatic play to build their understanding of animal defenses before they are able to make a connection with protective features in today's world—Session 2 of the guide.

In addition, this assessment identifies new words students incorporate into their storytelling and informal conversations. It is a great springboard for future writing on their dinosaur and the predator-prey concept.

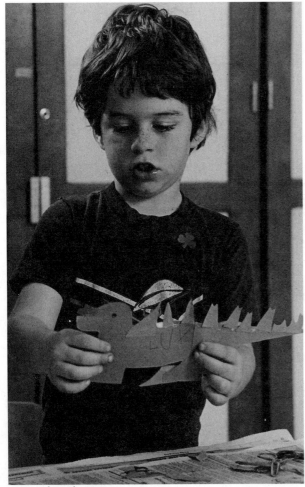

Animal Defenses

Animal Defenses

Constructing Animal Homes from *Build It! Festival*

Elementary school students have numerous opportunities for model-making throughout *Build It! Festival*. The Going Further activity for the Dowel Designs station challenges students to build three-dimensional structures to house stuffed animals. During Dowel Designs, students create two- and three-dimensional structures out of newspaper dowels. Teachers pose questions to guide students to make discoveries about the properties of geometric shapes. For example, young children discover the number of sides on two-dimensional shapes, or the number of faces on three-dimensional shapes. Older students investigate angles and vertices. In addition, students discover what shape provides the most strength and stability as they build larger structures.

Each student is asked to select one plastic or stuffed animal from the classroom or their home. Students discuss their animal's habits, environment, and special needs. Teachers provide an assortment of building materials and provide students with the following instructions.

ANIMAL HOMES

1. Build a home where your animal will live. You can use:
    - Newspaper dowels and tape
    - Straws and clay
    - Toothpicks and peas

2. Your house must be strong and safe for your animal. Be sure that it won't fall down!

3. Your house should be designed so that your animal will be comfortable in it.

4. After you build your home, write some information about it. Be sure to answer the following questions:

    ➤ What shapes did you use?

    ➤ Why did you choose the shapes?

    ➤ What special things did you add to your home for your animal?

Q What do I want to see?

The models and the written responses will demonstrate students' ability to:

➤ Recognize that some two-dimensional shapes are sturdier than others.

➤ Apply their knowledge of structural properties to build a model of a strong and safe animal home.

➤ Integrate their knowledge of animals with their knowledge of geometric constructions to add special features for their particular inhabitant.

➤ Use mathematical language to describe their structure.

➤ Use their knowledge of structural properties to articulate why they selected particular shapes for their animal home.

Q How do I evaluate the student work?

In this assessment, students demonstrate their knowledge through two vehicles—concrete models and written explanations. Teachers can observe students as they construct and modify their models and assess how well they are able to apply the concepts and principles learned through the Dowel Design activities. The construction process will indicate the degree to which students are able to:

➤ Apply prior knowledge in real-life situations.

➤ Distinguish between sturdy and flimsy two-dimensional shapes.

➤ Modify their design based on structural observations.

➤ Adapt their home to the unique characteristics of their animal.

The students' explanations will provide insight into how well they are able to:

➤ Articulate why they selected particular shapes to build their home.

➤ Use mathematical language to describe their structures.

Older students may be able to describe faces, vertices, and angles and articulate that two-dimensional shapes become faces of three-dimensional polyhedra.

The following responses from Grade 3 represent a typical range of student work for this assessment. Students worked in pairs to construct an animal home and write about their structure.

Build It! Festival

SAMPLE 1

In this example, the students are better able to express their knowledge through the concrete model than through their written explanation. The model contains strong evidence that the partners spent a great deal of time to plan and construct an animal home that is sturdy, due to consistent use of triangular shapes. However, their written description mentions only a limited range of both two- and three-dimensional shapes that were selected so the house would be "sturdy."

To build our house we used a lot of triangles, a hexagon, a pyramid, a flag, some letters, some stars, and 6 balconies around the sides. We chose these shapes because they were strong and it would make it sturdy. That is why we picked these shapes. Our house is special because it is very sturdy.

SAMPLE 2

In this example, a clear, step-by-step explanation accompanies a fairly uncomplicated structure. The written description utilizes a range of geometric and spatial vocabulary and a strong rationale for the use of triangular prisms ("it would be strong because triangles are strong"). The structure reveals less knowledge than the more elaborate written work.

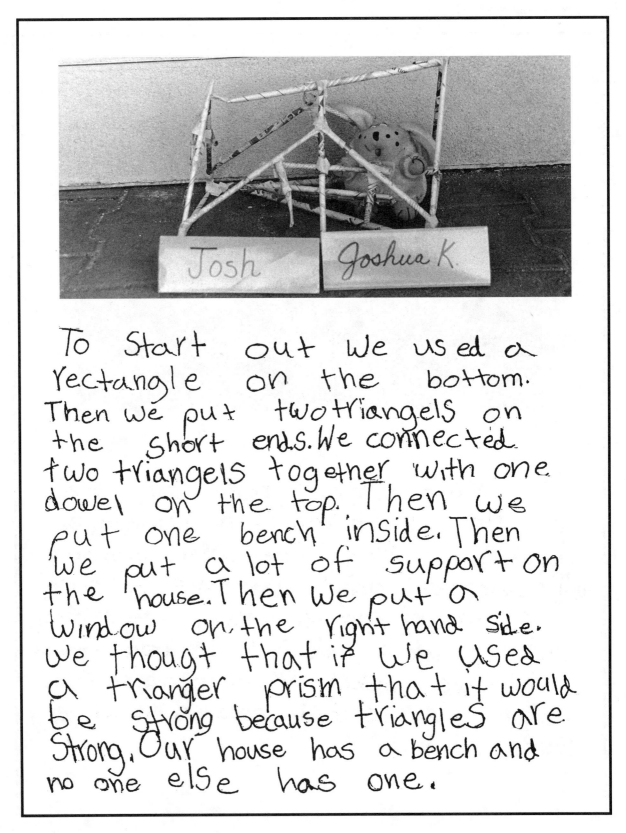

To Start out We used a rectangle on the bottom. Then we put two triangels on the short ends. We connected two triangels together with one dowel on the top. Then we put one bench inside. Then We put a lot of support on the house. Then We put a window on the right hand side. We thougt that if We used a trianger prism that it would be strong because triangles are strong. Our house has a bench and no one else has one.

SAMPLE 3

This two-story structure was clearly the most complex animal home that was built. It includes sitting areas for the two animals and a ladder (not visible in the photo) so the bear can climb up. The students informed us that the bird would fly through the window to get in. The written explanation utilizes standard ("rectangular prism") and nonstandard ("hourglass") geometric vocabulary and provides some detail about the process used to construct the home.

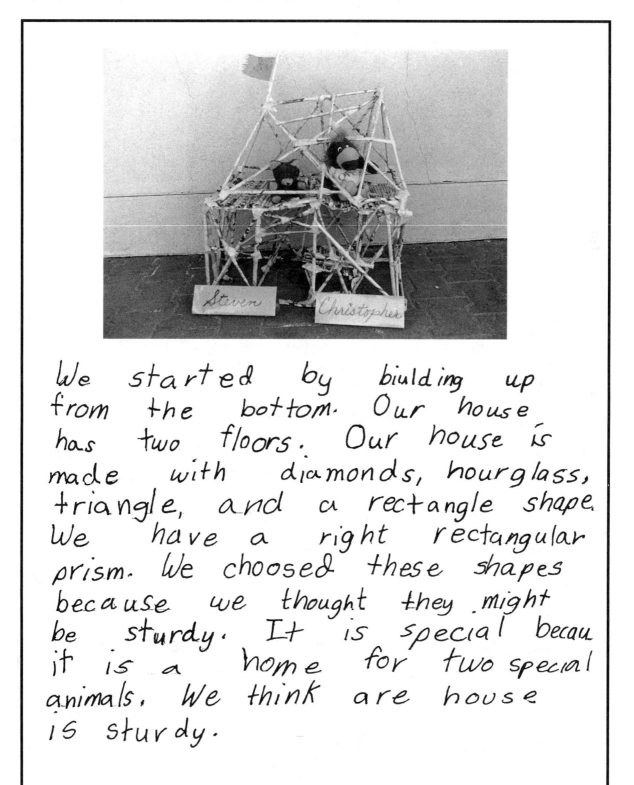

We started by biulding up from the bottom. Our house has two floors. Our house is made with diamonds, hourglass, triangle, and a rectangle shape. We have a right rectangular prism. We choosed these shapes because we thought they might be sturdy. It is special becau it is a home for two special animals. We think are house is sturdy.

SAMPLE 4

This structure is also elaborate and sturdy. The written description includes an extensive geometric rationale for why the shapes were chosen and modified throughout the construction process. For example, the builders added "cross supports" to make the right rectangular prism sturdier. The house also has features specifically designed for animals, e.g., an underground floor to "keep it moist and store food."

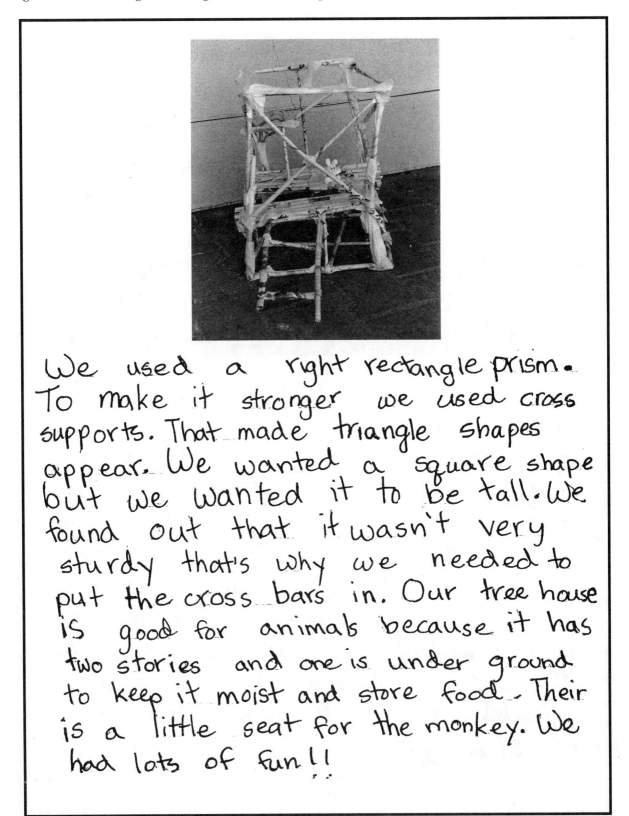

We used a right rectangle prism. To make it stronger we used cross supports. That made triangle shapes appear. We wanted a square shape but we wanted it to be tall. We found out that it wasn't very sturdy that's why we needed to put the cross bars in. Our tree house is good for animals because it has two stories and one is under ground to keep it moist and store food. Their is a little seat for the monkey. We had lots of fun!!

SAMPLE 5

This structure was unique in that it was the only home that did not have a flat roof. The written explanation shows sophisticated use of geometric terms and a clear rationale for the use of the pyramid shape. Several conveniences are added for the bears who will inhabit the house (chairs, beds, swings). In addition, the partners took care to be sure that the house provided ample room for the animals to "fit."

To build our house we used a hexagon to do the floor. Then we started to build up and we got a pyramid. To make the house sturdier we put supports on the outside of the house. We used a pyramid because the pyramid is stronger. We have an attic on the top. We have a bed on the second floor, and we have a chair on the first floor The reason that we think this house is special because our animals fit and the house is sturdy.

What insights have I gained?

The animal homes and explanations are testimony to the fact that students have more opportunities to succeed when assessments are broadened to include visual as well as written samples of work. Some students were best able to demonstrate their knowledge of geometry through their model of an animal home. Others provided extensive descriptions for less detailed structures. On a few occasions, both the structure and the explanation are elaborate.

The written work shows students have begun to utilize geometric terms to describe their homes. To enhance the descriptions, the structures can be used as vehicles to help students build related mathematical vocabulary. Teachers can have students work in small groups to share, compare and study the animal homes and address the questions posed at the beginning of the assignment, with modifications as follows.

➤ Name all the shapes you see in your structure. If you find a shape that you cannot name, ask other groups if they can name it.

➤ Study the other animal homes in your group. What works well in these homes? What changes might you make to your home now that you've seen others? Why did you make the changes?

Tree Homes

➤ What did you learn about what makes a structure sturdy? Are some shapes sturdier than others? What shapes are used in buildings and bridges? Why are those shapes used?

The assessment did not provide significant evidence that students were able to incorporate their knowledge of animals in the design of a home with specific features for their particular inhabitant. Often the size of the home was not in proportion to the size of the animal. For example, a home for a large bear only had a few inches for the animal to move around.

The animals were not entirely ignored in a few children's plans. These students created built-in seats, beds, and television sets for their animals. This could indicate a whimsical approach to the activity or the assumption that the animals had human characteristics!

In this particular class, the teacher emphasized the geometric aspects of the assignment rather than the fact that the homes should be suitable for particular animals. In many cases, the animals did not "arrive" until the structures were almost complete, too late in the process for adjustments!

This Animal Home's assessment activity is well-suited for integrated, thematic teaching in the elementary grades. Students could explore animal behavior and gain information through the *Tree Homes* GEMS guide, multimedia presentations, science texts, or various trade books. At the same time, they could read literature about animals. An excellent choice for older students would be the book *Mrs. Frisby and the Rats of Nimh* by Robert C. O'Brien (Atheneum, New York, 1971). In that children's book, some highly intelligent rats escape from a biology lab and a build an underground community.

As part of the unit, students can study geometric structures and then create homes that are well-suited for specific animals. This would integrate the subject areas of mathematics, science, language, and visual arts, and would provide students with an opportunity to incorporate knowledge they have gained both in and out of the classroom.

Other Assessment Opportunities in GEMS Using Model Making

Here are some other assessment opportunities in GEMS that use the assessment strategy of model making. Use this list to find specific opportunities that may inspire you to create your own uses of this assessment strategy.

➤ *ANIMAL DEFENSES*
At the end of the unit, students can design a defenseless form of an animal that lives in water. They then add defenses and behaviors that would assist this animal in its underwater home.

➤ *BUBBLE-OLOGY*
As a homework assignment at the end of Activity 1, Bubble Technology, students apply their knowledge of soap films to design and draw bubble makers for specialized uses.

➤ *BUILD IT! FESTIVAL*
After What Comes Next? students can use a variety of materials to create patterns. After Dowel Designs, students create and fly kites. After Symmetry, students create and decorate symmetrical masks.

➤ *BUZZING A HIVE*
Students build a paper model of a bee to use in dramas. Students can also draw the different phases of a bee's life cycle from egg to adult bee.

➤ *EARTH, MOON, AND STARS*
Students make star clocks to represent the rotation of the night sky every night and the change in constellations month by month.

➤ *FROG MATH*
Students design a unique button, drawing on their knowledge about real buttons. These models can then be used in classification activities.

➤ *GLOBAL WARMING*
In Session 7, students create an Effects Wheel to model the chain of cause-and-effect relationships that might occur from global warming.

➤ *GROUP SOLUTIONS*
In an extension for Bear Line-Ups, students create and draw their own bear line-ups. As they tackle the Searches section, groups of students are asked to draw a picture that fits all the clues in their envelope. As they explore the Maps section, students imagine a fictional place and create a map of it, complete with directional statements.

➤ *HIDE A BUTTERFLY*
In Session 2, the students assist the teacher to create a butterfly with coloration on the inside of its wings. They then design their own butterfly to complement their flower.

➤ *IN ALL PROBABILITY*
Students are asked to make models of two spinners, one fair and one unfair. Students are also challenged to design a die or dice of their own. Later in the unit, students design their own set of game sticks to play a Native American game.

➤ *LADYBUGS*
Students make models of ladybugs and use them in dramatic play about the predator-prey relationship and the life cycle.

➤ *MOONS OF JUPITER*
Students can apply the concept of scale to design a paper model of the Jupiter system.

➤ *OOBLECK: WHAT DO SCIENTISTS DO?*
During Session 3, students design a spacecraft to land on an ocean of Oobleck.

➤ *TERRARIUM HABITATS*
In Activity 2, teams of students design and build a habitat for small animals that live in or on the soil.

➤ *TREE HOMES*
Students make, modify, and use lots of models, starting with a model of a tree. In the unit this model can change as do real trees. Students make models of an owl and raccoons, and build a paper bag nest.

Explorations as an Assessment Strategy

Protected by the thick metal skin of the submersible submarine Alvin, the scientists peered out of the thick glass viewports. The light blue-green color near the surface of the ocean gave way to a deep royal blue and then an inky blackness as the submarine sank deeper and deeper into the abyss. As they approached the ocean floor the scientists turned on the brilliant headlights, and were amazed at what they saw.

Years later the Alvin's pilot on this expedition, oceanographer Dr. Kathleen Crane, would recall it as the most exciting discovery of her life. Volcanoes on land are inhospitable places, where intense heat and poisonous gases destroy all life. So the team expected that the volcanic vent at the bottom of the ocean would also be devoid of life. But when they had descended several miles to the bottom of the ocean where natural light did not penetrate, and water was heated to several hundred degrees by constant volcanic eruptions, they were amazed to discover giant clams, huge tube worms several feet in length, and all sorts of odd creatures never before seen by human eyes.

The discoveries on the ocean floor raised many fascinating questions: How could these plants and animals live where there was no light? Did they use heat energy from the volcanoes instead? How did they survive under the extreme pressures and heat conditions? Could such deep ocean vents have been the place where all life on Earth originated?

The exploration phase is, in many ways, the most exciting part of science and mathematics. It starts with an open-ended challenge and a rich environment. In the above example, the challenge was to visit a deep sea oceanic vent and see what is there. In the GEMS unit, *Oobleck: What Do Scientists Do?* the challenge is to discover the properties of an unusual substance. What is most interesting about this phase is that it evokes many new discoveries and raises interesting questions.

Despite its open-ended quality, exploration is part of the disciplined way of thinking that is characteristic of science and mathematics. Consequently, as our students explore in the classroom, we would like to see them improve in certain disciplined skills, and these skills specifically:

- Utilize all of their senses, and observe many different aspects of a new situation.

- Record their observations with an increasingly rich descriptive vocabulary and/or more detailed pictures.

- Compare observations with what they see or with what they know, and categorize new objects and events as a way of making sense of the phenomena.

- Recognize some object or event as something that they had not seen before; and describe their new discovery in a way that is clear and convincing.

- Record observations in a way that shows changes over an extended period of time.

- Go beyond simple observations to formulate questions and hypotheses, that might form the bases for later investigations.

- Make inferences that may be speculative, but which are supported with evidence.

An assessment program should provide opportunities for students to show how their exploration skills improve by placing them in new situations to explore. The challenge to the students needs to be sufficiently open-ended to evoke the students' creativity, yet clear enough to provide guidance in the kinds of responses that are desired.

A case study using explorations as an assessment strategy in *Investigating Artifacts* begins on the next page; and a case study using explorations as an assessment strategy in *Oobleck: What Do Scientists Do?* begins on page 139. Opportunities for explorations assessments in other GEMS units are on page 148.

Mystery Object from *Investigating Artifacts*

During Sessions 5 and 6 of *Investigating Artifacts*, students explore shoe box middens filled with earth and hidden "artifacts" at a simulated archeological site. Student teams then become anthropologists who describe and discuss the various artifacts they have excavated from their midden. As a whole group, the teams generate a list of artifacts on a board and speculate how the objects may have been used in the past. Students identify evidence that supports their inferences. Each student then selects one object and describes how it may have been used by past cultures.

To assess students' ability to explore an unknown object and to make and apply logical inferences and support them with evidence, teachers can select unfamiliar mystery objects. These objects are often found in kitchens, garages or classroom closets, or at the local thrift store. These objects should be sturdy and safe to handle.

One group of third graders explored an object found by their teacher when she first moved to her home. The rust-spotted object was silver and had handles and moveable arms. Students closely examined the object and wrote individually about the following assignment.

 What do I want to see?

This assessment task provides students with an opportunity to apply skills learned through midden explorations and demonstrate the following.

➤ Observe the characteristics of an object.

➤ Use writing and drawings to describe their observations.

➤ Make one or more inferences about how the object may have been used.

➤ Justify their inferences with evidence they have collected and their own prior knowledge.

 How do I evaluate the student work?

Evaluate the responses in terms of how well students were able to observe and communicate the characteristics of the mystery object and make logical, substantiated inferences about what it could be. You may wish to construct an evaluation checklist to assess each student's work, as illustrated on the next page. The checklist was used to evaluate the student work on the following pages. Each student had the same object to describe.

---

1. Use words and pictures to describe your object in detail.

2. How could people have used this object in the past?

3. Why do you think people used the object that way?

Investigating Artifacts

INVESTIGATING ARTIFACTS
MYSTERY OBJECT

Student's Name_____

The student described the object with:

❏ Extensive detail.

❏ Adequate detail.

❏ Minimal detail.

The student:

❏ Made several inferences about the object's **possible** former use.

❏ Made one inference about the object's **possible** former use.

❏ Was unable to make an inference about the object's **possible** former use.

The student's inferences were:

❏ Strongly supported by evidence gained during the exploration and/or prior knowledge.

❏ Adequately supported by evidence gained during the exploration and/or prior knowledge.

❏ Somewhat supported by evidence and/or prior knowledge.

❏ Unsupported by evidence.

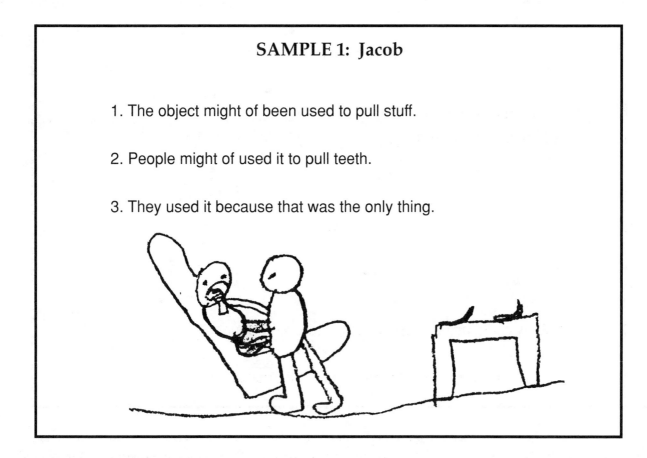

SAMPLE 1: Jacob

1. The object might of been used to pull stuff.

2. People might of used it to pull teeth.

3. They used it because that was the only thing.

Jacob is singularly focused on his notion that the object was used to pull teeth, as evidenced by the fact that he repeats the hypothesis as an answer to each of the three questions. His picture describes well how the object could be used, but does not provide information about its attributes. He also depicts a fairly modern setting (a dentist's office) to illustrate how an object was used in the past. Jacob may need additional support and experiences to focus on the question that is asked: describe an object, distinguish past from present, and/or justify his inferences with evidence.

The student described the object with:

☑ Minimal detail (Object was not described).

The student:

☑ Made one inference about the object's **possible** former use.

The student's inferences were:

☑ Somewhat supported by evidence and/or prior knowledge.

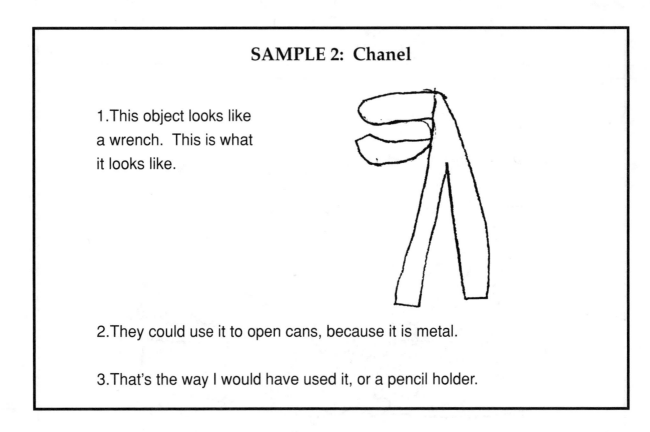

SAMPLE 2: Chanel

1. This object looks like a wrench. This is what it looks like.

2. They could use it to open cans, because it is metal.

3. That's the way I would have used it, or a pencil holder.

Chanel describes her object with words and pictures. Her inferences are based on prior knowledge and the fact that the object is metal. She makes the assumption that people in the past used the object just as she would use it in the context of the present! Chanel needs additional support to justify inferences and to increase her written vocabulary of attributes to describe an object. She, too, needs support to distinguish past from present.

The student described the object with:

☑ Adequate detail.

The student:

☑ Made several inferences about the object's **possible** former use.

The student's inferences were:

☑ Somewhat supported by evidence and/or prior knowledge.

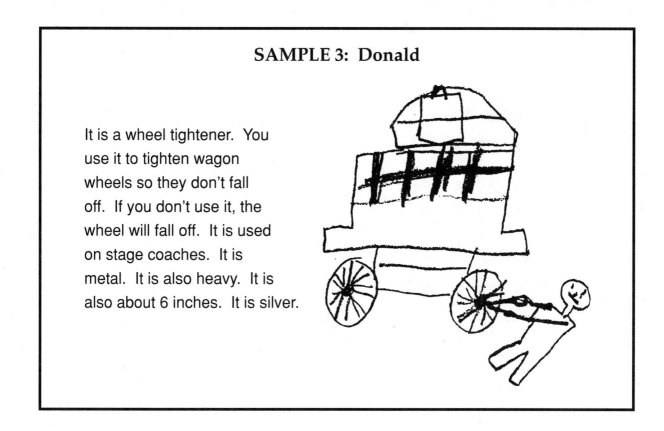

SAMPLE 3: Donald

It is a wheel tightener. You use it to tighten wagon wheels so they don't fall off. If you don't use it, the wheel will fall off. It is used on stage coaches. It is metal. It is also heavy. It is also about 6 inches. It is silver.

Donald describes the object's size, weight, color, and composition and provides a drawing to show its shape. His response shows a vivid sense of history and an ability to project back into the past. He provides a pictorial rationale for the use of his object; it depicts a person who grasps the object's handle to tighten a wagon wheel. Donald might be able to strengthen his written justification if he were asked to explain what features of the object made it particularly suitable to tighten wagon wheels.

The student described the object with:

☑ Extensive detail.

The student:

☑ Made one inference about the object's **possible** former use.

The inferences made were:

☑ Strongly supported by evidence gained during the exploration and/or prior knowledge.

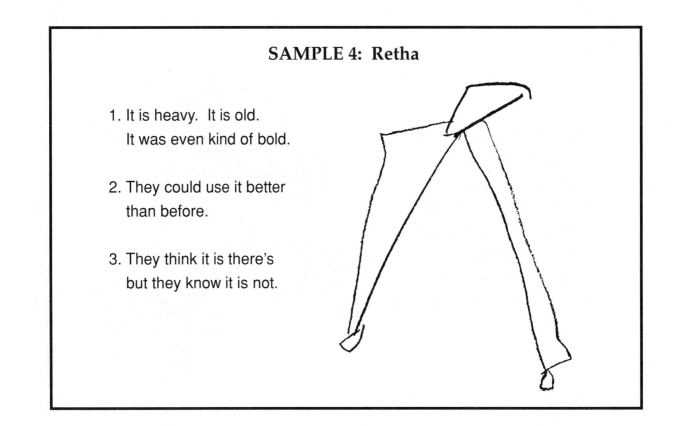

SAMPLE 4: Retha

1. It is heavy. It is old.
   It was even kind of bold.

2. They could use it better
   than before.

3. They think it is there's
   but they know it is not.

Retha begins to describe the object with words and a picture that depicts its moveable parts. However, she is unable to make an inference about how the object could have been used in the past. Her thinking is not clearly communicated in her response. Further questioning might lend insight into how Retha perceived the object as well her interpretation of the task. Once this information is revealed, an additional assessment could be made to determine which experiences would help Retha develop a more elaborate, focused response to the assignment.

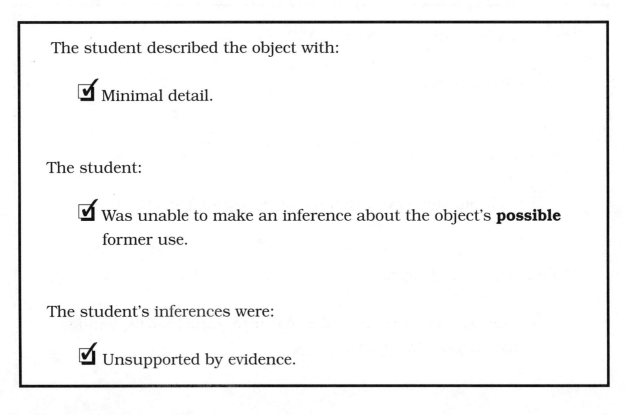

The student described the object with:

☑ Minimal detail.

The student:

☑ Was unable to make an inference about the object's **possible** former use.

The student's inferences were:

☑ Unsupported by evidence.

SAMPLE 5: Charlotte

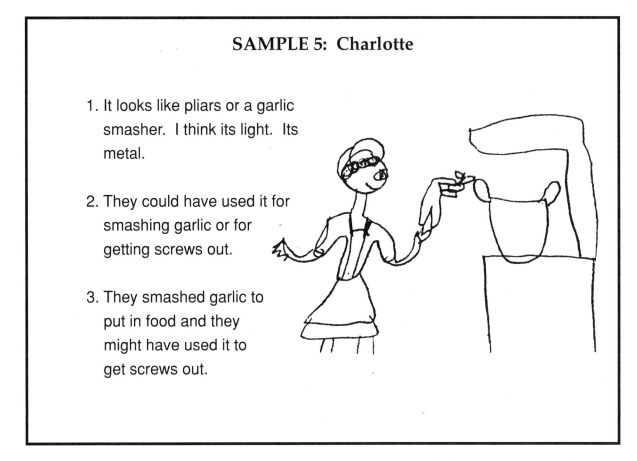

1. It looks like pliars or a garlic smasher. I think its light. Its metal.

2. They could have used it for smashing garlic or for getting screws out.

3. They smashed garlic to put in food and they might have used it to get screws out.

Charlotte uses pictures and words to depict her object, although she needs additional support to develop and/or use attribute vocabulary in her description. Her hypotheses are plausible and appear to be based on prior knowledge. Her illustration shows how the features of the object are particularly suited for garlic smashing!

The student described the object with:

☑ Adequate detail.

The student:

☑ Made several inferences about the object's **possible** former use.

The student's inferences were:

☑ Somewhat supported by evidence and/or prior knowledge.

SAMPLE 6: Ashley

Object # 2 is made out of metal. The people in the past could have used that object by snapping stuff or they could have used it by getting the food out of hot pots. I think they used it that way because I saw something like it before. The object tells me that they did a lot of work to make that object out of metal.

Ashley was the only student in the class to correctly hypothesize that the object was used as a handle for hot pots. Her justification is strongly based on prior knowledge because she informs us that "I saw something like it before." She exhibits an appreciation for the culture that created the object when she recognizes that "they did a lot of work" to fashion it from metal. Ashley uses only one feature (metal) to describe the object, perhaps because she is so focused on its use. However, she may need additional experiences to help her develop and use attribute vocabulary.

The student described the object with:

☑ Minimal detail.

The student:

☑ Made several inferences about the object's **possible** former use.

The student's inferences were:

☑ Strongly supported by evidence gained during the exploration and/or prior knowledge.

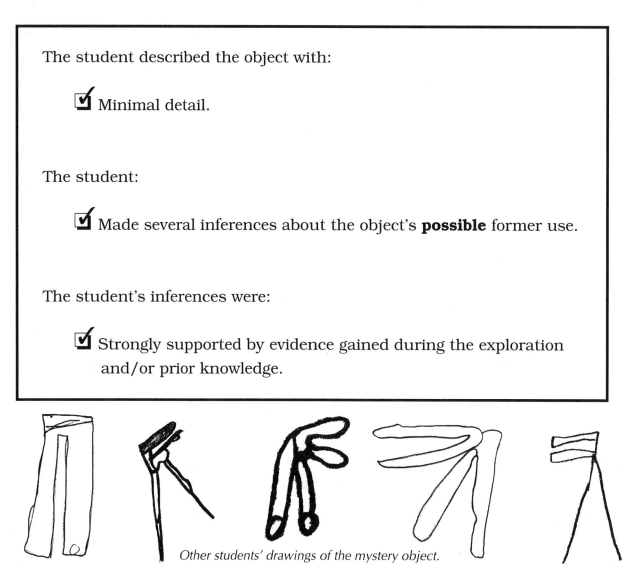

Other students' drawings of the mystery object.

SAMPLE 7: Stephanie

1. Object # 2 looks like a dinosure, and it is made out of grayish metal.

2. Long ago, it could have been used as some plyers.

3. People could have used it for screwing things together, or if a student is bad, teachers pinch thair ears so they could be quiet.

Stephanie uses a simile to describe her object ("like a dinosaur") and also includes the features of color and composition. She predicts that the object may have been used as a pliers or a tool to punish students. Her explanation is that "people could have used it for screwing things together." Stephanie needs to further develop and/or articulate a rationale for her inferences.

The student described the object with:

☑ Adequate detail.

The student:

☑ Made several inferences about the object's **possible** former use.

The inferences made were:

☑ Somewhat supported by evidence and/or prior knowledge.

 What insights have I gained?

Students were very enthusiastic about the assignment and almost all were able to describe their object with some detail and present a plausible hypothesis about its former use. However, the assessment indicated that a large number of students needed additional support to:

➤ Use rich attribute vocabulary to describe objects.

➤ Make realistic inferences about the past based on clues found in the present.

➤ Support inferences with evidence from their exploration of the object or prior knowledge.

To help students use rich attribute vocabulary, teachers may wish to plan a series of classification activities that require detailed descriptions of objects. For example, the class can play Guess My Object. In this game, one student selects an object, hides it behind a barrier, and uses a series of sentences to describe it. One sentence at a time is presented, until the class has enough information to guess the object. After the game, students can create a list of words to describe the object. Students can also play this game in pairs.

In this particular activity, the choice of object may have been a factor that limited the students' descriptions. For this assessment, we selected a simple object that was unfamiliar to the students, yet limited in easily identifiable attributes. It is possible that students would be able to describe a more complex object with greater detail.

Many primary grade students are unable to make realistic projections into the past. Very young children, in particular, find it difficult to conceive of "a week ago" or "last year." Therefore, the concept of "in the past" is relative to the child's experience of time. Some students see the past as "yesterday" or "when I was a baby," while others have the capacity to conceive that there were events that occurred, beyond their life experience, in a context that was entirely different than the present.

Investigating Artifacts

Teachers can help students understand the passage of time through a variety of activities. Young children can sequence recent events to establish a sense of "before" and "after." Older students can first create autobiographical timelines of their lives, before they attempt to understand historical timelines. Students can also interview people from other generations (parents, grandparents, friends) to gain a broader perspective of the past and how it relates to the present. Teachers might also frame this assessment in a more specific context. For example: "How might this object be used by people over 100 years ago?" or "How might your great great grandparents have used this object?"

Often students are better able to justify inferences with evidence when teachers consistently use questioning techniques to encourage reflection and active learning. For example, as students explore the unusual object, the teacher can focus their thinking with questions such as:

➤ If you lived a long time ago, how might you have used this object?

➤ What other uses could there be for this object?

➤ What about this object makes you think that it was used for ___?

➤ What do you know about how people lived long ago that makes you think they needed this object for ___?

➤ Who do you think used this object? What does this object tell you about the lives of the people who used it?

Results from this assessment can be considered as teachers plan related activities and units across the curriculum: in science, social studies, math, and language arts. For example, observation and classification skills are strengthened whenever a student is asked to describe something, whether it is an object, a character or setting from a book, a pattern of numbers, or geographical features. Likewise, students can justify inferences and reflect back in time as they explore topics in literature and history.

The Sand Task
from *Oobleck: What Do Scientists Do?*

Students explore the properties of an unusual substance that has the properties of both a solid and a liquid in the *Oobleck* GEMS guide. In the first session, students form small laboratory teams to learn how scientists describe the properties of a substance. They observe, hypothesize, and experiment with Oobleck to determine its unique qualities. During the second session, the lab teams hold a scientific convention to discuss and analyze their findings. Students challenge each other to define the properties of Oobleck more accurately and refine their communication skills.

To assess students' ability to apply their knowledge of properties in a new situation, we presented fifth graders with a sand exploration. To prepare for the task, the teacher provides pairs of students with:

- a small cup of sand
- an empty cup
- a stick for use as a probe
- a magnifying lens

In addition, each student receives a record sheet, as shown on the next page.

Students are told they are scientists whose job is to explore the sand. They may use any of the tools provided or other materials that they might find in the classroom in their explorations. Pairs of students investigate the sand and make a list of its properties. Each student makes an individual list on his or her record sheet (Part I: Investigating Sand) while the pair works together to explore the sand.

As in the *Oobleck* unit, the teacher then leads a class discussion where each team presents its ideas. The entire class discusses in detail one or more of the properties of sand that addresses whether or not sand should be considered a liquid, a solid, or both.

The students then work individually to answer Part II: Sand Questions on their record sheets.

Oobleck: What Do Scientists Do?

My Name _____

My Partner's Name _____

Part I: Investigating Sand

1. Work with your partner and use the materials at your table to explore the sand. Use your senses and what you discover as you explore to make a list of the **Properties of Sand**.

Part II: Sand Questions

Answer these questions. Use information you discovered when you explored the sand.

1. In what ways is **sand like a liquid**?

2. In what ways is **sand like a solid**?

Q What do I want to see?

This two-part assessment task provides students with an opportunity to apply skills learned through the *Oobleck* unit and demonstrate their ability to:

➤ Observe the properties of a substance.

➤ Record and communicate observations.

➤ Determine conditions under which sand behaves like a liquid or a solid.

➤ Describe how a substance can have properties of both liquids and solids.

Q How do I evaluate the student work?

Teachers may decide to group student work into three categories.

COMPLETE RESPONSES to this task would include the following qualities.

Part I
The record sheet includes a wide variety of both sensory and experiential observations (what they observed as they conducted simple manipulations with the sand). Language explicitly describes the students' findings.

Oobleck: What Do Scientists Do?

Part II
The students are able to respond extensively to the questions with detailed examples of what they did and observed with samples of sand. They present a strong, clear case to explain why sand has properties similar to both liquids and solids, under different conditions.

PARTIAL RESPONSES would include the following qualities.

Part I
The record sheet includes a limited list of sensory and/or experiential observations. The list may omit one or more essential qualities of sand (i.e., its color, its ability to pour). Students adequately summarize their findings but descriptions are limited to the more observable features of sand.

Part II
The students respond to the questions with limited insight and a few examples of what they did and observed with samples of sand. They maintain that sand has properties of both liquids and solids but provide only partial or unclear justification for their conclusion.

MINIMAL RESPONSES would include the following qualities.

Part I
The record sheet includes a short list of sensory OR experiential observations. The list may omit one or more essential qualities of sand (e.g., its color, its ability to pour). The descriptions provide little detail about the properties.

Part II
The students respond to the questions with minimal insight and few or no examples of what they did and observed with samples of sand. They may describe sand as similar to a liquid or a solid, but do not discuss the fact that sand could have both liquid AND solid properties. Or, they may agree that sand is like a liquid and a solid but do not support their conclusion with clear scientific evidence.

COMPLETE RESPONSE—1

PART I: PROPERTIES OF SAND

1. It is rough when you feel it.

   It's mixed with different kinds of rocks.

   It turns into mud, and feels slimy and sticky.

   If you dig a hole, it fills itself back up so it's like a liquid.

   It's made of really small pebbles.

   You can make shapes out it if it's wet so it's like a solid.

   It goes all over the place when you shake it or throw it.

   If you put water in it and shake it, it could turn back into a flat surface like ordinary water.

   It has an odor.

   If you put some sand in a bucket and a little water and leave it for a while, it will turn to the shape like the bucket. When you turn it over and let it drop, it will stay like the shape of the bucket and will look like cement.

PART II: (1) SAND LIKE A LIQUID AND (2) SAND LIKE A SOLID

1. Sand can be poured like a liquid, but it is not wet like a liquid. It splatters when you hit it like a liquid does. And, sand cannot freeze like a liquid can, and it cannot evaporate like a liquid can.

2. Sand grains by themselves are solid. Sand grains together are little solids, even though they can be poured like a liquid when they are put together in a container. Also, sand is made of tiny grains and the grains don't change shape like a liquid does.

In this response, the student uses sensory and experiential qualities to create an elaborate list of the properties of sand. Part II clearly compares and contrasts sand's properties to those of a liquid and a solid.

COMPLETE RESPONSE—2

PART I: PROPERTIES OF SAND

1. SIGHT — It looks like little tiny rocks, and bigger rocks through the magnifying glass. It is brownish and tannish.

   HEAR — If you put some sand in a cup and jiggle it around, you'll hear weird noises.

   SMELL — Sand smells like a new book being opened or a furniture store. It really smells like salt.

   TOUCH—It feels rough. It sticks on your hand when you touch it. It feels like little tiny rocks bunched together.

   TASTE—You can't taste it but when you put it in your mouth it feels weird.

PART II: (1) SAND LIKE A LIQUID AND (2) SAND LIKE A SOLID

1. Sand is like a liquid because you can put it in a cup with little holes and it will go through. A solid would not go through, but water, sand, gas and other liquids will. Also, when you put sand in your hand, it will drain, like water. Sand is also like a liquid when it's quicksand.

2. Sand is like a solid because the little tiny rocks don't change their shape, even when you pour sand. I also think sand is a solid because it used to be a big rock. I rubbed the sand and it was hard. Also, very few things can sink through sand unless you push them in.

In this response, the student presents an organized and detailed list of the properties of sand. Both sensory and experiential qualities are included. The conclusions in Part II are supported with references to the student's experiments with sand.

PARTIAL RESPONSE—1

PART I: PROPERTIES OF SAND

1. Rocky

   Soothing

   Dry

   Liquid

   Silky

   Sticky

   Chunky

   Kitty Litter

   Clumpy (like cream "o" wheat)

Thick when wet

Soft when dry

Smelling

Bottom of seas

Dark when wet

Light when dry

Like a beach

Sparkly

PART II: (1) SAND LIKE A LIQUID AND (2) SAND LIKE A SOLID

1. Sand is not like a liquid because it's just like miniature rocks. People say sand is like a liquid because you can pour it, but if you got a big huge rock and poured it, they would say it is not a liquid. I think that sand is simply just NOT like a liquid. If sand is dry and it is being poured and people say it is like a liquid, then if a rock is dry and it is being poured, then it should be like a liquid. If it isn't a liquid, I think that sand must be a solid.

2. Sand is a solid because it is made of rocks. If a rock is a solid, then I think sand is. Sand was made when two big rocks crashed into each other and became a whole bunch of tiny pieces. If sand is NOT a liquid because it is small, that means if you're a small person, you're NOT a person.

In this response, the student presents a extensive list of the properties of sand, but does not include references to his exploration of the substance. Part II presents a complex analysis of why sand is a like a solid not a liquid, but the student's thinking is sometimes unclear and relies on logic (and in some cases, flawed logic) rather than results from the exploration.

PARTIAL RESPONSE—2

PART I: PROPERTIES OF SAND

1. Big, sharp crystals, sparkly, powdery, colorful, see-through, sticky, has many shapes.

PART II: (1) SAND LIKE A LIQUID AND (2) SAND LIKE A SOLID

1. The reason I think sand is like a liquid is because you can pour it and when you put it in something like a colander, it would fall out. I also think it is like a liquid because it has water in it when you build something like a sand castle and water is a liquid.

2. Sand is like a solid because it has hard grains.

This student has compiled a limited list of the features of sand. Part II includes an explanation of why sand is like a liquid but falsely assumes that if a substance has water in it, it should be classified as a liquid. The explanation for why sand is like a solid needs elaboration.

PARTIAL RESPONSE—3

PART I: PROPERTIES OF SAND

1. Some grains are bigger than others. Some grains are almost transparent. Most grains are smaller than one centimeter. Rocky, lumpy, hard.
   Can be different shapes.

PART II: (1) SAND LIKE A LIQUID AND (2) SAND LIKE A SOLID

1. Sand is like a liquid because you can spread it out on a table, and you cannot spread out a solid.

2. Sand is like a solid because you can see a lot of tiny rocks when you use a magnifying glass.

This student presents a detailed list of the properties of sand and a partial explanation of why sand has properties of both a liquid and a solid. References to the student's exploration in both parts would strengthen this response.

MINIMAL RESPONSE—1

PART I: PROPERTIES OF SAND

1. Dusty, looks like dust, sort of looks like glass, tiny pebbles

PART II: (1) SAND LIKE A LIQUID AND (2) SAND LIKE A SOLID

1. Sand is like a liquid because it's different than a solid.

2. Sand is like a solid because if you make a sand castle, it would be easier to knock it down if it was a liquid, which it isn't.

This student limits the properties of sand to those that are visible. Part II contains vague justifications for the fact that sand can be both a liquid and a solid.

MINIMAL RESPONSE—2

PART I: PROPERTIES OF SAND

1. Rocky, Hard, Dirty, Nasty. It makes you have ring worms.

PART II: (1) SAND LIKE A LIQUID AND (2) SAND LIKE A SOLID

1. Sand is like a liquid because as you pick up the sand, it feels weird. It feels rocky but it's not because it's very soft.

2. Sand is like a solid because it is a little bit solid and a little bit liquid because its both. But it's still obvious that everything in it is liquid and solid. But, only one good scientist will know.

Few distinct properties of sand are mentioned in this response. The explanations in Part II reveal minimal understanding of the characteristics of liquids and solids.

What insights have I gained?

This assessment can be used to guide instructional decisions about how to structure scientific explorations or future implementation plans for the *Oobleck* unit. For example, in Part I of the assessment, all fifth grade students were able to name at least several properties of sand. The results indicated that they understood the scientific concept of properties, and were able to apply this concept to a new substance. However, students varied greatly in their ability to make precise observations; conduct explorations of sand and articulate their findings. The assessment indicated that a majority of students needed additional experiences that enable them to explore and describe the distinct features of a substance.

To address this need in the *Oobleck* unit, teachers can provide time for students to share their lists and expand them with input from their peers. Students can also describe the experiments they devised to determine the properties of sand. As students exchange ideas, they are likely to develop new methods to explore sand.

In Part II of the assessment, a majority of students were unable to formulate clear statements and support them with facts and observations from their explorations with sand. There are several ways to help students strengthen their ability to support their conclusions.

First, teachers can ask students to explain their thinking orally and/or in writing during all steps of mathematical problem solving or scientific exploration. We should not assume that just because a student knows the answer to a question, she can also explain the rationale for the answer. Students can be asked to show evidence that their conclusions are correct to a classmate or at a mathematical or scientific convention. This evidence can be self-assessed or evaluated by others and students can use this feedback to strengthen their contentions.

If appropriate, this assessment can be easily evaluated for use with a traditional grading system. Teachers can evaluate the responses and assign point values to each section of the assessment.

COMPLETE = 3 points
PARTIAL = 2 points
MARGINAL = 1 point
NO RESPONSE = 0 points

Thus, the total number of possible points for this assessment would be six (three for each section). Performance levels could be established with a range of "6" (exemplary) to "0" (no response) and assigned a percentage or letter grade value.

For example, some students may score well on one section but need improvement on another section. This student might develop a comprehensive list of the properties of sand, and score a "3" on Part I of the assessment. However, their analysis in Part II may need additional justification and thus would score a "2." The total for this student would be a "5" of a possible six points which could translate to an 83% score.

Although this method of assessment can be used as the basis of a traditional grade, it is far richer in the feedback it provides for the teacher and student. The activity shows how the students apply their abilities to explore new substances in a real-life situation. It shows how they use their senses, apply concepts and reflect on their discoveries to support their conclusions. The students will gain more information about their progress from a detailed analysis of what they did well than from a letter grade alone.

For all students, the concepts and skills involved in the Sand Task assessment go far beyond letter grades, the narrow definition of what a "property" is, or physical science understandings of matter. As with Oobleck, this seemingly simple observation and analysis of a substance (in this case, sand), exemplifies the essence of the nature of science, or "what scientists do." As students plan, conduct, record and discuss their explorations, they gain a direct, tactile, yet also quite sophisticated and practical understanding of how a scientist approaches the real world. Because student abilities and conceptual understandings grow and develop over time, explorations such as the Sand Task can be evaluated on many levels and presented at different grade levels.

Other Assessment Opportunities in GEMS Using Explorations

Here are some other assessment opportunities in GEMS that use the assessment strategy of explorations. Use this list to find specific opportunities and to inspire you to create your own uses of this assessment strategy.

➤ *BUILD IT! FESTIVAL*
For Create-A-Shape, students explore different ways to combine squares to form cubes. In Octahedron Exploration, they find as many ways as they can to build a polyhedron with eight faces.

➤ *CRIME LAB CHEMISTRY*
At the end of the unit, students use chromatography to analyze the pigments found in plants, colored markers, and candy coatings.

➤ *EARTHWORMS*
Students measure the pulse rates of other animals such as humans, rats, chinchillas, and daphnia. They then compare the results to their earthworm experiments.

➤ *GROUP SOLUTIONS*
After they complete the Coin Count section, students explore advertising flyers from supermarkets and make statements about what they've found.

➤ *LIQUID EXPLORATIONS*
In the opening demonstrations of the Ocean in a Bottle activity, students predict whether the various liquids might mix and explain what happens when they are poured together.

➤ *MAPPING ANIMAL MOVEMENTS*
Students use sampling techniques to map the movements of a variety of classroom animals.

➤ *MOONS OF JUPITER*
Students observe the slide simulation of the movement of Jupiter's moons over a period of nine nights. Then, they work in small groups to determine how long it takes each moon to circle Jupiter.

➤ *OF CABBAGES AND CHEMISTRY*
In Presto Change-O and Acid and Aliens, students explore how to neutralize mystery solutions as they navigate their way through an alien space craft.

➤ *TERRARIUM HABITATS*
Students observe earthworms, pill bugs, sow bugs, snails, and other creatures as they adjust to their new habitat over several weeks or longer periods of time. They then record their observations.

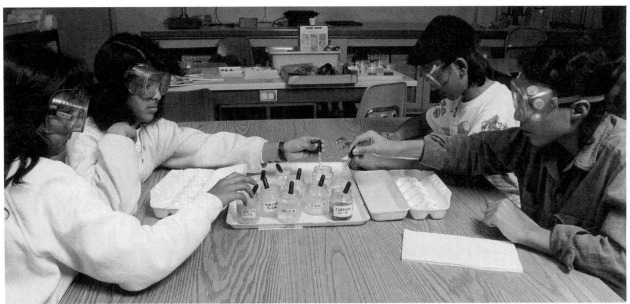

Of Cabbages and Chemistry

Experiments as an Assessment Strategy

The word experiment is used loosely in the English language to mean "messing around" or "trying something new." In science, however, the word experiment has a very precise meaning. All experiments are characterized by some sort of comparison. For example, if you bake a cake, it is not an experiment, even if it's your very first cake. But if you bake two cakes, one with oil and the other with butter, to determine the effects of different types of fat, you've conducted an experiment.

In his famous experiment, Galileo Galilee climbed the stairs of the Tower of Pisa to test his hypothesis that objects of different masses fall at very nearly the same rate of speed. He dropped two objects at the same time from the top of the tower. There were observers at the base of the tower to determine whether or not they struck the ground at the same time. Galileo compared the rate at which two objects of different masses fall.

It is necessary to control variables if we are to conduct fair and accurate experiments. All variables in the two comparison situations must be the same except for one. This variable is called the "test variable." In the cake baking experiment, the test variable is the *type* of fat. There must be exactly the same *amount* of each kind of fat and the same *kind* and *amount* of all the other ingredients. The identical procedure must be used to mix the ingredients, and the cakes must be baked at the *same temperature* for the *same amount of time*.

In Galileo's experiment, the test variable was the *mass* of the different objects. Galileo was quite careful to be sure that he dropped two objects of the same size and shape (only their mass was different), at the same time, and in the same manner. It is not always easy to control all variables in an experiment, and an experiment can still be valid when the variables are not perfectly controlled. However, it may be difficult to draw conclusions based on the results from experiments when more than one variable is present. Often, an additional experiment must be conducted to answer the initial question.

Experiments also involve a method to measure and verify an *outcome*. Galileo asked observers to compare the *time* at which each of the two objects struck the ground. This enabled him to calculate the rate of speed that each object fell, since he knew the height of the tower.

Sometimes it is hard to find a measurable outcome to help answer the original question or hypothesis. For example, a variety of factors may be considered to determine the quality of a cake—texture, color, height, moisture, number of calories, taste, and general appearance—and each factor will be evaluated with a different method.

Experiments can have a range of very specific to broad outcomes. The outcome depends on the question. A cake baker's question might be "Does using butter instead of oil make a cake look more yellow?" The outcome for this experiment would be a color comparison of the two cakes. However, the baker might want to know "What differences are there between a cake made with butter and a cake made with oil?" The baker then would want to consider a variety of factors and other differences that can be observed!

When students design, conduct, and analyze experiments, teachers have an ideal opportunity to observe and assess their abilities to:

- Describe the variables in a situation.

- Design a comparison situation in which all variables are controlled except the test variable.

- Conduct a controlled experiment—make observations, collect data, keep records, analyze data, and communicate results.

- Determine appropriate experimental outcomes.

- Critique an experiment for uncontrolled variables or irrelevant outcomes.

- Draw conclusions based on experimental results.

At science fairs, students display experiments that they have designed and conducted. Indeed, experimentation is the main focus of professional scientists as well! In some ways, experiments are the ultimate authentic assessment of a person's ability to "do science," just as a solo concert is for a violinist and a football game is for a quarterback. Each of these activities (the concert, the game, and the experiment) involve the use of a variety of skills, tools, and abilities.

Keep in mind that just as a violinist would need to practice and play for many years before delivering a high quality concert, so too does a student of science. In the same way, scientists continually refine their experimental approaches and techniques as they pursue answers to challenging questions. Even though student experiments may be unsophisticated, designing experiments, doing experiments, and reflecting on experiments offers a revealing window into your students' scientific reasoning. And like all things, more opportunities will result in more progress towards the grand goal of "doing science."

Younger students, in particular, may need support to design, conduct, and critique experiments, or even brainstorm the list of variables. Older students can be given opportunities to design their own experiments. GEMS units provide many age-appropriate opportunities for students to design, conduct, and/or critique experiments, and each of these is a potential window into your students' understanding.

A case study using experiments as an assessment strategy in *Chemical Reactions* begins on the next page. Opportunities for experiments assessments in other GEMS units are on pages 161–162.

Chemical Reactions

Chemical Reactions

CASE STUDY USING EXPERIMENTS
Heat Experiments from *Chemical Reactions*

In the *Chemical Reactions* unit, students observe and describe three chemicals: baking soda ($NaHCO_3$), calcium chloride ($CaCl_2$), and phenol red solution. They then mix them together in a ziplock bag. The result is a chemical reaction that turns yellow and produces gas, odor, and heat. In Session 2, students are challenged to design and conduct two experiments to determine which of the three reactants is necessary to produce the heat. They are reminded that one of the reactants is a solution of phenol red and water.

Students are given the Heat Experiments data sheet to record their plans, the results of those experiments, and their conclusions. The data sheet asks them to plan two experiments and compare their findings with results from the preliminary experiment (in Session 1) when they combined all reactants and heat was produced. The students are asked to determine the minimum number of reactants needed to cause the heat as they answer the following questions.

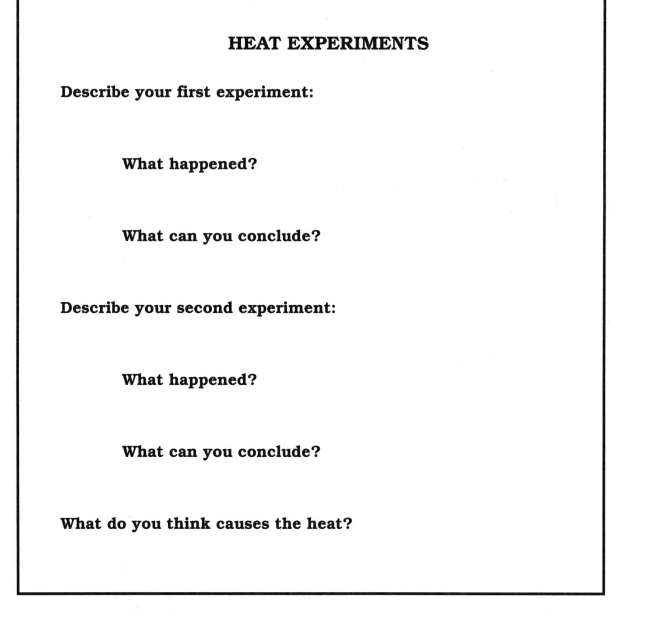

HEAT EXPERIMENTS

Describe your first experiment:

What happened?

What can you conclude?

Describe your second experiment:

What happened?

What can you conclude?

What do you think causes the heat?

What do I want to see?

This assessment task provides students with an opportunity to design and conduct experiments and draw conclusions from their results. They demonstrate their ability to:

➤ Design a controlled experiment in which only one ingredient is omitted, so there is ONLY one difference between the preliminary reaction and the comparison reaction.

➤ Design experiments that will provide information to help determine which reactants are necessary to produce the heat in this reaction.

➤ Record their experiments, results, and conclusions using chemical notation as appropriate.

➤ Use experiment results and reasoning skills to draw conclusions about what causes the heat.

 ## How do I evaluate the student work?

As indicated in the following sixth grade samples, most students were able to come to the correct conclusion, though not all were able to use logical reasoning or to support their conclusions with test results. Many student responses featured inadequate experimental designs. Students often would control variables, but they selected a test variable that did not help them answer the main question at hand. In addition, students recorded their results with varying degrees of clarity. Their attempts to use chemical notation varied widely.

As we reviewed the student work featured on the following pages, we developed a checklist to identify additional experiences that students needed in order to improve their ability to plan, conduct, record, and analyze experiments.

Areas for additional practice

❏ planning experiments that address a particular question

❏ designing controlled experiments

❏ keeping clear, detailed records of plans, results, and conclusions

❏ drawing conclusions from experiment results

❏ using scientific notation to record experiments and results

Areas for additional practice

☑ using scientific notation to record experiments
and results

Jonathan is very systematic in his approach. He first omits the baking soda and sees what would happen with a mixture of calcium chloride and phenol red. Based on his results, he correctly concludes that calcium chloride and phenol red make heat. He next explores the effect of the phenol red as he substitutes water for phenol red solution and combines it with calcium chloride. He makes the astute observation that this reaction is even hotter than the calcium chloride and phenol red solution and correctly concludes that phenol red does not create the heat. Rather, he states that water and calcium chloride produce the heat. Jonathan uses his own abbreviation for calcium chloride, C.C. rather than $CaCO_3$, within the context of an equation format to share what ingredients were combined and the results.

Sample 2: STEPHANIE

Describe your first experiment:
  P.R. + B.S. ——————> cold

What happened?
  P.R. + B.S. stayed cold. Changed hot pink.

What can you conclude?
  This mixture has nothing to do with the production of heat.

Describe your second experiment:
  C.C. + H_2O ——————> hot

What happened?
  The C.C. + H_2O became hot.

What can you conclude?
  This mixture provided the heat.

What do you think causes the heat?
  The C.C. and H_2O make heat for sure. It's possible that the P.R. when mixed
  with C.C. would cause heat, but we know that P.R. is not really a heat maker
  all by itself or without C.C. because of the first experiment we did. And P.R.
  is really a solution with water so that's another reason why water is probably
  what's needed, along with C.C. to make heat. We'd have to try mixing P.R.
  with C.C. to see if that gets hot. I think it would, but I still think that just
  means that water or a liquid like water is needed with C.C. to make heat.

Areas for additional practice

 designing controlled experiments

 using scientific notation to record experiments
  and results

Stephanie first decides to omit the calcium chloride and combine phenol red and baking soda. When the reaction's results are cold, she correctly concludes that this mixture has nothing to do with the production of heat. However, she does not control variables in her next experiment, when she combines calcium chloride and water. Her decision is based on the following logical, though faulty, reasoning: If phenol red and baking soda do not produce heat, perhaps the other two reactants will! When heat is produced in her second experiment, she concludes that calcium chloride and water provide the heat. Technically, she should conduct another experiment so all variables are controlled. However, she considers this in her final conclusion when she discusses the possibility that mixing phenol red and calcium chloride (which she didn't try) would result in heat. She speculates on the results of this reaction, and goes on to share her reasoning for her ultimate conclusion—that water, or a liquid like water, is needed with calcium chloride to make heat. Given the limitation of the two experiments, the combination she first chose, and the fact that she is aware of the weakness of her experimental design, hers is a good handling of the results. She implies that she would explore the unanswered questions if given an opportunity to conduct a third experiment. Like Jonathan, Stephanie uses chemical notation with some of her own abbreviations.

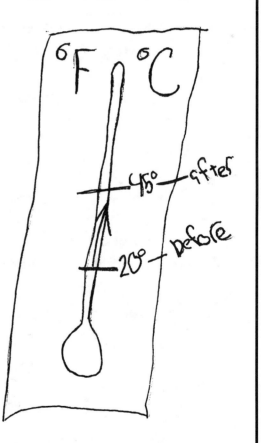

Sample 3: TYLER

Describe your first experiment:
red stuff, CC

What happened?
hot pink, really hot

What can you conclude?
that red and CC make heat

Describe your second experiment:
water, baking soda, CC

What happened?
fizzed, hot

What can you conclude?
that red stuff does nothing but change color

What do you think causes the heat?
CC + water = heat

Areas for additional practice

- ☑ keeping clear, detailed records of plans, results, and conclusions
- ☑ using scientific notation to record experiments and results

Tyler's plans, observations, and conclusions are minimally described and he refers to the phenol red as "red stuff." On the other hand, his planning and reasoning show sound scientific thinking. He first omits baking soda and determines that the phenol red and calcium chloride produce heat. For his second experiment, he removes the phenol red from the original reaction and mixes baking soda, calcium chloride and water. When this mixture also gets hot, he correctly concludes that the "red stuff" only affects the color, and therefore the calcium chloride and water produce the heat. At the end, he makes an effort at chemical notation, though he uses an equal sign (=) instead of an arrow (→).

Sample 4: EMILY

Describe your first experiment:
I mixed water, calcium chloride, and baking soda.

What happened?
It fizzed and got hot. It was hottest where the calcium chloride was.

What can you conclude?
The calcium chloride makes it hot.

Describe your second experiment:
mixing phenol red and calcium chloride

What happened?
It stayed pink but it got really hot. It didn't fizz and the bag didn't inflate.

What can you conclude?
The calcium chloride needs a liquid to conduct heat.

What do you think causes the heat?
Calcium Chloride

Emily substitutes water for phenol red in her first experiment. She notices the reaction is hottest near the calcium chloride and thus concludes that the calcium chloride makes it hot. This is a good hypothesis, but not a valid conclusion at this point. A more correct conclusion, based on the experiment results, is that phenol red does *not* cause the heat. Next, Emily combines phenol red and calcium chloride, a change of two variables in comparison to the last experiment. This new reaction also produces heat, but Emily does not conclude that baking soda is *unnecessary* for the heat. Rather, she states that calcium chloride needs a liquid to conduct heat. This conclusion is not based on experimental results, and it is only partially correct because aqueous liquids mixed with calcium chloride cause the heat. In addition, Emily's final conclusion (calcium chloride causes the heat) is incorrect because it omits the addition of water or a water-based liquid. She also does not use chemical notation.

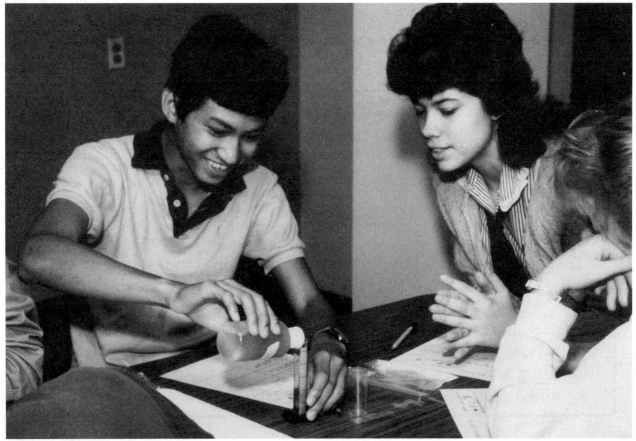

Chemical Reactions

Sample 5: KELLY

Describe your first experiment:
B.S. + C.C. + H_2O

What happened?
heat, bubbles, color change

What can you conclude?

Describe your second experiment:
C.C. + phenol red solution

What happened?
turned hot, pink, boiled

What can you conclude?
is water + C.C. or phenol + C.C.

What do you think causes the heat?
water + C.C.

Areas for additional practice

☑ planning experiments that address a particular question

☑ designing controlled experiments

☑ keeping clear, detailed records of plans, results, and conclusions

☑ drawing conclusions from experiment results

☑ using scientific notation to record experiments and results

Chemical Reactions

Kelly at first substitutes water for phenol red. Her observations of the reaction are perceptive, but she is unable to reach a conclusion. She then chooses to mix calcium chloride and phenol red solution. While technically the variables are controlled between this experiment and the original reaction—baking soda becomes the test variable—Kelly's conclusion is that water and calcium chloride, or phenol red and calcium chloride, cause the heat. These conclusions are not justified by her experiments nor is her final conclusion that water plus calcium chloride cause the heat. Her recording is minimal, though she does make an attempt to use chemical notation.

Sample 6: EVAN

Describe your first experiment:
put in baking soda and calcium chloride and water

What happened?
it fizzed, got hot, dissolved, and gave off a gas, smelled bad! there was less stuff in the bag at the end.

What can you conclude?
that the calcium chloride and baking soda need liquid to change

Describe your second experiment:
baking soda, phenol red, and calcium chloride

What happened?
it fizzed, got hot, dissolved, and gave off a gas, it was like watery lemon pudding

What can you conclude?
that the calcium chloride is the main reason why it is hot

What do you think causes the heat?
The C.C. and H_2O

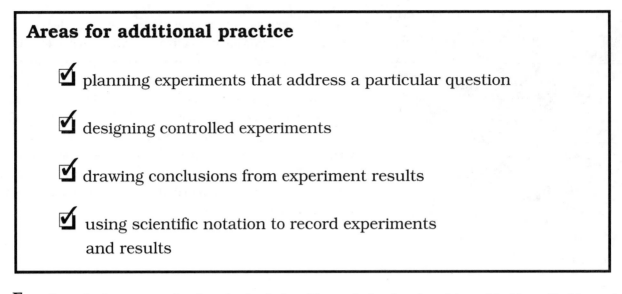

Areas for additional practice

☑ planning experiments that address a particular question

☑ designing controlled experiments

☑ drawing conclusions from experiment results

☑ using scientific notation to record experiments and results

Evan first substitutes water for phenol red solution. He concludes that the calcium chloride and baking soda need liquid to change. This conclusion, though correct, does not answer the question of what causes the heat. His second experiment is identical to the first and provides no additional information. Evan's final conclusion is correct, but it is either based on a hunch or observations of other students' results. It is clear from his records that Evan was so fascinated with the detailed results of his first experiment that he lost sight of the goal to determine the cause of the heat.

 What insights have I gained?

The checklist can help individual students focus on their areas of strength, as well as needs for improvement. To help the entire class develop strong scientific experimentation procedures, the teacher can pose a question and ask for experiments that would help answer the question. At each step of the way, the teacher can ask questions to guide student thinking.

➤ What is the test variable?

➤ Are the variables controlled?

➤ Is there a different experiment we could do which could give us more information about our question?

➤ How might I write down this plan?

The teacher or students could provide hypothetical results of the experiment and ask these questions.

➤ What conclusions can we draw?

➤ Are there any other conclusions that could be drawn from this same test result?

The responses provide information about the students' developmental readiness for the chemical reaction experiment activities. Learning to control variables requires the ability to reason on the abstract level. While sixth graders can be taught the definition and use of controlled variables, multiple experiences are required for students to internalize and apply the concept. When this GEMS activity is used in the future, teachers might ask student to conduct a third or fourth experiment in order to verify their conclusions. Likewise, students could work in pairs to prove their conclusions with test results.

In our sample group, very few students were able to use chemical notation to explain the plans and results of their experiments. This could be due to a number of things.

➤ Lack of teacher emphasis on scientific notation during the unit.

➤ Student discomfort with scientific notation.

➤ Unclear instructions for the task regarding the expectation that chemical notation should be used when students write about their experiments.

If the teacher believes that scientific notation is an important outcome for this unit, and the assessment results indicate that students did not use chemical notation, instruction and/or assessment expectations can be adjusted accordingly.

The responses also indicated that some students had misconceptions about the reaction. One student observed "boiling." While the chemical mixture was both hot and bubbling, it was not boiling (undergoing a phase change from liquid to gas). The teacher might choose to further explore this observation and ask the class whether the mixture was boiling or not, and why. Students could be asked to justify their assumptions with scientific reasoning.

An additional opportunity for follow-up is provided by the student who mentioned that there is "less stuff" in the bag. The teacher might ask, "Did the liquid disappear?" "Where did it go?" While the concept of conservation of mass may seem obvious once it is learned, many students predict that the bag will weigh less after the reaction has occurred! Students can discuss these questions and then predict how or if the weight of the bag might change before and after the reaction occurs; then use an analytical balance to test the students' hypotheses.

Make sure to double bag so you don't "disprove" the law of conservation of mass!

Other Assessment Opportunities in GEMS Using Experiments

Here are some other assessment opportunities in GEMS that use the assessment strategy of experiments. Use this list to find specific opportunities and to inspire you to create your own uses of this assessment strategy.

➤ *BUBBLE-OLOGY*
In Activity 2, students determine which brand of dish washing liquid makes the largest bubbles. Students design an experiment that tests the cleaning properties of various brands of dish washing liquid as a follow-up to Activity 2. In Activity 3, students are asked to identify uncontrolled variables as they redesign an experiment on the effect of glycerin on bubble size. In Activity 6, students conduct experiments to blow a bubble that will last as long as possible.

➤ *CHEMICAL REACTIONS*
Near the end of Part 2, students can conduct experiments to investigate what causes the yellow color, the gas, or the odor in the reaction.

➤ *CRIME LAB CHEMISTRY*
In a Going Further activity at the end of the unit, students use chromatography as a tool to analyze various brown candy smudges and solve the mystery of who used the candy machine.

➤ *EARTHWORMS*
In Session 2, students use the pulse-calculating technique from Session 1 to conduct a new series of experiments where they vary the temperature in the earthworms' habitats.

➤ *EXPERIMENTING WITH MODEL ROCKETS*
In Session 1, students watch their teacher launch a model rocket. They then design a rocket that differs from the teacher's model in only one respect.

➤ *FROG MATH*
Have students conduct a math experiment and explore what would occur if the Hop to the Pond game were played with three dice. How would the frogs be numbered? Which frogs do they think would win the most often? Why? What would the results be?

➤ *HOT WATER AND WARM HOMES*
In Sessions 1–3, students conduct experiments with the solar houses that they've constructed. In Sessions 4–5, they conduct experiments with solar water heaters.

➤ *IN ALL PROBABILITY*
Students can engage in a probability experiment by considering what might happen if game sticks

Involving Dissolving

were played with eight, rather than six, sticks. How would the outcomes change? How would it affect the game?

➤ *INVOLVING DISSOLVING*
Students think of as many words as they can to describe a mystery substance such as Kool-aid powder or Jello-powder. They then predict what might happen when the substance is mixed with cold water, and test their predictions.

➤ *MOONS OF JUPITER*
In Activity 2, the students experiment with impact craters in the classroom.

➤ *PAPER TOWEL TESTING*
In Sessions 2 and 3, students plan and conduct experiments to further explore the comparative qualities of paper towels. They can also design and conduct fair tests to evaluate other attributes of paper towels, such as softness or durability.

➤ *VITAMIN C TESTING*
In Session 4, Experimenting With Vitamin C Content, students conduct an experiment to determine how certain variables affect vitamin C content. In Session 3, students use the previous experiment to compare the vitamin C content in beverages they bring from home.

Hot Water and Warm Homes From Sunlight

Investigations as an Assessment Strategy

Investigations begin with a question to be pursued. The question can be broad or narrow. What is making these holes in the sand? Why does a flute sound different from a violin? How many blocks would it take to build a tower as tall as the ceiling? Why are these plants withered while the rest of the garden is thriving? How much money does it take to own and operate a car? How does the rain get up in the sky? Questions arise from students' natural curiosity about the world and what they encounter in their daily lives. This curiosity, if encouraged and supported, can lead to great discoveries.

Like detectives or police investigators who want to find out who committed a crime, scientific investigators use every tool and strategy at their command to find the answers to their questions. They may go to the library to look up pertinent information, explore relevant phenomena first hand, or perform experiments. The term "investigation" refers to the entire process, from formulation of the question to the point at which the investigator feels satisfied that the best possible answer has been found. Authentic student investigations come from *students'* questions and are open-ended in the directions they lead. However, many students learn how to conduct their own investigations when they first solve problems posed by the teacher.

An investigation undertaken by a second grader would look very different from one done by a group of eighth graders and teacher expectations should vary accordingly. Similar questions may be posed by younger and older students, but all children will develop methods for investigation that are developmentally appropriate for their age and experience.

For example, second graders might wonder how big a bubble they can blow. They could use a straw and blow a number of bubbles. They might wait for each bubble to pop and devise a way to measure the size (diameter or perimeter) of the bubble. If they are unable to blow a larger bubble after several additional tries, they will probably stop.

Eighth graders may have the same question but can be expected to explore bubble making with a variety of tools and several different bubble solutions. As they investigate, they will probably modify their plan several times until they succeed or understand why it cannot succeed.

Students utilize their knowledge of content as well as process skills as they construct their own pathways to explore a question. They make observations and collect and analyze data in order to draw conclusions. Investigations offer the teacher an opportunity to find out what students know and wonder; how they proceed to explore and construct more knowledge about a question; and how they respond when they encounter stumbling blocks. Students demonstrate the important scientific attitudes of curiosity and persistence, expectations and knowledge, as well as their ability to change and modify plans according to evidence and experience.

It may be helpful to think of investigations as the most inclusive category of student projects. To complete an investigation, students utilize a variety of tools. They often explore new areas, create models, plan and perform experiments, conduct research, collect and analyze data, and write reports.

An investigation is completed with a reconsideration of the original question in light of the results. In some cases, new questions may arise during the process that warrant further investigation. Thus the process begins again.

A case study using investigations as an assessment strategy for *Bubble Festival* begins on the next page. Opportunities for investigations assessments in other GEMS units are on page 172.

Searching for Bubble Solutions from *Bubble Festival*

In the *Bubble Festival* unit, students explore bubbles and soap film in many different contexts. A Going Further activity involves students in attempting to answer a question they have about bubbles. This is preceded by a chance for students to write or tell about their discoveries and questions about bubbles.

 What do I want to see?

This assessment task provides students with an number of opportunities.

➤ Articulate a question they have about bubbles—something they wonder about or a challenge they'd like to try.

➤ Come up with and articulate a plan to answer their question or challenge.

➤ Carry out their plan.

➤ Observe and evaluate the results of their plan.

➤ Modify their plan as necessary.

➤ Exhibit the important scientific attitudes of curiosity and persistence in pursuing their questions and challenges.

➤ Demonstrate an understanding of the properties of soap film and a variety of physical phenomena related to soap bubbles.

➤ Solve problems and use other process skills in this investigative context.

 How do I evaluate the student work?

Because the bubble challenge is an open-ended and unstructured investigation, it may not be useful to grade or tightly evaluate student performance. Rather, a teacher can observe students' curiosity, persistence, and see other scientific behaviors in action. Teachers gain information about students' abilities to formulate and articulate investigation plans and results. In addition, investigations can help reveal where students' past knowledge comes into play and where new knowledge is gained.

A teacher can choose to tightly evaluate student investigations *if* specific expectations are made clear to students, prior to beginning their investigations. For instance, a teacher of sixth graders could require that students modify their plans if they don't work at first. Students may also be asked to obtain information from firsthand exploration and experiments *as well as* from other sources such as the library.

The following example describes the step-by-step process for a second grade investigation of bubble making. We describe our observations of students as they conduct their investigations and include examples of students' writing to provide a window on their science and math knowledge, attitudes, and skills at one point in time. Throughout the process, the following questions were addressed.

• How well did students communicate their plans and the results?

• Were they able to modify their plans?

• Did particular children exhibit unusual curiosity and persistence for their age?

To introduce the activity, an open-ended bubble exploration session was conducted. At the end of the session, we asked student to reflect about three questions.

➤ What do you know about bubbles?

➤ What did you find out from your explorations?

➤ What did you see or do with bubbles?

These questions were intentionally open-ended and were more inclusive and enabling than more specific questions, for example, "How big was your bubble?" We also omitted the question "What did you learn about bubbles" because it can be intimidating to some students, especially those who are less aware of their own learning process.

The following list was generated by the students and is just the tip of the iceberg of their discoveries. During the discussion, nearly every child's hand was raised continuously as each wanted to share more about their experiences. Embedded in this list are important discoveries about bubble shapes: the colors on bubbles, methods of blowing bubbles, how two or more bubbles interact, and other insights.

Things We Discovered Today

- made a big bubble

- made a group bubble

- bubbles were mostly circles

- made a bubble on my hand

- I used my hand as a blower

- I transferred a bubble little by little from my hand onto the table.

- I saw reflections in the bubble.

- I joined two bubbles into one big bubble.

- We made a city of bubbles.

- made an egg-shaped bubble

- I put my hand in a bubble.

- when you blow a bubble, it spins and swirls

- started with a small bubble and made it larger

- you can pass bubbles back and forth

- rainbow colors switch when the bubble moves

- it looks like tar on the street (or like oil or acid fluid)

- the bubble was purple then ugly

- bubble looks different from different angles

Throughout the exploration, a GEMS observer noted that one student, who often plays an attention-seeking and disruptive role, was completely absorbed and involved in the bubble activities. When it came time to share discoveries, this child had much to say and her observations were particularly astute. During the discussion, her teacher encouraged the child to contribute to the discussion, and subtly helped to establish her as a "bubble expert," giving her an unaccustomed high status with her peers.

Students then were asked the following open-ended questions.

➤ What do you wonder about bubbles?

➤ What questions do you have about bubbles?

➤ What do you want to try tomorrow?

The following list was generated and recorded.

Things To Investigate Tomorrow

• Can I make a bubble from foam (by smushing)?

• Can we make bubbles with different shapes?

• Will more straws make a bigger bubble?

• Can I make a bubble in a bubble in a bubble?

• What if I smush a bubble between my hands — will it still be there?

• Can I blow a big bubble in the air with a straw?

• Can I blow a bubble through my finger and thumb?

• Can I touch a bubble without popping it?

The questions were designed to enable each student to find his own access point to contribute to this list, whether he was able to formulate a specific question or whether he was still thinking about what he wanted to try. Both are valid starting points for an investigation.

On the following day, the second graders were given a short time to write their responses to three questions.

➤ What do you want to try?

➤ What will you use?

➤ What do you predict will happen?

Students were reminded that spelling was not important for this task. Within ten minutes, all had completed their plans and had begun to blow bubbles, in a calm and focused way. They were on task and inventive. Some students persisted in addressing their challenges longer than others. Others created additional challenges, once they had answered their first question to their satisfaction. A sizable group of students quickly returned to open-ended exploration of the bubbles, with no particular challenge in mind. In retrospect, this particular class demonstrated that they ideally should have had more time to explore the bubbles before they began their investigation activity. At the end of the session, students were asked to go back to their papers and write what happened.

The following selections of student work offer insights into the ways that the students investigated bubbles. The insights are gained from observation, questioning during the investigation process, and students' written answers to the questions.

Julie selected a round tinker toy connector with one larger hole in the middle and several smaller holes around the edges. At first she tried blowing directly on the holes. When she was unable to make a bubble using this strategy, Julie blew through a straw aimed at each hole. This worked with the larger hole but not with the smaller holes. Julie's approach was systematic and thorough. She persisted until it worked. She wrote:

> I want to try making a bubble on my hand and close my hands together and open them. I also want to use a thing that is called a tinker toy. I predict that I will not blow a bubbel with the tinker toy.
>
> It pritty much worked exsept I had to use a straw insted of just air from my mouth and then it worked. I cud only blow threw the middel hole. The straw was too big for the other holes.

Julie does not report the results of her first investigation. She made a bubble about the size of an orange on one soapy hand, and then took another soapy hand and placed it on top of the bubble. She slowly pressed her hands together until there was no space between them. Then she repeatedly opened her hands to see if the bubble would form again. In each instance, the bubble was gone when she pulled her hands apart. When asked what she thought the problem was, Julie responded that the air from the bubble had escaped. When asked where the bubble was now, Julie responded that the outsides of the bubble were still on her hands!

Julie's description of the "deflated" bubble clearly demonstrates her intuitive understanding that a bubble is a thin layer of soap film that encloses air. As she pursued her question, Julie was able to think of a bubble as something with two parts (the soap film and the air) and to analyze what happened when she compressed the bubble by considering each part separately. Her response to the investigation sheds light on her concept of what a bubble is and also demonstrates a second grader's understanding of scientific systems and interactions.

Emily wanted to blow a large bubble dome on a table with four bubble domes nested inside of it. She began with five straws in her mouth to create these nested table bubbles. She predicted that three of these five bubbles would pop. As she attempted her challenge, she found her strategy did not work. When she blew through five straws simultaneously, she created clusters of many bubbles at a time. She wrote:

> I want to try to do 4 inside, inside, inside. I want to use 5 straws to do it. I predict that three bubbles will pop.
>
> All bubbles poped. I think that 5 straws were to much because it didn't werk and only one time I got one bubble. The rest of the times I got like 10, 5, 4, 12, 17 and so.

Emily had a reasonable plan, was able to execute that plan and even made good, quantitative observations about what happened! She then correctly speculated about the cause of the problem. She did not continue on to find a different strategy that might have worked to produce the result she wanted.

Joseph attempted a similar but more modest challenge. He wanted to blow three nested table bubbles. In spite of his prediction that he would be unable to accomplish his goal, Joseph was able to try a variety of strategies until he successfully made a bubble inside a bubble inside a bubble. His successful strategy was to blow a large table bubble, remove the straw, re-dip his straw in bubble solution, insert the wet straw through the wall of the bubble, and then blow a new table bubble by placing the soapy straw next to the surface of the table and blowing. He repeated this sequence of steps until he had blown three nested table bubbles. Joseph demonstrated persistence and focus as he pursued his goal. More information is gained from the observation than from his summary below.

> I want to try putting a bubul into another bubul. I will use straws. I predict that it won't work.
>
> First it dident work and then it did. I blue a bubul then I took the straw out and put it in a bububl and put the straw win and bloo another bubble in it.

Ryan also challenged himself to make nested table bubbles. Ryan is extremely active and is often disruptive in class. Ryan's teacher spent time at the table with him helping him get started. Ryan spent over half the class period working on this challenge—longer than most children. His teacher provided positive feedback for his persistence, and also gave him encouragement when necessary. Ryan had much more success than his paper below indicates, though he shows a striking understanding of his own limits and why he was unable to accomplish his goal.

> 4 inside, inside, inside, inside
> Can use the straw
> I think it will pop.
>
> It didn't work because i was blowing to hard and i got destrackeded.
> and i moved to much.

Anna was very excited about her idea. She wanted to try to make a square bubble by using a bubble manipulative she had once seen—a square-shaped frame made with straws connected by string. (This is referred to as a "bubble window" in the *Bubble Festival* guide). At first, she was convinced that she'd be unable to do it, because she didn't have string "or even know how to make something like that." With a few prompts from the teacher, she found some yarn and scissors and constructed her string and straw apparatus. When she had difficulty threading the limp yarn through the thin straws, Anna asked for transparent tape and taped the strings to the straws! This inventive technique proved to be the flaw of Anna's investigation! She quickly realized her next challenge when she saw that the size of her square-shaped frame was larger than the small bowls of bubble solution. Again, Anna concluded that her investigation wouldn't work.

Anna had a quick consult with the teacher who challenged her with the question "How will you solve that problem?" Anna then independently found a larger container and filled it with bubble solution. When she went to see if her string and straws frame would make a square bubble, the tape quickly lost its stickiness in the bubble solution and her square frame fell apart. Anna described the problem to the teacher. After some discussion, Anna agreed that her initial plan was best—to string the yarn through the straws. However, she had no interest in trying it!

In general, Anna persisted and used good problem-solving skills for a second grader. While her first tendency was to conclude that things wouldn't work, she responded positively to prompts from the teacher and was able to do what she needed to overcome the first three or four hurdles! In this situation, Anna did not persist beyond the first failed trial of her investigation. Her curiosity about her original question was not strong enough to motivate her to solve what she perceived to be a big problem with her investigation equipment, as illustrated in her written response on the next page.

I want to try to make a scware bubble. I am going to use a straw and string witch looks like this:

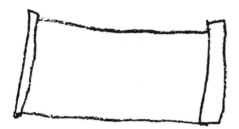

I perdict that it will look like this:

My thing fell apart. I think it was not a good one. The string fell apart first. Then the straws.

Bubble Festival

Bubble Festival

Marcus used a familiar tool for a new purpose when he decided to investigate whether bubbles can be blown with scissors. When he dipped the closed scissors handles in the bubble solution and blew, he was able to make bubbles. As he described in his paper, opened scissors did not work.

> I'm going to try to blow a buble with a scissors. I want to use scissors.
> I think it will work.
>
> It worked really good. First I just blew and it worked. then i tryed to do it when it was open. it did not work.

Though it is not evident from his writing, Marcus was extremely systematic in his approach. We observed Marcus as he closed the open scissors, little by little, stopping at each interval to test whether he was able to make a bubble. He attempted to find the threshold at which the handles were close enough to make bubbles. Other student responses show a range of approaches and varying degrees of success.

Pasand used his body as a nonstandard measuring tool as shown in his description of the size of his bubbles.

> I will try to make a bubble as big as me. I will use a straw and my hand. I predict that I won't make a bubble as big as me.
>
> I could not make it work because the bubble kept poping. But I could make bubbles as big as may head.

Herman modified his goal during his investigation. After he attempted to cover the table with one large bubble, he instead managed to cover the surface with many small bubbles, as he summarizes.

> I want to try to make a bubble that is as big as the table. I will use a straw. I predict that the bubble will pop.
>
> It worked good. Insted I made a lot of bubbles.

Anita had a similar goal and conceded that she could only make a bubble half the size of the table. She wrote:

> Covering the table with a bubble. Three straws. I think it will not work.
>
> It didn't work becuas wen I bluw a bubble it got only meedium and then popet. But I did make a bubl have the size of the table.

Anita, Herman and Pasand all learned things about the limits of bubble size. This knowledge will enable them to correctly predict a variety of other size-related questions.

Alice formulated a question that involved cooperative learning. She became an expert at "passing" bubbles from her straw to another. In order to do this, she gained an intuitive understanding of some of the differences between large and small bubbles. In discussion with the observer, she noted that big bubbles are floppy and have very thin "outsides." Small bubbles have thicker "outsides" and are therefore less fragile. Her direct experience helps her begin to understand that smaller bubbles do not undulate or change shape when they are manipulated with a straw, and thus they are easier to pass from one straw to another.

> I want to try to blow a big bubble
> on the straw and pass it back and
> fourth to another person. I will
> use a straw. I will pass a big
> bubble and then it will pop.
>
> I culdent blow a big bubble so I
> did it with little bubbles.

 ## What insights have I gained?

Investigations can emphasize important learning qualities that aren't often explicitly recognized with more traditional assessment tools. An observant teacher will gain information about students' level of curiosity, willingness to take risks, organizational approaches, persistence in problem solving, and their ability to cooperate with others who are working on similar tasks. In primary grades, teacher observations are essential to the evaluation process, as students will likely be unable to express the full breadth of their experience in writing.

Investigations also validate a variety of learning styles. For example, in the second grade classroom, students who were least focused in traditional classroom activities were extremely persistent and successful in the bubble investigations. This is often the case when teachers move beyond rote learning and adopt student-centered approaches to mathematics and science curriculum.

Curiosity and persistence are key elements of successful investigations at all grade levels. To encourage these qualities, the teacher might choose to provide students with positive feedback about curiosity and persistence as students share their investigations.

It is important that students have opportunities to investigate at the earliest grade levels. This will help them bring greater skill and increased motivation to investigations in later years. Thus investigations are not only useful to help you discover what your students can do; they are also learning experiences in themselves.

Bubble Festival

Other Assessment Opportunities in GEMS Using Investigations

Here are some other assessment opportunities in GEMS that use the assessment strategy of investigations. Use this list to find specific opportunities and to inspire you to create your own uses of this assessment strategy.

➤ *ANIMALS IN ACTION*

At the end of Session 2, students are introduced to the term *hypothesis* and are guided to develop sample hypotheses based on the animal behaviors they observe. In Session 3, teams investigate animal behavior, and are asked to design their own experiment to test their hypotheses. In Session 4, teams conduct the investigations they designed.

➤ *BUILD IT! FESTIVAL*

In the What Comes Next? activity, students utilize their knowledge of polygons to investigate whether any four sided polygons can tessellate.

➤ *EARTHWORMS*

Students conduct other pulse rate experiments with earthworms as a Going Further activity at the end of the guide.

➤ *IN ALL PROBABILITY*

After they conduct the Penny Flip activity, students describe the results of their investigations and then analyze the data from the entire class.

➤ *INVESTIGATING ARTIFACTS*

Devise a What's Hidden in a Real Midden? assignment, to build upon and extend the Famous Finds page. Each team can research a famous find and select five artifacts unearthed at the site. Other teams can ask questions and attempt to figure out more about the discovery and determine the exact location and culture.

➤ *MAPPING ANIMAL MOVEMENTS*

Have students design and conduct other animal mapping investigations at home with pets, backyard animals, with their own family, or in the classroom.

➤ *MAPPING FISH HABITATS*

In Session 4, students plan and conduct their own aquarium investigations. The teacher can ask each team to write a description of the investigation. The description should include any habitat changes, predictions, and procedures.

➤ *RIVER CUTTERS*

Assign student teams to design a different dripper system to model the dripping of raindrops onto the soil. Teams can draw their own dripper system and use any materials/mechanisms. The one condition is that the system should drip.

Earthworms

Conventions, Conferences, and Debates as an Assessment Strategy

Scientific conventions, conferences, and debates in the classroom can all be excellent assessment forums, just as they, in the real world, serve as active forums for communicating on major issues.

At a scientific convention, scientists and mathematicians meet to share their ideas with the larger science and mathematics community. They learn about each others' research and argue, debate, and critically evaluate each others' work. The purpose of these conventions is to critically evaluate each others' findings, and to seek better understandings of the natural world. It is through this kind of forum, as well as the publication of research papers, that scientific and mathematics communities advance and refine knowledge. In the GEMS unit *Oobleck: What Do Scientists Do?*, students hold a scientific convention to discuss and refine the "laws of Oobleck." The ability to clearly communicate ideas, critically evaluate them with respect to the larger field of knowledge, and convince others is essential in science. This becomes evident when attending a scientific convention or reading about a controversial subject in a scientific journal.

Issue-oriented conferences, debates, hearings, and town meetings are among our most important and visible social forums. At a conference various people with different perspectives meet to share their ideas on a matter of common concern. Conferences are often held to clarify the key issues and problems in a field—be it health care, science education, computer networks, or corporate management—to exchange information about the issues and problems, and, if at all possible, propose solutions that might be acceptable to many of the groups involved. Depending on the topic, some of these forums also involve scientists, mathematicians, and engineers speaking about their areas of expertise on matters of public concern, such as health and safety issues, environmental impact of new initiatives, and issues related to technology. This is an important interface between science and society, where knowledge can be used to protect and improve our society. In the town meeting in *Acid Rain*, students gather to represent different community members and interests, seeking to solve problems caused by or related to acid rain.

By participating in classroom conferences, town meetings, and debates, students are able to demonstrate their understanding of key issues and problems. They can also improve in their abilities to recognize alternative points of view, to communicate ideas clearly, to speak persuasively, and to critically evaluate the ideas of others. There is a strong connection to real-world issues and processes, as well as the immediate and compelling need to communicate knowledge and ideas to one's peers. In classroom conferences, peer-teaching abounds, both within and between groups of students.

For the purposes of assessment, a classroom conference, a scientific convention, a town meeting, or a debate share many common attributes because they all allow you to trace the growth of your students' abilities to assimilate ideas and communicate them to others in the context of a simulated real-world group meeting. It may be useful, however, to draw some distinctions. A scientific convention is generally attended just by scientists (or students acting as scientists) who critique each others' findings in order to advance scientific knowledge. A conference is often a meeting of people with different perspectives and viewpoints who come together to air these viewpoints and perhaps come to some mutual understandings. A debate is an opportunity for advocates of a defined position to exercise their skills to persuade others. The goal of a debate is to convince others that you are right, not necessarily to arrive at mutual understandings or to learn more about the natural world. Conferences, scientific conventions, and debates are all useful strategies for teaching, learning, and assessment.

Students benefit tremendously by participating in their own conventions, conferences, and debates. There is a strong connection to real-world issues and processes as well as the immediate and compelling need to communicate knowledge and ideas to one's peers. In classroom conferences, peer teaching abounds, both within and between groups of students.

Being able to see students in action at a classroom convention or conference provides teachers with ideal opportunities to assess their students' abilities to:

- Demonstrate and apply their knowledge about a subject area.

- Demonstrate ability to listen carefully and be non-judgemental.

- Communicate their viewpoints to others clearly and persuasively.

- Critically evaluate their own and other people's ideas.

- Synthesize a variety of viewpoints.

- Modify their opinions and findings based on input from others.

A case study using conventions, conferences, and debates as an assessment strategy (via a World Conference) in *Global Warming and the Greenhouse Effect* begins on the next page. Opportunities for conventions, conferences, and debates assessments in other GEMS units are on page 182.

Global Warming and the Greenhouse Effect

Global Warming and the Greenhouse Effect

Global Warming and the Greenhouse Effect

CASE STUDY USING CONVENTIONS, CONFERENCES, AND DEBATES

World Conference from *Global Warming and the Greenhouse Effect*

Groups of students take on the role of different interest groups, including automobile manufacturers, island nations, agriculturalists, conservationists, and wood and paper producers. They spend several sessions preparing for a World Conference on Global Warming in which they present their points of view and solutions to either cope with a warmer world or to reduce the amount of carbon dioxide in the atmosphere.

 What do I want to see?

In their preparatory notes, students should demonstrate that they:

➤ Understand the viewpoint of the interest group they represent.

➤ Have ideas about how to prevent or reduce global warming, and/or adapt to a warmer world.

➤ Work cooperatively with everyone in group-making contributions.

Through their participation in the World Conference, students should demonstrate their abilities to:

➤ Explain the greenhouse effect.

➤ Explain why many scientists believe the greenhouse effect in the Earth's atmosphere, and the increase in greenhouse gases, may cause global warming.

➤ Refer to one or two controversies about global warming: whether or not global warming has actually been observed, uncertainty about how great an increase in global temperature there may be, or disagreements about the possible effects.

➤ Speak in a clear and persuasive way.

➤ Make insightful comments and/or raise challenging questions to other groups.

➤ Show in their comments that they understand the viewpoints of other interest groups.

➤ Present reasonable ideas for how their interest group could assist in efforts to reduce carbon dioxide production, or find ways to adapt to a warmer world.

➤ Interact constructively with the other groups, listening to what they have to say and responding to their concerns.

➤ Propose one or more solutions that might reduce the increase in greenhouse gases and might be acceptable to other groups. Demonstrate understanding of the need for a **global** solution. Consider more than their own viewpoint when discussing possible solutions.

 How do I evaluate the student work?

The teacher chose to evaluate the work of groups of eighth grade students in two ways.

1. During the World Conference, he stood in the back of the classroom taking notes on individuals' and groups' presentations, especially in light of the above criteria. He also videotaped the World Conference so he could refer back, if necessary, to specific students' or groups' presentations.

2. He collected writing that students had done to prepare for the conference. To help students understand the basis for evaluating the work, the main criteria were discussed ahead of time with them. They were also told that this project would represent a significant portion of their grade for the semester and that assessment would depend on both their groups' written preparation notes and their performance in the World Conference.

Here, and on the following pages, are samplings of some of the initial preparatory student work. The assignment was to write a brief description of their group's views and come up with questions for the other four groups.

CONSERVATIONISTS

One of the feared effects of global warming is the melting of the polar ice caps. Which in turn raises the sea level. This may have effects on the island nations.

We are especially worried about the rain forest. We would like a planting program to be supplied by all countries but nothing can happen without the help of others. We want immediate reduction in the amount of greenhouse gases being produced, and laws that will make this happen, especially those in major countries. We want commitment of countries and industries.

(to the island nations) Are the island nations prepared for what could happen?

(to the wood and paper manufacturers) What happens when the section of the forest that you are chopping wood runs out? Do you keep on taking more of the forest?

(to the agriculturalists) Do they have the info to cut the input of CO2 into the atmosphere?

(to the auto makers) What proof do you have to back up your statement that you want to make cars that people who want to protect the environment will buy?

Teacher Notes

Too focused on rain forests. Definitely a related topic, but they didn't address global warming directly. Didn't state their own position. Need to stress for next preparation session. Question to the agriculturalists not clear. Other questions good. Tough question to auto makers.

AUTOMOBILE MANUFACTURERS

DEBATE! SPEACH We at the automobil company feel a need to produce quality cars, and we also need to build cars to fit the need of you, the people. We have been recently asked by the legislation to produce more pollution-efficient cars and factories. By doing this we would need more money, and that would cost more money for the buyer. This would increase the firering and termination of more employies, because of need for money.

To the island nations: What kinds of things do you use on your island such as motor boats?

To the paper manufacturers: What did you say you do with the waste wood and papers? Do people really need as much paper as you make?

To the agriculturalists: Why do you think it's our faugt when your animals aren't helping either? All the blame shouldn't go to us. We don't feel we need laws to protect trees which take up space. We could make more freeways for the cars.

To the conservationists: What have you done to help pollution?

Teacher Notes

Auto makers group worked well together to come up with position statement. Tone of defensiveness and attacking others, though pointed questions OK. Need to think about what <u>they</u> might do to ease pollution, etc. Interesting comment on economics, though not clearly stated.

WOOD AND PAPER PRODUCERS

We are an important part of the economy. We employ loggers and other workers in sawmills in the timber industry. We have been accused of not respecting the environment and wasting wood, but we ask you—don't people need our products? People need wood for houses, for furniture, and paper is needed for books and newspapers, so we believe we perform a useful service to others.

Of course we are in favor of replanting programs, and we have no wish to overly damage the environment. But we are not at all sure about whether or not global warming is really happening, and how much we have to do with it!

To the conservationists, we ask how are we sure that the Greenhouse Effect is going to cause major changes—what evidence, proof, do you have?

To the automobile manufacturers—what do you think you're doing to the environment?

Teacher Notes

They raise key question—whether or not global warming is an issue. Great question about evidence. Worked well together, though Carolyn tended to dominate a bit. Tone more aggressive than other groups, hostile, defensive, not as geared to working with other groups to solve problems, etc. Stress this for next time.

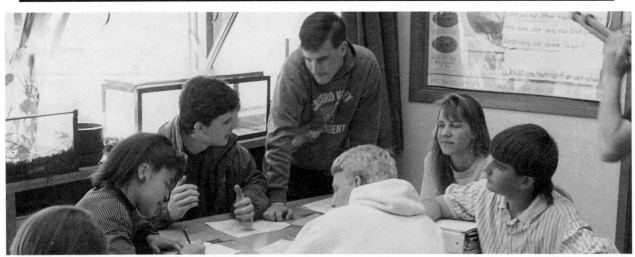

Global Warming and the Greenhouse Effect

ISLAND NATIONS

Green Island Nations *(presented in rap-style)*

The rising sea
Has threatened our own life
Our freshwater and gardens
Have nearly died

We are part of an island nation
We are part of an island nation

Those hurricanes
Devastate my mind
They have grown more frequent
In my time-line

We are part of an island nation
We are part of an island nation

The greenhouse gases
Have clogged our throats
Now we have to leave
In our small boats

We are part of an island nation
We are part of an island nation

If you will stop
All of this bad stuff,
We just can't thank you
Can't thank you enough!

We are part of an island nation
We are part of an island nation

The moral is—the greenhouse effect is messing a lot of people up and you need to stop producing greenhouse gases.

Directed to the conservationists—what have you done for us lately?

Directed to the Wood and Paper Producers—what have you done to help? You need to help recycling real bad.

Teacher Notes

Group didn't work as well together as some others. Two wrote down song/rap; two others had some input on song but mostly did questions. Questions slang/amusing but lack specific content. All in group should work on these before conference. Great to see Leroi and Caitlin so enthusiastic!

AGRICULTURALISTS

We are the agriculturalists. We are very worried because if the climate changes then our livlihoods depend on our farms and animals and if the climate changes it could alter our production & distribution of our crops and income. But we're in a delemma because on the other hand our sheep and horses create menthane threw the menuer which contributes to the greenhouse affects. Maybe if we change their diet & try to do more research on how we can use meXthane to produce more energy around our farms.

We also contribute to the amount of CO_2 in the air by cutting down our trees, so we would like to research how we can cut down on that process. We are glad that the Wood & Paper Producers can at least use the wood that we cut down so it doesn't go to waste. It would help us if the automobile makers would try to find a way to cut down on exhaust so our crops don't die.

Teacher Notes

Group did not list questions, needs to do so before conference! Worked well together in group and included (spelling aside) the issue of animals and methane. Good sense of interconnection between the groups, cooperative tone—need to emphasize that to some of the other groups.

Global Warming and the Greenhouse Effect

In addition to the notes on the five different groups attending the "World Conference," the teacher made more general notes on the class as a whole, as well as notes on how well the presentations were given and received.

General Teacher Notes

"Some groups cooperated well in writing a brief statement and brainstorming questions, while in others (Island Nations, Conservationists) too much of work done by smaller number. Use notes to give feedback to each group as they continue to prepare for conference. Need to address issue of casting blame on other groups for the problem. Some questions for other groups overly hostile, defensive. Already suggested groups should look for ways to compromise and work together, but that point could have been made more clearly as student teams began work. Tricky line here—on one hand, it's logical that groups hold some conflicting positions, on the other hand, decision making, problem solving in the real world have to involve negotiation. A good real-life lesson.

On the Presentations

"Intense interest and involvement of the class as a whole . . . Carolyn, Paul, Latifah, Graciela, oral skills excellent, pleased to see Graciela so confident and strong, she likes being an environmentalist!

"Manuel—quick responses to the questions directed at his group (auto makers), graceful way of agreeing with position of other group, stressing care about the environment, but maintaining own position, etc.

"Many others definitely challenged, trying hard, displaying real improvement in ability to speak clearly in front of the class.

"A few (Albert, Stephanie) confused global warming and the ozone hole, and no one contradicted them.

"Great debate, started mainly between the conservationists and wood and paper producers, with lots of others chiming in—on whether or not global warming is really happening or are changes in temperature part of a natural cycle? Variety of opinions and good evidence introduced.

"Five or six students referred directly to portions of unit to support positions. Colin especially talked about comparing CO_2 in car exhaust and other gases—pretty hard for auto makers to respond! Rebecca, Leroi, both referred to the story of Noua's Island. Caitlin and Tawnisha, the effects wheel activity. Real advance for Caitlin, connecting science to real life, really getting into the plight of the islanders—and performing the rap with Leroi—simply fantastic, can't wait to see them again on the video!

"Attempted arguments of some students (Isabel, Alan, Chris, maybe Rosa) indicate they may not fully understand what is meant scientifically by greenhouse effect—seemed confused when others talked about higher levels of carbon dioxide and increased global temperature. Also, a few students still seem to think problems are in a particular place, or caused by a specific industry, etc.—don't realize fully the global nature of the issue, and the interconnections between all interest groups."

Q What insights have I gained?

The intensity of emotion and level of knowledge displayed by the large majority of students, as seen in the classroom observations, student writing, and the video, was impressive. Information sheets provided in the guide to each interest group definitely influenced some of what they wrote and spoke, but several groups went far beyond these in preparing and presenting their cases. Some referred to a world environmental conference going on at the time; others cited information from magazine and newspaper articles to support their positions.

In the important realm of unexpected outcomes, the teacher was overjoyed to read the rhyme/rap creation and witness its outstanding performance by two somewhat challenging and less involved students.

Although clarified during the unit, students still had difficulty distinguishing between global warming issues and the "hole" in the ozone layer. This confusion is also a common misconception in the general population. It needs to be further clarified in next week's debriefing discussions with students and stressed next time the unit is presented. The teacher decided not to hold students accountable in grading for this confusion, and to explain that to them, when he stresses that grades will be based on participation, teamwork, and the knowledge/creativity students displayed over the course of the entire project.

Most importantly, notes and observations suggest the need for an increased emphasis throughout the last several sessions, and especially right before students start preparing for the conference, on **coming up with mutual solutions, rather than casting blame.**

The debate on whether or not global warming is an actual phenomenon emerged as a strong way to focus discussion. Perhaps the limerick on the back cover of the GEMS guide could be handed out to students after the world conference and they could dramatize it for extra credit.

The teacher also considered preceding the entire unit with the GEMS guide *Hot Water and Warm Homes from Sunlight*, to attain further clarity on the greenhouse effect, as well as for its other environmentally related content.

He was especially pleased to see how students used the hands-on and other experiences they'd had in the unit to better articulate their positions in the debate. The general high quality of the conference presentations indicated how successful students were in applying their new science and mathematics learning in a more social studies-oriented context, and from a particular point of view. That level of success was a joy to behold!

Other Assessment Opportunities in GEMS Using Conventions, Conferences, and Debates

Here are some other assessment opportunities in GEMS that use the assessment strategy of conventions and debates. Use this list to find specific opportunities and to inspire you to create your own uses of this assessment strategy.

➤ *ACID RAIN*
Students conduct a town meeting on acid rain, taking the roles of manufacturers, politicians, fishing people, and local residents.

➤ *CHEMICAL REACTIONS*
Students could conduct a scientific convention, sharing the results of their experiments.

➤ *INVESTIGATING ARTIFACTS*
Students could conduct a public hearing on the environmental impact of building a shopping center on the site of a Native American midden.

➤ *MYSTERY FESTIVAL*
Students could enact a trial at which groups of students present evidence for why they think a certain suspect is responsible for the disappearance of Felix.

➤ *OOBLECK: WHAT DO SCIENTISTS DO?*
Students conduct a scientific convention to determine the natural laws of Oobleck, or students engage in a debate: is it a liquid or a solid?

➤ *RIVER CUTTERS*
Students could conduct a public forum on the results of their investigations of the effects of constructing dams and/or burying toxic waste near the river site.

Applications as an Assessment Strategy

The assessment strategies of exploration, experimentation, and application highlighted in this handbook reflect the three stages of "the learning cycle" as described in a seminal paper by Karplus and Atkin in 1962. GEMS guides generally follow this cycle of activity because it helps students construct new knowledge as they sharpen their scientific and mathematical thinking skills.

As recommended by Karplus and Atkin, GEMS guides begin with open-ended **explorations** of real phenomena, so students can become familiar with the new terrain, and raise some initial questions themselves. The exploration phase concludes when students describe their discoveries, discuss and debate their initial findings, and raise new ideas and questions with teacher encouragement. In stage two, the teacher **introduces new concepts and methods that help the students make sense of their observations**, or answer some of their initial questions. Often this more disciplined study takes the form of experiments. This stage concludes when students report on the results of their experiments and investigations. The purpose of stage three is to help the students consolidate and utilize their knowledge by challenging them to **apply what they learned to new situations.** As they apply their new knowledge and methods, students may explore new phenomena or raise new questions, so the learning cycle begins again.

By asking students to apply what they know, teachers can observe as students utilize knowledge and process skills to solve problems, master challenges, and make new discoveries. Often students recognize the relevance of content and process knowledge during this application phase of learning. When an activity requires application of knowledge, teachers learn whether students are able to apply concepts in new and/or real-life situations. This makes applications a valuable and natural assessment strategy.

Applications can be close or distant transfers of the knowledge, skills, and concepts gained from GEMS guides. For example, in *Height-O-Meters*, students use the triangulation technique to measure the angular height of the flagpole, or other tall object in or near

their school, and the height of balls thrown in the air. This is a close transfer, a replication of the procedure in a concrete and familiar situation. A distant transfer occurs when students apply the technique of triangulation to determine the location of a forest fire. Instead of visualizing a vertical triangle formed by the top and bottom of the flagpole and the observer, the students can only solve this problem if they visualize a horizontal triangle formed by the two observation towers and the forest fire. While this problem situation is more difficult than finding the altitude of another vertical object, students who can solve it have not simply learned a rote method; they have learned to use triangulation as a very powerful general concept, applicable to all sorts of different situations.

When tasks require student to apply their knowledge and skills to new situations, teachers can gain information about their students' abilities to:

- Grasp the essential concepts, methods, and techniques that were presented in the unit.

- Utilize concepts, techniques, and methods in math and science in new situations.

- Apply the full range of scientific processes—observing, comparing, categorizing, communicating, relating, hypothesizing, inferring, etc.—to real-world problems.

- Recognize that a great many real-world problems can be solved through scientific concepts and methods.

A case study using applications as an assessment strategy in *Fingerprinting* is on the next page. Opportunities for applications assessments in other GEMS units are on pages 193–194.

Fingerprint Comparison from *Fingerprinting*

Students explore the similarities and variations of fingerprints in the *Fingerprinting* GEMS guide. First, they use pencil, paper, and tape to produce their own fingerprints. They create their own scheme to classify ten different fingerprints and then are introduced to the standard arch-loop-whorl system of classification. Last, they apply this classification system to solve a mystery.

To assess students' ability to produce and compare fingerprints, we presented fifth graders with tape, scratch paper, magnifying lenses, and #2 pencils. We asked them to complete the following assignment (see the next page) at the end of the unit.

 What do I want to see?

This assessment task provides students with an opportunity to apply skills learned during the *Fingerprinting* unit and demonstrate their ability to:

➤ Use the graphite-tape fingerprinting technique.

➤ Use rich attribute vocabulary to describe their own thumbprint and another print.

➤ Use the classifications of arch, loop, and whorl to analyze fingerprints.

➤ Compare two prints and describe their differences and similarities.

 How do I evaluate the student work?

Students will need to produce a clear fingerprint in order to describe and compare it with the model provided. However, the emphasis of this assessment is to observe, describe, and compare fingerprints. Therefore, students were not penalized if they had not perfected the graphite-tape fingerprint technique. The form below was used to evaluate student responses that appear on the following pages.

FINGERPRINT ASSESSMENT

DESCRIPTIONS OF FINGERPRINTS					
Minimal					Extensive

COMPARISON OF FINGERPRINTS					
Minimal					Extensive

USE OF STANDARD CLASSIFICATIONS					
Minimal					Extensive

Name _____ Date _____

Use tape and a pencil to make a print of your left or right thumb.

Put the print in the empty space below.

↓

Use words to describe the patterns and lines you see in this print. Use what you know about fingerprints to list as many descriptions as you can!

Use words to describe the patterns and lines you see in your print. Use what you know about fingerprints to list as many descriptions as you can!

Tell how these two fingerprints are different:

Tell how these two fingerprints are alike:

RESPONSE 1

The description of the fingerprints is extensive and thoughtful. The comparison of the fingerprints is minimal. The arch-loop-whorl classification is used with detail in the description but omitted from the comparison.

FINGERPRINT MODEL	STUDENT'S FINGERPRINT
This fingerprint is a loop. The loop starts from the right and moves its way up and to the left. It goes in a little and drops right back out. It looks different.	This fingerprint is a whorl. A whorl goes round and round until at one point, it stops way in the middle. I like this print because it's never been noticed by me before. I just realized I had a whorl!
THE PRINTS ARE DIFFERENT . . .	**THE PRINTS ARE ALIKE . . .**
They have different shapes.	They're both fingerprints.

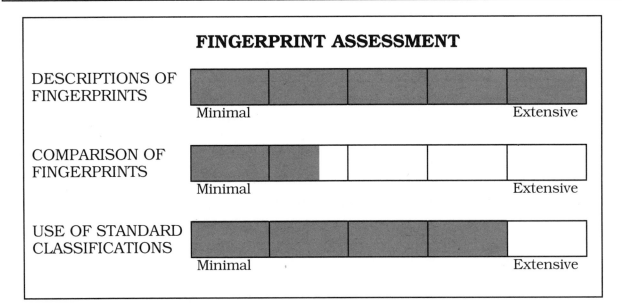

FINGERPRINT ASSESSMENT

DESCRIPTIONS OF FINGERPRINTS
Minimal   Extensive

COMPARISON OF FINGERPRINTS
Minimal   Extensive

USE OF STANDARD CLASSIFICATIONS
Minimal   Extensive

RESPONSE 2

The description of the fingerprints includes details of the origination points of the loop and whorl. The comparison of the fingerprints lacks detail.

FINGERPRINT MODEL	STUDENT'S FINGERPRINT
This is a loop and it started on the right.	It's a whorl and it started from the bottom.
THE PRINTS ARE DIFFERENT . . .	**THE PRINTS ARE ALIKE . . .**
One is a loop and one is a whorl. They are different. One is made with tape.	They're both fingerprints and there are lines.

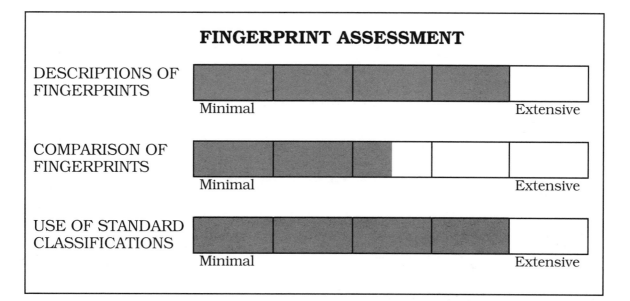

FINGERPRINT ASSESSMENT

DESCRIPTIONS OF FINGERPRINTS — Minimal / Extensive

COMPARISON OF FINGERPRINTS — Minimal / Extensive

USE OF STANDARD CLASSIFICATIONS — Minimal / Extensive

RESPONSE 3

This student describes two strikingly similar fingerprints in detail but has incorrectly applied the standard fingerprint classification system in her response. She uses the arch, loop, whorl vocabulary to describe the shapes of individual lines in the print. However, she has not demonstrated understanding of the concept that forensic scientists classify **entire** prints as either arches, loops, or whorls.

FINGERPRINT MODEL	STUDENT'S FINGERPRINT
I see a loop, a couple of arches, but no whorls. This looks kind of like my right thumb.	It's a whorl and it started from the bottom.
THE PRINTS ARE DIFFERENT . . .	**THE PRINTS ARE ALIKE . . .**
They aren't really different. They look the same except mine is a little larger.	Well, they both have a loop, some arches, but no whorls. I'm beginning to think the one on the left is MY fingerprint.

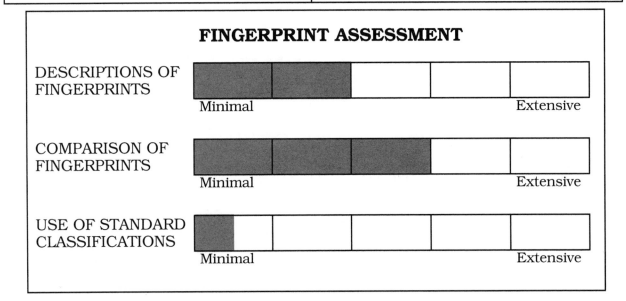

RESPONSE 4

This student's description of the fingerprints is fairly extensive while her comparison of the fingerprints is extremely detailed. The high quality of the comparisons illustrates that use of standard classifications is helpful, though not essential, to a precise description. It is clear, however, that the student understands and can apply the classifications of loop and whorl.

FINGERPRINT MODEL	STUDENT'S FINGERPRINT
This fingerprint goes up and turns back down. It seems to curve like a road. The pattern is a loop.	My fingerprint turns around like a whirlpool. it goes around like a spiral. The pattern is a whorl.
THE PRINTS ARE DIFFERENT . . .	**THE PRINTS ARE ALIKE . . .**
The two fingerprints are very different by the patterns. The pattern on the left starts at one point and loops around and goes the same direction from where it started from. The other pattern starts at one point and goes around and around.	These two fingerprints are alike from the top curves. They go around their main spot, the middle. These patterns are alike from the humps at the top and also the humps on the top kind of look like hills.

FINGERPRINT ASSESSMENT

DESCRIPTIONS OF FINGERPRINTS
Minimal ▮▮▮▮☐ Extensive

COMPARISON OF FINGERPRINTS
Minimal ▮▮▮▮▮ Extensive

USE OF STANDARD CLASSIFICATIONS
Minimal ▮▮☐☐☐ Extensive

RESPONSE 5

This response contains few details in the description or the comparison of the fingerprints. The student does not mention specific characteristics or standard classifications of the prints. Rather, a limited view is presented by comparisons of what the print "looks like."

FINGERPRINT MODEL	STUDENT'S FINGERPRINT
It looks like a whirlpool.	Hairball, mask, basketball

THE PRINTS ARE DIFFERENT . . .	THE PRINTS ARE ALIKE . . .
One looks like a whirlpool and the one I did looks like a hairball.	Basketball, ball

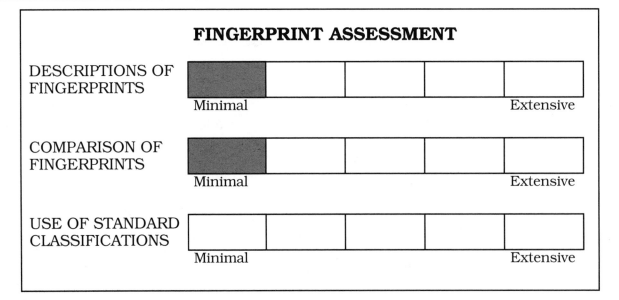

FINGERPRINT ASSESSMENT

DESCRIPTIONS OF FINGERPRINTS	▓				
	Minimal				Extensive
COMPARISON OF FINGERPRINTS	▓				
	Minimal				Extensive
USE OF STANDARD CLASSIFICATIONS					
	Minimal				Extensive

RESPONSE 6

This response superficially describes the fingerprints, makes vague comparisons between the two prints and makes only one reference to the standard arch-loop-whorl classification system.

FINGERPRINT MODEL	STUDENT'S FINGERPRINT
Looks like my print on my ring finger on my left hand, lines are together.	Lines are separated, lots of lines, lines are small.
THE PRINTS ARE DIFFERENT . . .	**THE PRINTS ARE ALIKE . . .**
My print's lines are separated, the next one's lines are together.	Both are loops, have lots of lines.

FINGERPRINT ASSESSMENT

DESCRIPTIONS OF FINGERPRINTS	Minimal			Extensive
COMPARISON OF FINGERPRINTS	Minimal			Extensive
USE OF STANDARD CLASSIFICATIONS	Minimal			Extensive

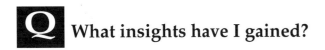

Q What insights have I gained?

Students varied greatly in their ability to describe their fingerprints and use their understanding of the standard classification scheme to classify and compare prints.

In this group, some students appeared more comfortable with the arch-loop-whorl classification system. However, only a few students in the class demonstrated no knowledge or incorrect knowledge of these classifications. It seems clear that the large majority class was developmentally ready to understand and use classification schemes.

Although a range of responses is likely to occur in any assessment task, we realized that a large number of students need additional experiences where they could hone their observation skills and build the necessary vocabulary to notice detailed differences between fingerprints or other objects. These experiences could be provided as part of the Going Further activities suggested in the *Fingerprinting* unit, which include group brainstorming, additional discussion, and ample writing time for students to list the distinguishing features of particular fingerprints and compare how the prints are similar or different. Students could also work in pairs to edit and strengthen their descriptions and comparisons.

The scientific processes of observing, communicating, comparing, and ordering are also explored in several GEMS guides at this grade level, most notably *Investigating Artifacts*, *Mystery Festival*, and *Of Cabbages and Chemistry*. These processes are also utilized in other curriculum areas. For example, students are often asked to describe and compare characters from literature in language arts.

Mystery Festival

Investigating Artifacts

Of Cabbages and Chemistry

Other Assessment Opportunities in GEMS Using Applications

Here are some other assessment opportunities in GEMS that use the assessment strategy of applications. Use this list to find specific opportunities and to inspire you to create your own uses of this assessment strategy.

➤ *COLOR ANALYZERS*
In Session 1, students use colored light filters to decode secret messages. In Session 2, students apply the knowledge they gained in the last session to create their own secret messages that can be decoded with colored light filters.

➤ *CONVECTION: A CURRENT EVENT*
Students work individually or in pairs to figure out, based on what they have learned, what causes winds around the globe. They use their understanding of convection to predict which way they would expect the wind to blow for someone who lives in the United States and for someone who lives in Australia.

➤ *EARTH, MOON, AND STARS*
After the unit is completed, students have an opportunity to apply their knowledge of moon phases. When the moon is visible in the sky, they predict where the moon will be the next day or the next week. When the moon is not visible, they explain where it is now.

➤ *EXPERIMENTING WITH MODEL ROCKETS*
In Sessions 5 and 6, students apply their knowledge of measurement with altimeters as they determine the angular height of their rockets and calculate linear altitudes.

➤ *FROG MATH*
Students apply their ability to estimate during weekly challenges at a classroom estimation station. They make estimates, write about which estimate they think is the closest, and why.

➤ *GROUP SOLUTIONS*
Students create their own cooperative logic problems.

➤ *HEIGHT-O-METERS*
Students first use their Height-O-Meters to measure the angular height of the flagpole or some other tall object in or near their school, and the height of balls thrown in the air. They then apply the technique of triangulation to determine the location of a forest fire.

➤ *HIDE A BUTTERFLY*
Students search for real butterflies that may or may not be camouflaged during a class hike or at home.

➤ *HOT WATER AND WARM HOMES FROM SUNLIGHT*
Students write a manual on how to build a new house with an explanation of how the reader might save energy if the house is planned carefully.

➤ *IN ALL PROBABILITY*
Students change the rules of the Race Track game so that another horse or horses have a better chance of winning.

➤ *INVOLVING DISSOLVING*
Students dissolve other substances (powders, crystals, and other solids) and draw or write about their methods and observations.

➤ *LIQUID EXPLORATIONS*
Students apply what they learned about liquids in the Swirling Colors activity to help a pirate determine which liquids are salt water and which are freshwater without tasting them.

➤ *MAPPING ANIMAL MOVEMENTS*
Students use what they learned in mapping activities to study threatened species and their habitats.

➤ *MORE THAN MAGNIFIERS*
At the conclusion of the unit, students locate the lenses on a variety of cameras, telescopes, magnifiers, and projectors. They then describe the function of each lens and predict how the effects of the instrument would be different if shorter or longer focal length lenses were used.

➤ *OF CABBAGES AND CHEMISTRY*

In Session 4, students use their new found understanding of the indicator properties of cabbage juice to determine whether a substance is acidic, basic, or neutral.

➤ *QUADICE*

After mastering the game of QUADICE, students are shown sets of numbers that represent fictitious rolls of the dice. They are asked to decide if they'd rather be the adder, subtracter, or divider, and articulate the reasons for their choice.

➤ *TREE HOMES*

Students figure out one or more ways to sort a variety of shoes. They are challenged to use words, pictures or Venn diagrams to show their sorts.

Liquid Explorations

Height-O-Meters

Teacher Observations as an Assessment Strategy

Teacher observations often reveal important information about students to supplement evidence from tests, class work, homework, projects, and other assessments. As teachers, we observe our students working day in and day out, and we may sometimes forget that teacher observations are a valid and enormously valuable assessment strategy.

As our students engage in the learning process, we can observe and document learning modalities, work habits, problem-solving strategies, and group interactions. Documentation can be in the form of anecdotal reports, checklists, notes, or focused assessment strategies that have been designed for a particular purpose such as to determine the percentage of time that students productively work on a task during a given period, to note levels of cooperative behavior, to gain a sense of student understanding of control of variables. There's no one "correct" way! There are a multitude of effective ways, depending on the purposes, the backgrounds and experience of students, not to mention your own teaching styles and preferences!

For example, we know one sixth grade teacher, Mr. Q, who, together with the other sixth grade teachers at his school, uses ongoing teacher observation as one important way of assessing student learning. They decided that rather than using a checklist format, they preferred to make more open-ended comments about student behaviors and skills that they observed. They agreed on a list of student learning characteristics that could serve as their main criteria. These could be used for all teachers at their grade level and would provide essential and concrete information over time. Among the main categories of student progress they decided to focus on were whether, and in which ways, a student:

- Makes good observations and communicates these to others.

- Is curious and asks inquiring questions.

- Is persistent.

- Demonstrates good logical thinking.

- Uses problem-solving techniques.

- Makes an effort to control variables.

- Draws conclusions and makes inferences based on evidence.

- Works cooperatively with other members of a team.

- Is able to follow procedures and work safely.

Agreeing on these criteria helped all of them focus on and keep constantly in mind what they collectively considered to be important in empowering students in science and mathematics. It also allows for plenty of individual variation in how each teacher approaches the task. In this case, each teacher kept a clipboard just for the purpose of recording these observations. Whenever there is a time in a science or mathematics activity when students are working in their groups, Mr. Q grabs his clipboard and circulates, writing down quick comments about student skills and behaviors he notices. He has a stack of mailing labels on his clipboard, on which each student's name is copied. As he observes something of note, he jots it down on the mailing label with that student's name. When the mailing label becomes full, he later sticks it to a page in that student's science and math portfolio and then places a new sticker on the clipboard. Ms. T, one of the other sixth grade teachers, prefers a system where she uses masking tape to attach index cards in a staggered manner, so the cards can be flipped one by one. Ms. B copies seating charts and writes on those. Later she cuts them up and tapes appropriate portions to a page in each student's portfolio.

To each her or his own, but together these teachers documented important aspects of the science and mathematics learning progress of each of their sixth-grade students. Their methods are open-ended, informal, time-efficient, yet chock full of useful information.

A case study using teacher observations as an assessment strategy in *Group Solutions* begins on the next page. Opportunities for teacher-observation assessments in other GEMS units are on page 200.

Teacher Observations and Student Self-Evaluation from *Group Solutions*

Ms. S, a second/third grade teacher, used a combination of **teacher observations** and student **self-evaluation** to help her assess individual and group cooperation skills as demonstrated through *Group Solutions* logic activities. First, she modeled a problem from the Coin Count section, where students use clues to determine the number of pennies in a cup. Then all groups got materials and started working. Ms. S moved from group to group and compiled notes about what the children were doing. Later she asked students to complete a self-evaluation form.

 ## What do I want to see?

Ms. S's goals were to assess how groups worked together and what the role of each group member was in that dynamic. She wanted to know students' perceptions about themselves as group members and their overall level of cooperation in the activity. Through the assessment, she also hoped to help students focus on specific cooperative behaviors that contributed to productive group interaction.

Group Solutions

Here are the notes for her anecdotal report for Group 1, which consisted of Michelle, Juan, Keisha, and Andrew.

Group 1

Sharing clues. Michelle leaves group, throws her clue card on table, moves chair away—upset. Keisha, Juan, Andrew keep going, use her card. Keisha concerned, looks over, but Michelle makes a face. I just observe, think about intervening, but don't. Michelle stays away, bangs foot against desk, etc. Rest of group solves puzzle, records solution. Need to get back to this!

During this one day, Ms. S was able to make notes about four of her eight groups. She made observations about the remaining four groups the next day as they continued to work on cooperative logic problems.

How much observation can be done during any one class period of course depends on each classroom situation, on the purpose, focus, and detail of the notes, and on the specific activities involved. Responding to student questions, helping those having difficulty, and navigating all the other tasks and duties of modern-day teaching can, to put it mildly, extend the timeline for such observations. Nonetheless, activity-based science and math, with its emphasis on students working together to make their own discoveries, and perhaps especially the intense student interest in the cooperative puzzles of *Group Solutions* definitely does allow for many golden opportunities for teacher observation.

After the two days of her own observation, Ms. S distributed a self-evaluation form to all students. She asked each group to complete the group form together, each placing a tally mark where they think it should go. She then had them write individually about three things they liked about working in their group and three things they didn't like.

The four responses from Group 1: Keisha, Michelle, Juan, and Andrew, are summarized in the chart below with their comments corrected for spelling. Of the other seven groups in the class, six functioned fairly well, while Group 7 had difficulties similar to those of Group 1.

GROUP 1 **About Our Group**	★	★★	★★★
We listened to each other.	I		III
Everyone had a turn.	I		III
We shared the materials.	I		III
We checked to be sure we were right.			IIII
Our group was fair to everyone.	I	I	II

Three Things I Liked About Working In My Group	**Three Things I Didn't Liked About Working In My Group**
MICHELLE Nothing	They don't work together. They are mean. They did nothing.
JUAN They're all my friends. We do good to each other. They're in my group to help people.	We sort of didn't listen too well.
KEISHA The group I work in is great. I know the people in my group. I like my group.	One of us didn't help. She was upset.
ANDREW Everyone shared. Everyone was honest. And we listened.	One kid was mad.

Q What insights have I gained?

For the most part, the students' self-evaluation validated Ms. S's observations and provided additional insights. For instance, in Group 1, though three of four students give a 3-star rating to almost all of the cooperative behaviors, Michelle's perceptions consistently differed from that of her peers. The other three group members apparently believed that the group worked well for them, and did not include Michelle's perspective in their overall rating. However, Andrew and Keisha did show insight into Michelle's situation in their comments about what they didn't like about working in their group: "One of us didn't help. One kid was mad." Through the self-evaluation and over time, Michelle found words to express her discontent, though was unable to do so while the activity was in progress.

Because this form of assessment is ongoing throughout the instructional process, Ms. S was able to use the information to structure subsequent *Group Solutions* sessions. She decided that she wanted the students to develop more of an awareness about behaviors and attitudes that contribute to inclusiveness and harmony in cooperative groups. After students completed the self-evaluation, she convened the entire class and the following discussion ensued.

Ms. S
How many groups feel that they worked well together? (Six of eight groups raise their hands enthusiastically. Two groups do not.)

Ms. S
What helped you work together?

TAMIKA
We didn't grab the cards.

PAUL
We shared the money and the glue.

STEFFI
We listened to each other.

MANNY
We didn't yell. We talked it out.

Ms. S
What made groups not work well together?

MICHELLE
Not sharing! My group didn't share with me!

Ms. S
Do you want to tell us what happened?

MICHELLE
They were mean! They didn't share the pennies. The money was all on Keisha's desk and I couldn't reach it.

Ms. S
What did you do?

MICHELLE (shyly):
I got mad. I gave them my clue and went away.

Ms. S
Everybody think of one thing you could do if this happened to you. (She waits a minute and then calls on several volunteers, starting with Michelle.)

MICHELLE
I could have told them I couldn't reach the pennies. I could have asked them to move closer.

TYLER
I could remind everybody that each person needs to have a turn with the pennies.

PAUL
I could tell the teacher.

Ms. S
Now everybody think of one thing that the other members of the group could do to help someone who is having trouble participating.

KEISHA
I knew Michelle was mad. I could have given her some of the pennies. I was going to move them but there was a hole in the middle of our desks, and I was afraid they'd fall on the floor.

198   INSIGHTS—Teacher Observations

ALICE

We could tell the grabby kids they have to share.

Ms. S

Do you think that ALL of us could work better together next time?

The entire group agreed. In subsequent sessions, Ms. S rewards groups that cooperate by letting them spend longer doing the *Group Solutions* logic problems.

 What insights have I gained?

For Ms. S, the results of her observations influenced key instructional decisions about GEMS units. These decisions eventually led to more equitable and productive participation in *Group Solutions* and other activities that involved cooperative work. Most GEMS units involve students working in groups, so this strong emphasis in *Group Solutions* and other cooperative learning activities can help prepare students for more complex tasks and interactions when doing activity-based science and math in later grades. Being able to work together cooperatively is of course extremely beneficial in many school settings, not to mention the family, the work place, and other social interactions.

Involving students in reflection about themselves, their peers, and how they work together was a powerful way to address some of her goals for her students' behavior. The students in Ms. S's class have been given plenty of experience in reflecting on their own performance and so have gotten increasingly adept at completing the forms and articulating their thoughts. Both her observation notes and the students' group and self evaluations may also be useful to her in sharing specific information with parents in a concrete way.

Group Solutions

Other Assessment Opportunities in GEMS Using Teacher Observations

Here are some other assessment opportunities in GEMS using the assessment strategy of teacher observations. Use this list to find specific opportunities and to inspire you to create your own uses of this assessment strategy.

➢ *COLOR ANALYZERS*
This guide provides good opportunities to assess student learning by observing what the students do, rather than just what they say. For example, in Activity 2 students create their own secret messages. When these go up on the wall, look at the techniques that the students have used. Did they use blue, purple, and green for the content of the message? Did they use red, yellow, or orange to disguise it? Have they invented means of embedding their messages in pictures or words that serve as a distraction?

➢ *FROG MATH*
Teachers can observe students as they sort and classify buttons during free exploration in Session 1 and Guess the Sort in Session 2. Look for growth in student ability to make discoveries in an open-ended setting, observe similarities and differences among buttons, and use logical-thinking skills to create multiple sorts of a given set of objects.

➢ *IN ALL PROBABILITY*
Teachers can observe students as they flip pennies, spin a variety of spinners, and use dice throughout the unit. Listen for comments that indicate each student's awareness of probability as they predict likely results in each of the mathematical experiments. Look for student growth in the ability to recognize and communicate that certain results are more likely to occur than others, based on probability.

➢ *INVESTIGATING ARTIFACTS*
Students categorize, sort, and classify. Through observation during these activities, you can assess how well they understand Venn diagrams or how well they are inventing and following their own rationales for sorts. There is also an opportunity to see who has sorted the same objects in more than one way, as well as how well groups are cooperating, communicating, and sharing.

➢ *MOONS OF JUPITER*
The final activity, in which students create bases on one of the moons, is a wonderful opportunity for teachers to see what students have learned in the unit. Walk around the classroom with a clipboard and jot down examples of comments and ideas that show that the students understand what it might be like to live and work on one of the moons, as well as knowledge about the features, or other information they've gained through the unit.

➢ *PAPER TOWEL TESTING*
Students plan and conduct controlled experiments. A good way to assess how well students understand the concept of controlled experimentation is to listen to their responses to each others' experiments, and to note any critical comments or suggestions in which they identify variables that may not have been controlled. Opportunities to take notes during students' discussions of each others' experiments also appear in many other GEMS units.

> "Not everything that counts can be counted,
> and not everything that can be counted counts."
>
> — *Quotation reportedly posted on Albert Einstein's office wall* —

Outcomes

This section contains **Selected Student Outcomes** for every teacher's guide in the GEMS series. The GEMS guides appear in alphabetical order. For each GEMS guide, we include a concise description of **Built-In Assessment Activities** that are already part of the unit, and **Additional Assessment Ideas**. Both the Built-In and Additional assessments are keyed to the student learning outcomes listed for that guide. (The numbers of the related Selected Student Outcomes appear in parentheses following each assessment suggestion.)

The student learning outcomes listed for each guide are not intended to be all-inclusive—there are many other learning outcomes that could be elaborated. We have chosen those we considered most central to the unit. With differing curricular emphases, you may want to come up with your own student learning outcomes, based on your own needs and unique ways that you present GEMS activities. Similarly, the Built-In and Additional assessments represent many, but far from all, of the assessment opportunities that interweave throughout GEMS activities. We encourage you to come up with your own and tell us about them!

Hide A Butterfly

ACID RAIN

Selected Student Outcomes

1. Students articulate the causes of acid rain and how it affects living organisms, ecosystems, and materials.

2. Students formulate thoughtful questions about acid rain.

3. Students demonstrate a working knowledge of acids, bases, neutrals, neutralization, the pH scale, and buffers.

4. Students recognize that lake pH is the result of a larger system of interacting parts.

5. Students explore possible solutions to the problem of acid rain and identify issues that relate to their solutions.

6. Students improve their ability to solve problems, think critically, and make decisions.

Built-In Assessment Activities

Pick Your Brain

In Session 1, students write down what they've heard about acid rain and what they wonder about the topic. A class list is compiled and, in subsequent sessions, this list is revisited and modified to accurately reflect the new information students have gained. Through this process, teachers see how students revise and expand their knowledge throughout the unit. Teachers may choose to have students reflect individually about acid rain at one or more points in the unit. (Outcomes 1–5)

This activity is a Case Study on page 92.

Startling Statements

In Session 3, students play a game called Startling Statements. First, they guess the answers to various questions with startling answers. Students then poll their classmates and summarize the range of responses. This activity enables teachers to assess students' current ideas about each of these questions. Teachers may wish to ask students to write a response to one or more of the questions later in the session based on what they learn in the game. (Outcomes 1, 3, 4)

Town Meeting

During Sessions 5 and 7, the class prepares for and conducts a town meeting about the problem of acid rain in fictional Lake Town. Groups of students assume the roles of various special interest groups. They analyze the problem from their perspective and develop appropriate solutions to address their particular issues. Each group has an opportunity to question other groups during the town meeting. During the debate, teachers can assess students' understanding of the causes and effects of acid rain; their knowledge about how acid rain affects lakes as part of a larger ecological system; and their ability to identify issues and solutions. A teacher can also observe how well students solve problems and think critically. (Outcomes 1–6)

ACID RAIN

Grades 6–10

Eight Sessions

Students gain scientific inquiry skills as they learn about acids and the pH scale, make Fake Lakes, determine how the pH changes after an acid rainstorm, present a play about the effects of acid rain on aquatic life, and hold a town meeting to discuss solutions to the problem. They also play a Startling Statements game and conduct a plant-growth experiment. Students are encouraged to analyze complex environmental issues for themselves.

Skills

Observing, Measuring and Recording Data, Experimenting, Classifying, Drawing Conclusions, Synthesizing Information, Role Playing, Problem Solving, Critical Thinking, Decision-Making, Brainstorming Solutions

Concepts

Acid, Base, Neutral, pH, Neutralize, Buffering Capacity, Ecosystem, Environmental Issues, Controversy in Science, Relationship Between Scientific and Social Issues, and Effect of Acid Rain on Plants, Animals, and Lakes

Themes

Systems and Interactions, Models and Simulations, Stability, Patterns of Change, Evolution, Scale, Energy, Matter

---

Sorting Out Solutions

In Session 8, students pretend they are the president and share their personal solution to the problem of acid rain. After their plans have been presented and discussed, students have an opportunity to critically assess the solutions and decide which they would choose. Students can also write about the solution they feel is best, explain their reasoning, and describe how they would modify that plan in response to other ideas. (Outcomes 5, 6)

Everything You've Always Wanted To Know About Acid Rain

In Session 8, students review the list of questions and statements to clarify any current misconceptions or uncertainties they may have about the scientific or social issues of acid rain. Students are given the opportunity to generate additional questions about the topic as well as to brainstorm ideas about possible experiments that could be done to explore answers to their questions. (Outcome 2)

Additional Assessment Ideas

Lake County

In a Going Further activity at the end of this unit, students write a story about a fictional region called Lake County. The teacher supplies students with a map that includes lakes and their pH's. Students' stories must explain why each lake has a certain pH. While students are encouraged to be creative, their stories must take into account the system of variables that determines lake pH. (Outcomes 1, 4)

Acid Authors

In another Going Further activity at the end of this unit, students write their own plays about acid rain, or add an additional scene to the play in Session 6. These plays should illustrate causes, effects, and solutions to acid rain. (Outcomes 1, 3, 4, 5)

Create a Comic Strip

Have students create a comic strip that explains, step-by-step, how acid rain is formed or how a lake becomes acidic. (Outcomes 1, 3, 4)

Write a Letter to a Third Grader

Ask students to explain to a third grader about acid rain, both the bad news (its adverse effects on our earth) and the good news (that there are solutions and progress being made). Tell them that the third grader doesn't know what acid rain is, but has heard that it is bad and is wrecking our ecosystem. (Outcomes 1, 3, 4)

Acid Rain

ANIMAL DEFENSES

Selected Student Outcomes

1. Students identify the defensive structures and behaviors that dinosaurs used to protect themselves.

2. Students apply their knowledge of defensive structures to create a model of a defended animal.

3. Students demonstrate their knowledge of the predator-prey relationship through dramatic play.

4. Students use their knowledge of prehistoric defenses to help them understand animal defenses in today's world.

Built-In Assessment Activities

Defense!

In Session 1, students see drawings of dinosaurs and then watch a drama about a defenseless animal. They are asked to identify body structures and behaviors that helped to defend the dinosaurs. During the drama, students are asked to name additional structures and behaviors that would help protect the defenseless animal. Throughout the session, teachers can listen to the students' responses; watch for rich, descriptive language and note their observations next to each student's name on a class list. (Outcome 1)

ANIMAL DEFENSES
Preschool–K
Two Sessions

In this unit, children add defensive structures to an imaginary defenseless animal. In a classroom drama, the animal encounters a *Tyrannosaurus rex*. In the second session, the children learn about the defenses of modern-day animals.

Skills
Observing, Identifying, Creative Thinking, Using Scissors (optional)

Concepts
Animal Protection, Predator-Prey, Distinction between Defensive Structures and Defensive Behaviors.

Themes
Systems and Interactions, Models and Simulations, Evolution, Scale, Structure, Diversity and Unity

---

Make a Defended Animal

In Session 1, students design their own defended animal as they add paper horns, spines, teeth, and wings to a cutout defenseless form. The teacher circulates among the class, poses questions, and asks students to explain the decisions they made about their creatures. Student learning can be measured by their oral descriptions and the complexity and detail of their model. (Outcomes 1, 2)

This activity is a Case Study on page 113.

My Animal in Action

In the final activity of Session 1, students use their defended animal in an action-packed confrontation with *Tyrannosaurus rex*. As they observe the dramatic play, the teacher can listen and assess the degree to which students are able to describe the animal's structures and behaviors, and how each defense functions as protection. (Outcomes 1, 3)

Animal Defenses Today

In Session 2, students create scenarios with toy animals to illustrate the structures and behaviors that protect animals common to today's world. These scenarios will illustrate whether students are able to generalize their knowledge about prehistoric defenses to help them understand animal defenses in their own world. (Outcome 4)

Additional Assessment Ideas

Once Upon a Time

During Session 1, students can write or dictate stories about their defended animal and then perform these stories for classmates and families. (Outcomes 1, 3)

Underwater Defenses

At the end of the unit, have students design a defenseless form of an animal that lives in water. Encourage them to add defenses and behaviors that would assist this animal in its underwater home. (Outcomes 1, 2, 3 , 4)

ANIMALS IN ACTION

Selected Student Outcomes

1. Students describe *observable* animal behaviors and distinguish between observable behaviors and *assumptions* about the behaviors.

2. Students develop and refine hypotheses regarding animal behavior.

3. Students design and conduct animal behavior investigations.

4. Students develop responsible attitudes and behaviors toward animals.

Built-In Assessment Activities

Evidence and Inference

In Session 1, The Animal Corral, students are introduced to the difference between observable behaviors and assumptions made about those behaviors. Later, in Session 2, Stimulus and Response, students observe how those same animals react to changes in their environment. They are asked to share the behaviors they observe. The teacher can listen to their ideas and note whether they make accurate observations or inferences. (Outcome 1)

Hypothesize and Design an Experiment

At the end of Session 2, students are introduced to the term *hypothesis* and are guided to develop sample hypotheses based on the animal behaviors they observe. Next, in Session 3, Small Critters in Action, teams further investigate animal behavior and are asked to design their own experiments. The experiment must have a hypothesis to be tested. Students plan together and complete an Animal Behavior Experiment Sheet. During the planning time, the teacher can circulate among the teams, listen to their ideas and review their written plan. (Outcomes 2, 3)

ANIMALS IN ACTION
Grades 5–9
Five Sessions

While observing animals in a large classroom corral, the class experiments with the physical environment and adds different stimuli. Teams of students generate hypotheses, conduct experiments, and hold a scientific convention to discuss their findings. Investigations that students can do with classroom animals include: How do animals move? What do they prefer to eat? How do they respond to light and sound? These questions are addressed through behavior experiments students conduct with rats, crickets, guinea pigs, cardboard boxes, and common classroom objects. Students learn to distinguish between direct observations and assumptions, as they differentiate evidence (what they observe) from inference (conclusions they draw from their observations).

Skills
Observing, Comparing, Communicating, Relating

Concepts
Biology, Animals, Objective Observation, Animal Behavior, Humane Treatment of Animals, Stimulus and Response

Themes
Systems and Interactions, Patterns of Change, Structure, Diversity and Unity

Animals In Action

Experiments in Action

In Session 4, Team Experiments, student teams conduct the investigations they designed. The teacher can observe how the plan is implemented and if it is true to the design. Team cooperation, effort, and attitudes toward animals can also be evaluated. (Outcomes 3, 4)

Drawing Conclusions

In Session 5, The Scientific Convention, teams report outcomes of their investigations to the class. They are expected to participate in discussions of other team's research. The teacher observes how teams report and analyze their results. The teacher can also note the quality of questions and responses generated by classmates. (Outcomes 1, 2, 3)

Additional Assessment Ideas

Design a Hypothesis

Similar to the "wolf" hypothesis in Session 2, give students an observed behavior of an animal such as "Robins gather on a lawn after it has been watered." Next, ask questions such as "What ideas do you have to explain their behavior?" "What is an example of a hypothesis that could explain this behavior?" As a follow-up to the discussion, students design an experiment that embodies the ideas of a "fair test." (Outcomes 2, 3)

Students Become Teachers

Have the students conduct the animal corral activity with younger students, emphasizing observation, assumptions, stimulus, response, and gentleness toward animals. The teacher observes her students as teachers and notes how they communicate concepts and attitudes. (Outcomes 1, 4)

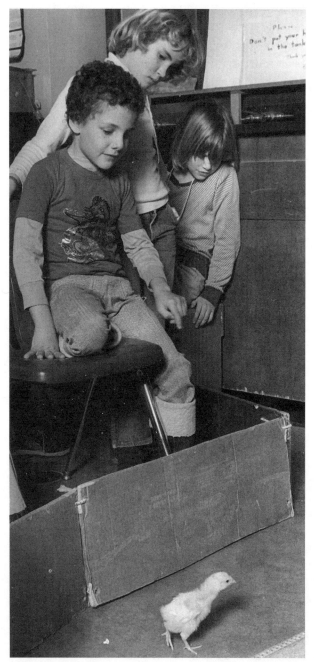

Animals In Action

Animals In Action

BUBBLE FESTIVAL

Selected Student Outcomes

1. Students discover the properties of soap film and a variety of physical phenomena related to soap bubbles.

2. Students generate their own questions about bubbles.

3. Students devise ways to answer their questions about bubbles.

4. Students improve their ability to make careful observations.

Built-In Assessment Activities

Discoveries and Questions

In the Closure: Sharing Discoveries and Writing and Bubbles sections of the guide, students tell, draw, and/or write what they discovered and what new questions they have after they explore a bubble station. The teacher can ask activity-specific questions to allow students to share specific findings from each station in the festival. As students write or tell about their discoveries and questions at various points during the festival, the teacher can observe increased detail in students' observations. (Outcomes 1, 2, 4)

Letters from the Bubble-Wise

In the Going Further sections that follow each activity; and in the Closure: Sharing Discoveries; and Writing and Bubbles sections, students are invited to share their bubble wisdom with others. Students can write a letter to a friend or cartoon character and explain how to blow a bubble, or older students can write a letter that describes how someone can use color to learn about a bubble. The letters provide information about students' ability to communicate what they have discovered about bubbles. (Outcome 1)

Additional Assessment Ideas

Bubble Investigations

Set up a session where your students can attempt to answer a question they have about bubbles. Younger students can decide on a question as a class and together search for the answer. Older students can work individually or in pairs. (Outcome 1, 2, 3)

This activity is a Case Study on page 164.

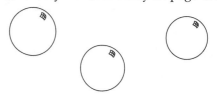

BUBBLE-OLOGY

Selected Student Outcomes

1. Students discover the properties of soap film and the ways that soap film creates bubbles and then apply this knowledge in a variety of situations.

2. Students learn to distinguish fair and unfair elements of a test.

3. Students improve their ability to design controlled experiments.

4. Students explain how evaporation and surface tension impact a liquid's ability to make bubbles.

5. Students predict how air currents affect bubbles in a variety of situations.

6. Students apply their knowledge of color patterns to predict when a bubble will pop.

BUBBLE-OLOGY
Grades 5–9
Ten Sessions (Six activities)

Students combine fun with an exploration of important concepts in chemistry and physics through imaginative experiments with soap bubbles. Students devise an ideal bubble-blowing instrument, test dishwashing brands to see which makes the biggest bubbles, determine the optimum amount of glycerin needed for the biggest bubbles, employ the Bernoulli principle to keep bubbles aloft, use color patterns to predict when a bubble will pop, and create bubbles that last for days.

Skills
Observing, Measuring and Recording Data, Experimenting, Classifying, Drawing Conclusions, Controlling Variables, Calculating Averages, Graphing Results

Concepts
Technology, Engineering, Chemical Composition, Substances, Properties, Surface Tension, Hygroscopicity, Optimum Amount, Bernoulli's Principle, Aerodynamics, Pressure, Patterns, Light and Color, Interference, Air Currents, Evaporation, Environments

Themes
Systems and Interactions, Stability, Patterns of Change, Scale, Structure, Matter

---

Built-In Assessment Activities

Design a Bubble Maker

As a homework assignment at the end of Activity 1, Bubble Technology, students design and draw bubble makers for specialized uses. The teacher can see how students apply their knowledge of soap films as they describe their bubble makers to the class. (Outcome 1)

Designing Other "Fair Tests"

In Activity 3, The Chemistry of Bigger Bubbles, students are asked how they would design the experiment so it is a fair comparison. The teacher can see how students identify uncontrolled variables, and how they devise a plan to control those variables. (Outcomes 2, 3)

Predicting the Pop

In Activity 5, Predict-A-Pop, students are challenged to apply what they've learned to invent a method for counting down, to the second, when their bubbles will pop. As students repeat this procedure, the teacher can observe how students use finer and finer observations to modify their predictions. (Outcome 6)

Longer-Lasting Bubbles

In Activity 6, Longer-Lasting Bubbles, students are challenged to apply what they've learned to blow a bubble that will last as long as possible. The teacher can see what factors students consider as they design systems to maintain bubbles. Teachers can also observe whether students use fair or unfair tests to approach this challenge. (Outcomes 1–6)

Additional Assessment Ideas

Dishwashing Tests

In the Going Further suggestion for Activity 2, Comparing Bubble Solutions, students design an experiment that tests the dishwashing properties of various brands of dishwashing liquid. The teacher has the opportunity to observe how students identify variables and plan an experiment that has controls for those variables. (Outcomes 2, 3)

The Ideal Bubble Solution

Students can make recommendations to the product development specialist at a toy company that plans to produce bubble toys. Their advice needs to include discussion of the following two points.

1. Why water needs soap in order to make bubbles that last.

2. Why bubble solution with glycerin makes sturdier bubbles.

(Outcome 4)

Sharing Bubble Discoveries

Students can write a letter to someone who has never blown soap bubbles before. They can include five different things they learned about bubbles such as tips for blowing table bubbles, how to blow the biggest bubble, how to keep a bubble in the air, how to make a bubble last long, or anything else that will let the person know about the properties of bubbles. (Outcomes 1, 4, 5, 6)

Bubble Maker Video Commercial

If your class has access to a video camera, have students write, design, narrate, and produce a short commercial to advertise their originally designed bubble maker. The commercial should explain to the viewer why the bubble maker makes the kinds of bubbles it does. (Outcome 1)

Bubble-ology

Bubble-ology

BUILD-IT! FESTIVAL

Selected Student Outcomes

1. Students learn to recognize names and properties of two- and three-dimensional shapes.

2. Students use spatial visualization to construct models.

3. Students improve their ability to find and articulate patterns, make predictions, and draw logical conclusions.

4. Students develop cooperation and communication in mathematics.

BUILD IT! FESTIVAL
Grades K–6
Nine Activities

This GEMS festival guide includes a wide assortment of classroom learning station activities that focus on mathematics, especially relating to construction, geometric challenges, spatial visualization, and many real-life skills and careers. Preliminary activities, which involve students in free exploration of the materials, are the foundation for such mathematical challenges as Create-A-Shape, Dowel Designs, Polyhedra, Symmetry, Tangrams, and What Comes Next? Background on geometry is provided. Depending on the stations chosen, required materials may include pattern blocks and polyhedra. Template patterns for folding and constructing shapes and creating tangrams are provided.

Skills
Observing, Building Models, Communicating, Finding and Articulating Patterns, Cooperating, Predicting, Finding Multiple Solutions, Drawing Conclusions, Constructing Geometric Definitions, Problem Solving

Concepts
Shape Recognition, Polygons, Polyhedra (edges, faces, vertices), Spatial Visualization, Surface Area, Pattern, Symmetry, Congruence, Similarity, Architectural Design, Tessellations

Science Themes
Structure, Scale, Models and Simulations, Diversity and Unity

Mathematics Strands
Geometry, Logic and Language, Number, Discrete Mathematics, Functions

---

Built-In Assessment Activity

Free Exploration

Free exploration is advised before all activities in this guide. As students explore materials, the teacher can informally assess what skills and knowledge the children bring to the activity. They can observe students' use of mathematical language, ability to construct models, find patterns, cooperate, and communicate. (Outcomes 1, 2, 3, 4)

Additional Assessment Ideas

Write about Architect/Builder

The Going Further activity following the Architect/Builder activity requires students to build a structure with pattern blocks. They then write directions for their partner to recreate the structure. The teacher can learn the extent of students' ability to use geometric and spatial terms to describe structures clearly. (Outcomes, 1, 2)

Feel-y Box 3-D Geometry

As a Going Further suggestion for the Create-A-Shape activity, students reach into a box, touch a shape, and guess what shape it is. The teacher can assess how well a student can translate the feel of a shape to its properties. (Outcome 1)

Paper Jackets

As another Going Further suggestion for the Create-A-Shape activity, students investigate surface area as they use grid paper to cover three-dimensional shapes. The teacher can assess students' spatial visualization skills. (Outcomes 1, 2)

Cube Challenge

As another Going Further suggestion for the Create-A-Shape activity, students investigate different ways to combine squares to form cubes. The teacher will notice students' ability to transfer two-dimensional properties into three-dimensional properties. (Outcomes 1, 2)

Structures to Inhabit

The Going Further suggestion for the Dowel Designs station challenges students to build and write about three-dimensional structures to house stuffed animals. The teacher will gain insights about students' knowledge of structural properties. (Outcomes 2, 4)

This activity is a Case Study on page 119.

Fly a Kite!

Dowel Designs includes a Going Further suggestion in which students create and fly kites. The teacher can use this activity to assess students' knowledge of structural properties of three-dimensional objects. (Outcomes 2, 4)

Octahedron Exploration

As a Going Further suggestion for Polyhedra, students find many ways to build a polyhedron with eight faces. The teacher can observe how students apply their knowledge of structure, faces, and angles to solve this discrete mathematics problem. (Outcomes 2, 3, 4)

Challenge Me!

In the Going Further suggestion for Fill-A-Shape, students fill a shape with a specified number of pattern blocks. The teacher can observe students' spatial skills as well as their knowledge of edges, angles and equivalence with pattern blocks. (Outcomes 1, 2, 3, 4)

Grid Designs

Symmetry includes a Going Further suggestion in which students use a grid to create one half of a design, and then complete the design symmetrically. The teacher assesses their understanding of symmetry. (Outcomes 1, 2, 3, 4)

Symmetrical Masks

In the Going Further suggestion for Symmetry, students create and decorate symmetrical masks. If these masks are described and sorted in a whole class activity, the teacher can observe students' level of understanding of different types of symmetry. (Outcomes 1, 3)

Build and Build Again

What Comes Next? features a Going Further suggestion in which students use a variety of materials to repeat patterns. The teacher observes the students' ability to articulate and generalize patterns. (Outcomes 1, 2, 3, 4)

Tessellating Quadrilateral

In the Going Further suggestion for What Comes Next?, students investigate whether any four-sided polygon can tessellate. The teacher can assess students' understanding of tessellations and the properties of polygons. (Outcomes 1, 2, 3)

Identifying Shapes

A Going Further suggestion for Tangrams requires younger students to identify and name certain shapes. The teacher can assess their ability to define and recognize shapes. (Outcome 1)

Non-Regular Geometric Shapes

In another Going Further suggestion for Tangrams, students create unusual polygons with the tangram pieces. The teacher can observe the students' ability to apply their knowledge of polygons in a new situation. (Outcomes 1, 3, 4)

Build It! Festival

BUZZING A HIVE

Selected Student Outcomes

1. Students identify structures and behaviors that help the honeybee survive in the wild.

2. Students articulate how and why bees collect pollen and nectar from flowers.

3. Students describe the different jobs that bees perform in their hives during their lifetime and the activities that occur inside the hive.

4. Students identify honey and beeswax as two products that come from bees and are helpful to people today.

5. Students gain knowledge about the life cycle of a bee.

6. Students are able to identify bee predators.

BUZZING A HIVE
Grades K–3
Ten Sessions

In this extensive unit, students learn about the complex social behavior, communication, and hive environment of the honeybee by making paper bees, a bee hive, flowers with pollen, and bee predators. In making their own paper bees, they learn about bee body structure. They also role-play bees in a beehive drama, perform bee dances, and learn how bees communicate directions. Another portion of the activities focuses on bee metamorphosis. Students also learn about bee predators and honey robbers, hear a "Bee Enemies" story, and make a paper skunk. They role-play guard bees and learn how bees work together to protect the hive. Live bees are not a part of this unit.

Skills
Observing, Comparing, Matching, Communicating, Role Playing

Concepts
Biology, Entomology, Honeybee Structure, Pollen, Nectar, Hive, Metamorphosis, Life Cycle, Enemies, Protection, Social Organization, Cooperation, Communication, Flight Pattern

Themes
Systems and Interactions, Models and Simulations, Stability, Patterns of Change, Evolution, Structure, Energy, Matter, Diversity and Unity

---

Built-In Assessment Activities

Getting to Know Honeybees

In Lesson 1, The Honeybee, students study a honeybee drawing, share their personal experiences with bees, and may view live bees outdoors or closely examine dead bees. Students also build a paper model of a bee to use in dramas. During these activities, the teacher can look for perceptive student responses such as "Bees have a stinger to protect themselves from enemies," or "My bee has lots of eyes to see all around." The paper models are a tool to assess what students understand about bee structure. (Outcome 1)

Honeybees and Flowers

In Lesson 2, Bees and Flowers, Pollen, and Nectar, students are introduced to the relationship between bees and flowers as they participate in a variety of multi-sensory activities. They observe real flowers, collect real pollen, sip juice for nectar, and taste honey. Next, they use a model flower and bee to enact dramas where bees collect pollen and nectar. The teacher can question the students during the activities, and listen to their thoughts and ideas. Observations of the planned and spontaneous bee dramas can also provide valuable information about what the students have learned. (Outcomes 1, 2)

Bee Jobs

Through activities in Lessons 1–4, students are introduced to the many jobs that bees perform during their lifetime. During Lesson 4, Young Bees Drama, students use their bee and hive models to review bees' jobs and choose a job for their bees. The teacher can listen for detailed descriptions of the various bee jobs and evidence of new vocabulary related to bee life such as bee bread, larva, wax, collecting pollen, nectar, and queen bee. (Outcome 3)

Bees and People

In Lessons 2–4, students learn that bees make honey from nectar and that bees make the wax for their honeycomb. They also see how bees use the hexagon shape to build a strong hive structure. To relate what bees do to their own life experiences, students taste honey, touch items made from beeswax, and collect everyday items built with the hexagon shape. The teacher can lead a discussion about how bee products are used by people or she can challenge students to bring in items from home that contain honey, beeswax, or the hexagon shape. Parents can help their children make a list of such items that they find at the grocery store. (Outcome 4)

Additional Assessment Ideas

Bee Books

Use drawings in the guide and student drawings as the basis for student writing and/or dictation about honeybees. The stories can be fanciful tales mixed with ideas from honeybee life and natural history. (Outcomes 1–6)

Beekeepers and Living Hives

At the end of the unit, invite a beekeeper to talk with your class or visit a living hive at a science center. Listen to the quality and kinds of questions and responses that come from the students. (Outcomes 1–6)

Bee Metamorphosis

Ask students to draw the different phases of a bee's life cycle, from egg to adult bee. (Outcome 5)

Bee Enemies

In Lesson 5, Role-Playing Guard Bees, students learn about bee defenses. Ask students to draw a picture and tell about, "The Day the Honeybee Hive Was Raided." (Outcome 6)

Buzzing A Hive

Buzzing A Hive

Buzzing A Hive

CHEMICAL REACTIONS

Selected Student Outcomes

1. Students improve their ability to use a variety of senses to make and describe careful observations.

2. Students explain that evidence such as changes in color; and production of a gas, heat, or odor are all clues that chemicals are reacting.

3. Students develop appropriate vocabulary to demonstrate their understanding of concepts that relate to chemical reactions.

    ➤ When chemicals *(reactants)* react, new substances *(products)* are created.

    ➤ In an *exothermic* reaction, heat is released. In an *endothermic* reaction, heat is absorbed.

4. Students improve their ability to conduct experiments in which they change only one variable at a time.

5. Students improve their ability to draw conclusions and make inferences based on evidence.

Built-In Assessment Activities

What Causes the Heat?

In Part 2, students investigate what causes the heat in the reaction. The teacher has the opportunity to see what experiments students plan and what conclusions they draw from these experiments. (Outcomes 4, 5)

This activity is a Case Study on page 151.

What Causes the Color Change? the Gas? the Odor?

Near the end of Part 2, students investigate what causes the yellow color, the gas, or the odor in the reaction. Teachers can observe how students use their skills and reasoning as they conduct experiments, draw conclusions, and make inferences based on the results. (Outcomes 4, 5)

Additional Assessment Ideas

Observing and Describing

Ask students to carefully describe something. This could be a lemon, a piece of chalk, a pile of flour, Epsom salts, or a substance or object that has many characteristics. Challenge them to use as many senses as they can to create a detailed list of the item's attributes. This assessment can be done before and/or after students have participated in the activities from this guide. The teacher can evaluate the detail and quality of students' observations and note how many senses the student used to describe the substance/object. (Outcome 1)

Comic Strip

Challenge students to design a comic strip that depicts, step-by-step, what occurred in the ziplock bag experiment and what they discovered. Explain that this comic strip will be used to teach other students about chemical reactions, reactants, and products. Teachers can note how students include these ideas and related vocabulary and concepts in their comic strips. (Outcomes 2, 3)

CHEMICAL REACTIONS
Grades 6–10
Two Sessions

An ordinary ziplock bag becomes a safe and spectacular laboratory, as students mix chemicals that bubble, change color, get hot; and produce gas, heat, and odor. They experiment to determine what causes the heat in this chemical reaction. This exciting activity explores chemical change, endothermic and exothermic reactions, and is a great introduction to chemistry. The activity has often been adapted for lower grade levels.

Skills
Observing, Recording Data, Experimenting, Making Inferences

Concepts
Chemistry, Evidence of Chemical Reaction, Endothermic/Exothermic Reactions, Chemical Safety

Themes
Systems and Interactions, Stability, Patterns of Change, Energy, Matter

---

COLOR ANALYZERS

Selected Student Outcomes

1. Students gain understanding about light and color as they learn how to make secret messages and why colored light filters work to decode secret messages.

2. Students learn light comes from only certain sources, and in order to see something, light must bounce off of the object and come to our eyes.

3. Students use a diffraction grating to discover that white light actually has many different colors in it, and black light is the absence of color. They discover the colors come from the light, and not from the plastic diffraction grating.

4. Students are able to explain why objects appear to be certain colors.

Built-In Assessment Activities

Inventing Secret Messages

In Session 1, students use colored light filters to decode secret messages. In Session 2, they create their own secret messages. These messages provide an

---

COLOR ANALYZERS
Grades 5–9
Four Sessions

Students investigate light and color while experimenting with diffraction gratings and color filters. They use color filters to decipher secret messages, then create their own secret messages. The front and back covers of the book can be used for classroom activities. A class set of red and green filters and diffraction gratings is included.

Skills
Observing, Comparing, Describing, Classifying, Inferring, Predicting, Recording Data, Drawing Conclusions

Concepts
Physical Science: Properties of Light and Color, Color Filters, Diffraction Gratings

Themes
Systems and Interactions, Energy, Matter

---

opportunity for the teacher to find out if students can properly apply the rules they learned about filtering. For example, red filters transmit red light, but stop all other light. To further assess students' ideas about light and color, the teacher can ask them to explain why their messages "work." (Outcome 1)

Colors of the Rainbow

In Session 3, students use crayons to draw the colors they see through the diffraction grating. The drawings will show the students' perceptions of the order of colors and their orientation. With this information, the teacher can determine whether or not students are looking through the diffraction grating correctly. The discussion at the end of the activity helps the teacher learn about students' understanding of the colors in white light. (Outcome 3)

What Happened to the Stripes?

In Session 4, students look at a sheet of paper with red stripes. They are asked to explain why the stripes disappear when viewed through a red filter. The students' justifications illustrate the degree to which they have understood how light helps us see things. Their reasoning can also provide evidence of their knowledge about how colored filters function. (Outcomes 1, 2, 3)

Why Does an Apple Look Red?

The suggested questions in Session 4 are designed to help your students reflect on what they've learned so far, and discover how people perceive color. By listening to their responses, the teacher can determine how well the students have understood that all colors originally come from light sources, and that the reason an apple appears red is because it reflects only red, and absorbs all other colors. (Outcomes 1, 2, 3, 4)

Additional Assessment Idea

Mystery Box

As a Going Further at the end of the unit, students create a box with a hole. Although the box is brightly colored inside, it appears black when students look at it through the hole. If your students have understood the previous lessons, they can provide a good explanation for this paradox. (Outcome 2)

CONVECTION: A CURRENT EVENT

Selected Student Outcomes

1. Students observe and record the movements of water in a pan and apply their understanding of convection currents to draw inferences about the movement of the water.

2. Students articulate that convection currents are caused by uneven heating, predict when and where a convection current may occur, and determine how it is likely to flow.

3. Students apply the concept of a convection current to explain heat distribution in a room, local and global wind patterns, and the cause of continental drift.

Built-In Assessment Activities

There's a Convection Current On Your Desk!

In Session 1, students create convection currents in pans of water and record their observations. During this activity, the teacher can visit each group to determine how carefully the students observe and record what they see. (Outcome 1)

CONVECTION: A CURRENT EVENT
Grades 6–9
Three Sessions

Students explore this important physical phenomenon by observing and charting the convection currents in liquid. They explore convection in air and generalize their findings to describe wind patterns. Convection is related to the ways heat moves and to the movement of magma inside the earth.

Skills
Observing, Recording, Making Inferences, Applying, Generalizing

Concepts
Heat, Heat Transfer, Convection, Diffusion, Fluids, Wind, Ocean Currents

Themes
Systems and Interactions, Models and Simulations, Stability, Patterns of Change, Evolution, Scale, Structure, Energy, Matter, Diversity and Unity

---

The Whole Picture

In Session 2, the students combine their observations and, with the teacher's help, describe a complete convection current. At the end of the activity, they are asked to solve a problem concerning a submarine that is stuck at the bottom of the ocean. If the students can solve the problem by steering it over a warm ocean vent, then they are aware of at least part of the convection current. To create an individual assessment activity, the teacher can have her students write their ideas about the problem individually before and/or after they discuss it as a class. (Outcome 2)

Applying the Concept of Convection

In Session 3, the students apply the convection concept as they complete a series of three activity sheets, each of which moves the concept to a larger and more abstract scale. The teacher can evaluate the students' answers on the activity sheets to determine how well the students are able to apply the concept of convection. (Outcome 3)

Additional Assessment Idea

Global Wind Patterns

The Behind the Scenes background section of the guide describes how convection is responsible for global wind patterns. As an assessment activity, ask students to work individually or in pairs to figure out, based on what they have learned, what causes winds around the globe. Challenge them to use their scheme to determine which way they would expect the wind to blow for someone who lives in the United States and for someone who lives in Australia. To give students a hint, draw a picture of the Earth and the Sun on the board. It is unlikely that students will come up with the complex pattern of winds described in the background section. Look for students describing a single large convection current in which air rises near the equator (where it is warmest), and falls at the poles. Such a pattern would suggest southerly winds in the United States and northerly winds in Australia. (Outcome 3)

CRIME LAB CHEMISTRY

Selected Student Outcomes

1. Students can explain that chromatography is a technique used to separate mixtures into their parts. They understand that the "colors" they see in a chromatogram are the "parts" that were mixed together to make the test substance (the mixture).

2. Students demonstrate their ability to use paper chromatography to separate substances from a mixture.

3. Students identify variables in chromatography tests and can explain why different groups may have different results in an experiment.

4. Students are able to explain why certain solvents do not cause a mixture to separate.

Built-In Assessment Activity

Questions

At various points throughout the activity, the teacher can ask key questions such as: "Where do the colors come from?" "Which ink contained the greatest number of pigments?" "Why might different groups have gotten different results?" "Why didn't pen number six move up the paper?" Student responses can reveal their understanding. Some teachers like to ask these questions more than once during the unit, thereby seeing students' progress in understanding. (Outcomes 1, 3, 4)

Additional Assessment Ideas

Colored Pens and Plant Pigments

In two Going Further activities at the end of the unit, students use chromatography to analyze the pigments found in different substances. In one activity, students determine what pigments were combined to create the colors of ink in a variety of watercolor markers. In another activity, they observe which solvents cause plant pigments to move up the test strip, and how many different pigments can be separated from the plant. Through these activities, the teacher can observe the students' ability to perform chromatography tests and interpret the resulting chromatograms. The plant pigment activities offer the teacher an opportunity to observe how well students can apply their understanding of solubility and solvents. (Outcomes 1, 2, 4)

Candy Chromatography

In another Going Further activity at the end of the unit, students use chromatography as a tool to analyze various brown candy smudges and solve the mystery of who used the candy machine. The teacher can observe how the students perform the tests, interpret the chromatograms, and use evidence to make inferences about who the culprit might be. (Outcomes 1, 2, 4)

Tell the Story of a Chromatogram

Show students a chromatogram made from black ink. Ask them to explain how it was made, where the colors come from, what the colors are, and what the colors tell us. Show a second chromatogram made from the same substance that looks similar but has differences. Explain that this is a chromatogram of the same ink, made by a different person. Ask students to explain how two chromatograms of the same ink could have different appearances. (Outcomes 1, 3)

CRIME LAB CHEMISTRY
Grades 4–8
Two Sessions

Challenged to determine which of several black pens was used to write a ransom note, students learn and use paper chromatography. Several mystery scenarios are suggested, with intriguing characters. In a special Going Further activity, students use "candy chromatography" to solve an additional mystery.

Skills
Experimenting, Analyzing Data, Making Inferences

Concepts
Chemistry, Chromatography, Separating Mixtures, Pigments, Solubility

Themes
Systems and Interactions, Stability, Patterns of Change, Structure, Energy, Diversity and Unity

---

DISCOVERING DENSITY

Selected Student Outcomes

1. Students explain, in their own words, why some liquids can be layered.

2. Students develop and articulate a working definition of density—a material is more dense than another material if one cup of that material weighs more than one cup of the other material.

3. Students learn to use the mathematical equation for density to calculate the density of various salt solutions.

4. Students apply their knowledge of density to real-life situations.

5. Students are able to visualize and draw a model that depicts substances of different densities at a super-magnified level.

Built-In Assessment Activities

Students' Concepts of Density

Throughout the unit, students demonstrate their understanding of density in the context of an activity.

DISCOVERING DENSITY
Grades 6–10
Five Sessions

Students attempt to layer various liquids in a straw, leading them to explore the concept of density. The teacher introduces the formula for determining density. Students have fun creating secret formula sheets, while reinforcing their practical understanding of this important concept. A final session includes Puzzling Scenarios as students explore real-life connections of density.

Skills
Measuring, Observing, Predicting, Using Proportions, Calculating Density

Concepts
Densities of Liquids

Themes
Systems and Interactions, Models and Simulations, Stability, Patterns of Change, Scale, Structure, Matter, Diversity and Unity

---

At the end of Session 1, students discuss the results from their experiments with mystery liquids. At the end of Session 2, they apply the concept of density in everyday situations. Teachers can assess students' understanding of density as they explain why the liquids layered, or how the layering technique could be used to tell more about different liquids or gases. Teachers can also ask students to write down their thoughts during each activity to see how their understanding of density develops as the unit progresses. (Outcomes 1, 2, 4)

Super-Magnifying Eyes

Twice during the unit, students are asked to imagine that they have super-magnifying eyes and to draw what things might look like with their powerful vision. At the end of Session 3, they draw different salt solutions. In Session 5, students draw what they think they would see on a molecular level when compar-

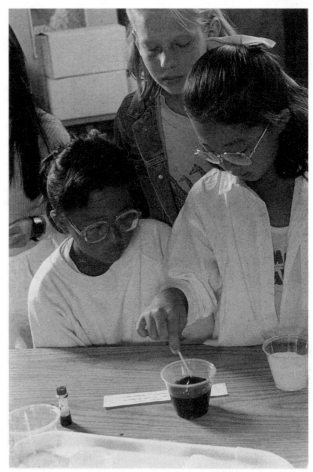

Discovering Density

ing the density of hot and cold water. These drawings provide insight into each student's thinking. This technique can be used regularly as an assessment of students' understanding of "invisible" things. (Outcome 5)

Puzzling Scenarios

In Session 5, students apply concepts of density to solve puzzling scenarios. Teachers can use each group's solution and the resulting class discussion to assess students' understanding of the concept of density and their ability to apply that knowledge. These scenarios can also be assigned to individual students. (Outcome 4)

Additional Assessment Ideas

Letter to a Younger Student

Tell students that a first grader came into the classroom and saw liquids that were layered in straws. The first grader wondered how the layering was possible and what the experiment had to do with science. Ask them to write a letter to this student, explaining why the liquids layered and how understanding density

can help them learn more about the world. Encourage students to use drawings and/or diagrams in their letters. (Outcomes 1, 2, 4, 5)

More Complicated Density Calculations

A Going Further activity for Session 4 challenges students to calculate the densities of solutions with various volumes. The teacher can assess students' abilities to utilize the mathematical equation for density. (Outcome 3)

Discovering Density

Discovering Density

EARTH, MOON, AND STARS

Selected Student Outcomes

1. Students are able to make systematic observations of the sky and create models to explain their observations.

2. Students are able to reconcile what they have been told about the Earth's spherical shape with its flat appearance.

3. Students are able to apply the concept of gravity to explain what happens to people and objects on or inside the Earth.

4. Students use a concrete model of the Earth, Moon, and Sun to explain phases of the moon and eclipses.

5. Students locate constellations in the night sky; describe how they move during the evening; and explain this movement in terms of the rotation of the Earth on its axis.

6. Students pose and answer some of their own questions about the Earth, Moon, and stars.

Built-In Assessment Activities

What Are Your Students' Ideas?

To find out students preconceptions about the Earth, Sun, stars, and Moon, questions are suggested at the beginning of most activities. For example, in Session 3 they are asked to describe phases of the moon, and to explain why phases occur. (Outcome 1, 4)

Questionnaire About the Earth's Shape and Gravity

In Session 2, students are asked to fill out a questionnaire about the Earth's shape and gravity. Collect the papers after individual students have completed them, before they are allowed to discuss their ideas with others. The students then discuss those concepts in small and large groups. After the unit is completed, give the questionnaire again, to see how much students have learned. (Outcome 2, 3)

This activity is a Case Study on page 102.

Setting Your Star Clock Alarm

In Session 5, students create a Star Clock and find out how to use it. To assess their understanding, use a large cardboard version of a Star Clock. Ask your students to set their Star Clocks for a specific time, such as 6:00 a.m., and to note the positions of the stars at that time. Then move the hands of the large clock in front of the class, and ask students to make a ringing noise when the stars have reached the position that they will have at the preset time. (Outcome 5)

Additional Assessment Ideas

Predictions

After the unit is completed, when the moon is visible in the sky, ask your students to predict where it will be the next day or the next week. When the moon

---

> ### EARTH, MOON, AND STARS
> Grades 5–9
> 15 Sessions
> Six Activities
>
> Students learn about astronomy and answer questions such as:
> "If the Earth is a ball, why does it look flat?"
> "Why does the moon change its shape?"
> "How can I find constellations and tell time by the stars?"
> Activities include observing and recording changes in the sky and creating models to explain observations.
>
> **Skills**
> Creating/Using Models, Synthesizing, Visualizing, Observing, Explaining, Measuring Angles, Recording, Estimating, Averaging, Using Instruments, Drawing Conclusions, Using a Map
>
> **Concepts**
> Astronomy, History of Astronomy, Spherical Earth, Gravity, Moon Phases, Eclipses, Measuring Time, The North Star, Earth's Daily Motion, Constellations, Horizon, Zenith
>
> **Themes**
> Systems and Interactions, Models and Simulations, Stability, Patterns of Change, Evolution, Scale, Structure
>
> **Mathematics Strands**
> Number, Measurement, Pattern, Geometry

is not visible, ask: "Where is the Moon now?" "Why can't we see it?" This will reveal the knowledge students retain and can apply beyond the duration of the unit. (Outcomes 1, 4)

Letter Writing

Ask your students to write a letter to a younger student explaining why people think the Earth is really round, even though it looks flat; or why the moon goes through different phases. You will gain information about the accuracy of students' conclusions as well as their ability to clearly communicate what they know. (Outcome 2)

What Do You Wonder?

Have your students work in small groups to brainstorm further questions they have about the Earth, Moon, and stars. Discuss their ideas about possible answers to these questions. (Outcome 6)

Earth, Moon, and Stars

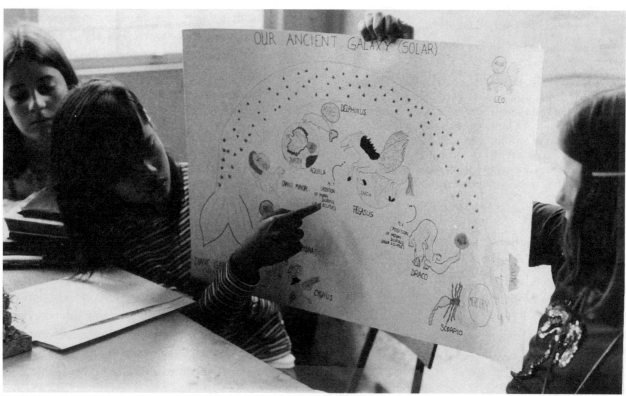

Earth, Moon, and Stars

EARTHWORMS

Selected Student Outcomes

1. Students describe the structures and behaviors of an earthworm that help it to survive underground.

2. Students are able to measure and calculate the pulse rate of an earthworm.

3. Students improve their ability to create, interpret, and explain graphs to support their discoveries.

4. Students gain an understanding of cold-blooded animals (animals whose body temperature is regulated by the temperature of the environment).

Built-In Assessment Activities

Earthworms Up Close

In Session 1, Observing Worms and Session 3, Graphing the Data, students closely observe their earthworms. They identify structures and note behaviors. They then discuss the results of the tempera-

---

EARTHWORMS
Grades 6–10
Three Sessions

Earthworm heartbeat patterns are safely investigated in living earthworms in this GEMS unit. Students observe blood vessels in worms, and observe and record the pulse rates. The students experiment to discover the responses of earthworms to different temperatures, and graph the results. In discussing why earthworms respond as they do, students learn about cold-blooded animals, the concept of adaptation, and circulatory systems.

Skills
Observing, Measuring, Experimenting, Predicting, Averaging, Graphing, Interpreting Data, Inferring

Concepts
Circulatory Systems, Pulse Rates, Cold-Blooded Animals, Effects of Temperature

Themes
Systems and Interactions, Stability, Patterns of Change, Evolution, Structure, Energy, Diversity and Unity

---

ture/pulse rate experiments. Teams share their ideas about earthworm adaptations to life underground as well as to life in a habitat subject to great temperature changes. Some classes may discuss how cold- and warm-blooded animals have different responses to environmental changes. The teacher can listen to discussions and assess their grasp of earthworm adaptations and the quality of conclusions students draw from their data. (Outcomes 1, 3)

Earthworm Pulse

In Session 2, Worms at Different Temperatures, students use the pulse-calculating technique from Session 1 to conduct a new series of tests where they vary the temperature in the earthworms' habitats. The teacher can observe each team's procedure and review the data sheets that are completed for each test to determine whether the tests have been conducted and recorded properly. (Outcome 2)

Analyze the Data

Teams organize their data, from Session 2, on a graph in Session 3, Graphing the Data. They have an opportunity to explain their data and show how it supports their answers to the questions on the data and graphing sheets. The teacher can ask questions to help students make inferences about earthworm behavior as it relates to changes in the environment. The teacher can listen for explanations supported by the data, observations made during the experiments, or during outdoor observations of earthworms. (Outcomes 1, 3)

It's An Earthworm's Life

In the concluding activity of Session 3, students are guided through a discussion relating the results of their data to the real-life challenges that earthworms experience. The concept of an animal being cold-blooded is introduced by the teacher, using animals such as lizards and snakes as examples. The teacher could ask students to explain (verbally or in writing) why an earthworm would be considered cold-blooded. The teacher can evaluate the responses for clarity and how well the explanations are supported by the data. (Outcomes 1, 3, 4)

Additional Assessment Ideas

More Earthworm Investigations

Use the Going Further suggestions for students to conduct other pulse rate experiments with earthworms. (Outcomes 1, 2, 3)

Adaptations in Other Animals

Have the students measure the pulse rates of other animals such as humans, rats, chinchillas, and daphnia. They then can compare the results to their earthworm experiments. (Outcomes 1, 2, 3)

Earthworms

Earthworms

EXPERIMENTING WITH MODEL ROCKETS

Selected Student Outcomes

1. Students improve their ability to plan a controlled experiment.

2. Students design, conduct, and interpret the results of a controlled experiment with model rockets.

3. Students use scale drawings to calculate the height of their model rockets in flight.

4. Students apply the concept of controlled experiments in other subject areas.

5. Students learn how to build and launch model rockets safely; and can explain the basic principles on which they work.

Built-In Assessment Activities

Designing Controlled Experiments

In Session 1, students watch their teacher launch a model rocket. They then design a rocket that differs from the teacher's model in only one respect. In this

---

EXPERIMENTING WITH MODEL ROCKETS
Grades 6–10
Seven Sessions

Controlled experimentation is introduced in this series of exciting rocketry activities. Students experiment to see what factors influence how high a model rocket will fly by varying the number and placement of fins or the length of the body tube. Safety and teamwork are stressed. Because students use Height-O-Meters to measure rocket altitudes, it is necessary to complete the *Height-O-Meters* GEMS unit before doing these rocketry activities.

Skills
Planning and Conducting Controlled Experiments, Measuring in Degrees and Meters, Graphing, Interpreting Data

Concepts
Rocketry, Space Science, Technology, Triangulation, Models

Themes
Systems and Interactions, Models and Simulations, Stability, Patterns of Change, Structure, Energy, Matter

---

pre-assessment task, teachers can evaluate the written plans to see if students are able to creatively design a controlled experiment to test a variable of their choice. (Outcome 1)

Building and Launching Rockets

In Sessions 2–5, the students build and launch their rockets. During this time, students focus on how to complete the multiple steps involved in construction and to safely prepare and launch the rockets. At each step in this process, the teacher can observe the students' projects to determine the successes and difficulties that they encounter. If the rocket is built according to the instructions, it should fly straight, but the altitude will depend on the particular design. After the launch, students should be able to describe the various phases of launch and why the rockets work. (Outcome 5)

Launching and Calculating Altitudes

During Sessions 5 and 6, the students measure the angular height of their rockets and calculate linear altitudes. This is a good assessment to see if students learned how to use scale drawings to calculate height when they previously studied in the GEMS guide *Height-O-Meters*. (Outcome 3)

Interpreting and Discussing Results

During the last sessions, the students draw conclusions, report results, and question each other in a convention. Students' performance in this discussion will indicate whether they are able to apply the concept of a controlled experiment to properly interpret results and draw valid conclusions. (Outcome 2)

Additional Assessment Ideas

Pre- and Post-Tests

These two tests assess students' abilities to design, critique, and interpret controlled experiments in two different subject areas: car design and plant growth.

The two tests on the next two pages—Experimenting With Cars, and Experimenting With Plants—are parallel. Both test the same abilities to design and critique experiments, by determining whether or not variables are controlled, but they use different

Experimenting With Cars

Vern and Lisa are auto engineers who work for a car manufacturing company. Their job is to find out how to get new cars to go as far as possible on one gallon of gas.

1. Lisa wants to see if a SMALL engine or a BIG engine gets more miles per gallon.

Car #1 has a SMALL engine and WHITE WALL Tires.
Car #2 has a BIG engine.

Which tires should she put on car #2?

    A. WHITE WALL tires?
    B. RADIAL tires?

Why?

2. Vern's experiment also compared SMALL and BIG engines.

Car #1 has a BIG engine and WHITE WALLS. It gets 35 mpg.
Car #2 has a SMALL engine and RADIALS. It gets 50 mpg.

Does this prove that a SMALL engine gets more miles per gallon than a BIG engine?

    A. Yes! a SMALL engine is better!
    B. No! We don't know which is better!

Why?

3. Vern and Lisa did one more experiment to see which KIND OF GAS is best.

Car #1 has a SMALL engine and WHITE WALL Tires, and used BRAND A gas. It gets 43 mpg.
Car #2 has a SMALL engine and WHITE WALL Tires, and used BRAND B gas. It gets 50 mpg.

    A. Yes! Brand B is better!
    B. No! We don't know for sure which brand is better!

Why?

Experimenting With Plants

Marty and Elise are space biologists who collected plants from a planet called Folia. Their job is to find out how to get the Folian plants to grow on board their spaceship.

1. Elise wants to see if FOLIAN soil or EARTH soil is best for growth.

    Plant #1 has FOLIAN soil and BLUE light.

    Plant #2 has EARTH soil.

Which kind of light should she use on Plant #2?

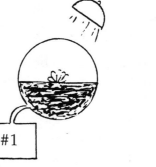

    A. RED light.
    B. BLUE light.

Why?

Plant #1   Plant #2

2. Marty's experiment also compared FOLIAN and EARTH soil.

    Plant #1 has FOLIAN soil and BLUE light. It grew 1 inch.

    Plant #2 has EARTH soil and RED light. It grew 2 inches.

Does this prove that FOLIAN soil is better than EARTH soil?

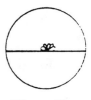

    A. Yes! FOLIAN soil is better!
    B. No! We don't know which is better!

Why?

3. Elise and Marty did one more experiment to see which FERTILIZER is best.

    Plant #1 has FOLIAN soil, a RED light and fertilizer type Y. It grew 1 inch.

    Plant #2 has FOLIAN soil, a RED light and fertilizer type Z. It grew 2 inches.

    A. Yes! Brand Z is better!
    B. No! We don't know for sure
        which brand is better!

Why?

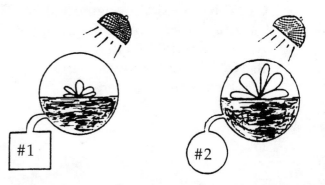

subject matter. **These tests can be used as pre-post tests for any science unit in which students are expected to improve in their abilities to control variables.**

Before the unit, give one test to half the class and the other test to the other half of the class. Be sure to record who takes which test! After the unit, give the Experimenting With Plants test to everyone who took the Experimenting With Cars test before, and vice versa. When you give the tests, tell the students that just circling "A" or "B" isn't enough. The most important thing is for them to explain **why** they circled that letter!

To evaluate student performances on these tests, staple together the pre- and post-tests for each student, and compare answers. Again, the answer circled is not as important as the rationale that students give for the answer. Following is a typical set of pre-post test answers from a student who did not know about controlling variables before the GEMS activity was conducted, learned the concept during the activity, and then took the post-test.

PRE-TEST Experimenting With Cars	POST-TEST Experimenting With Plants
A. White Wall tires. **Why?** Because they're the best tires.	**A.** Blue Light. **Why?** Because it should have the same kind of light.
A. Yes! The small engine is better. **Why?** Because it went 50 miles.	**B.** No! We don't know which is better. **Why?** Because the plants had different kinds of light.
A. Yes! Brand B is better! **Why?** Because the car with B gas went 50 miles and one with A gas only went 43 miles.	**A.** Yes! Brand Z is better! **Why?** Because both plants had the same kind of soil and the same kind of light. Only the fertilizer was different. The one with Z grew more.

FINGERPRINTING

Selected Student Outcomes

1. Students develop rich attribute vocabulary to describe fingerprint patterns.

2. Students articulate similarities and differences between fingerprints.

3. Students use the standard arch-loop-whorl system to classify fingerprints.

4. Students improve their ability to distinguish evidence from inference.

Built-In Assessment Activity

Solving the Crime

In Session 3, Solving the Crime, students use the standard arch-loop-whorl fingerprint classification system to solve a mystery and make inferences. During the session, the teacher can observe how students apply the standard fingerprint classification system to classify fingerprints for each suspect. The evidence that students use to support their inference is also observable. (Outcomes 3, 4)

FINGERPRINTING
Grades 4–8
Three Sessions

Students explore the similarities and variations of fingerprints in these fingers-on activities. Students take their own fingerprints, devise their own classification categories, then apply their classification skills to solve a crime. The mystery scenario "Who Robbed the Safe?" includes plot and character sketches.

Skills
Observing, Classifying, Drawing Conclusions, Making Inferences

Concepts
Fingerprints, Standard Fingerprint Classification System, Problem Solving

Themes
Systems and Interactions, Stability, Evolution, Diversity and Unity

---

Additional Assessment Ideas

News Reporters

In the Going Further activity for Session 3, students are invited to write newspaper articles about the crime, draw pictures, and create stories about each of the suspects. Teachers can ask half of the students to write their stories based on evidence, where any inference made is qualified. The other half of the class can be asked to write their stories for a tabloid newspaper, where evidence is secondary and wild inferences are welcome. Selected articles can then be read aloud, and the class can determine whether the article is based mostly on evidence or mostly on unfair inference. Individual papers and class discussion provide the "evidence" on which the teacher can assess students' ability to distinguish factual evidence from unfair inference. (Outcome 4)

Fingerprint Comparison

Have students use the tape and graphite method to make their own thumbprint and use attribute vocabulary to describe its attributes. They then compare their thumbprint to another print on the page and describe how the two prints are similar and different. This task provides the teacher with the opportunity to observe students' mastery of the graphite-tape fingerprinting technique, students' ability to

Fingerprinting

use rich attribute vocabulary to describe two thumbprints students' ability to compare two prints, and whether students are able to use the classifications of arch, loop, and whorl in context. (Outcomes 1, 2, 3)

This activity is a Case Study on page 184.

Guess Whose Thumb!

The teacher secretly makes a copy of a student's thumb (from the data sheet in Session 1) and invites the class to ask "yes" or "no" questions to see if the thumbprint is theirs. This activity gives the teacher an opportunity to hear how students articulate vocabulary to describe fingerprints, articulate similarities and differences, and whether students use arch-loop-whorl vocabulary to help them communicate in the task. (Outcomes 1, 2, 3)

My Thumb

Before and after the unit, students make a print of their own thumbs and write about the patterns they see. The teacher can observe how the students' descriptions change and what vocabulary they use to describe their thumbs. (Outcomes 1, 3)

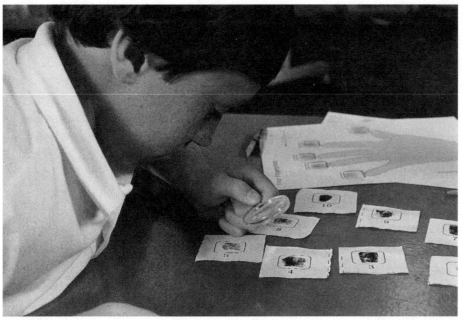

Fingerprinting

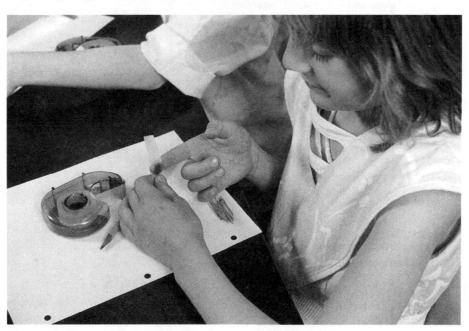

Fingerprinting

FROG MATH

Selected Student Outcomes

1. Students demonstrate their understanding that objects have a variety of attributes and may be sorted in many ways. They are able to make observations, sort and classify objects, and record and interpret their observations.

2. Students apply number sense to make reasonable estimates.

3. Students learn what a strategy is and are able to describe strategies that they use. They use logical reasoning to define, verbalize, test, generalize, and refine their strategies.

4. Students are able to recognize that probability is directly related to mathematical patterns that occur when one die and two dice are rolled.

Built-In Assessment Activities

Button Factory

In Session 1, students describe a button for their partner to draw. The teacher can observe how students use vocabulary to articulate attributes, how they listen to their partners' descriptions, and their ability to transfer the description to create a picture. (Outcome 1)

Guess the Sort

In Session 2, groups of students sort buttons and record their methods of classification. Then, they observe other groups and guess how their classmates sorted the buttons. The teacher observes how well students sort the buttons, how accurately they articulate their own methods of sorting, and how they use language and logical reasoning. (Outcome 1)

Dice Pre-Assessment

In Session 6, students tell or write what they know about dice before they play the Hop To The Pond game. From this activity, the teacher can gain a sense of students' knowledge and misconceptions about dice. The teacher can use this information to adjust the lesson so that it is appropriate to the students' experience level. (Outcome 4)

Additional Assessment Ideas

Estimation Station

In a Going Further activity following Session 4, students focus on a weekly estimation station, at which estimates are collected throughout the week. At the end of the week, before the actual unveiling and counting, the teacher may have the students write about which estimate they think is the closest, and why. The teacher can observe students' ability to make and articulate their estimates. (Outcome 2)

Write a Letter

In the Going Further activity that follows Session 5, students write (or dictate) a letter to tell a friend or

---

FROG MATH
Grades K–3
Six Sessions

This series of lively mathematics activities jumps off from one of the well-known Frog and Toad stories. From free exploration of buttons, sorting and classifying, and a Guess the Sort game, students go on to design their own buttons, and use a graphing grid to organize data. Students "guesstimate" the number of small plastic frogs in a jar and the number of lima beans in a handful to develop the valuable life skill of estimating. A Frog Pond board game helps students develop strategic-thinking skills. The Hop to the Pond game is an experiment in probability and statistics. Emphasis throughout is on student cooperation. Many extension and age modification suggestions are included.

Skills
Observing, Cooperating, Logical Thinking, Problem Solving, Collecting and Interpreting Data, Sorting and Classifying, Using Geometric Vocabulary, Noticing and Articulating Patterns, Graphing, Estimating, Predicting, Developing and Testing Strategies

Concepts
Literature and Art Connections to Mathematics, Classification, Number, Place Value, Pattern Recognition, Estimation, Probability and Statistics

Themes
Diversity and Unity, Models and Simulations, Systems and Interactions, Structure, Scale

Mathematics Strands
Number, Geometry, Patterns and Functions, Statistics and Probability, Logic

---

famous person about how to win the Frog Pond game. The teacher can assess how clearly the students understand the workings of the game, as well as how thoroughly they can articulate their strategies for winning. (Outcome 3)

Betting on the Winning Frog

In the Going Further activity after the Hop to the Pond game, students write their thoughts about which frog is most likely to win the race. This activity can be used to assess students' understanding of probability and how they apply their knowledge of probability to formulate a winning strategy. (Outcomes 3, 4)

Button Treasure Hunt

Have each student draw a button and put their own name on the back of the button. They then write words or sentences to describe the button on an index card. At the end of a school day, gather all the designed buttons and cards. Hide each button somewhere in your classroom. The next day, give students a card, and challenge them to find the button described on the card. Students can check their accuracy by asking the student whose name appears on the found button. After students have completed the task, have them list the steps they took to find the button, state how they knew it was the correct button, and think of words they could add to the description of the button. (Outcome 1)

This activity is a Case Study on page 84.

Estimation Jar

Create an estimation jar with a number of items appropriate to the developmental level of the students. Have the students record their estimate of items on a strip of paper; then pour out the contents of the jar. Have students write a new estimate under their original guess. Next, count out some of the items and have students record a new estimate. Finally, count the remainder of the items and have students write the actual answer. The paper strips will reveal each student's original guess, and how they refined their estimates as more information was provided. (Outcome 2)

Who Goes First?

Present students with the rules to a simple game, such as Tic-Tac-Toe. Ask them to write about whether they would want to go first, or second, and why. (Outcome 3)

Three Dice Hop

Discuss with students what might happen if the Hop To The Pond game were played with three dice. How would the frogs be numbered? Which frogs do they think would win the most often? Why? Have students write about their ideas. They then can play this version of the game, and share their results and insights. (Outcome 4)

Frog Math

GLOBAL WARMING AND THE GREENHOUSE EFFECT

Selected Student Outcomes

1. Students are able to explain and debate the major issues that relate to global warming.

   ➤ How the Earth's global temperature is changing during the current century.

   ➤ How the present climate relates to climatic changes thousands of years ago.

   ➤ The greenhouse effect and its impact.

   ➤ How carbon dioxide creates a kind of greenhouse effect in the Earth's atmosphere.

   ➤ How carbon dioxide can be detected and monitored.

   ➤ The sources that contribute to increasing carbon dioxide in the atmosphere.

   ➤ The relative amounts of greenhouse gases contributed by different countries.

2. Students are able to discuss some of the possible consequences of a warmer world and recognize the uncertainty of these predictions.

3. Students formulate their own opinions about what, if anything, should be done to slow the production of carbon dioxide and other greenhouse gases.

4. Students formulate thoughtful questions about global warming and the greenhouse effect.

Built-In Assessment Activities

What Have You Heard?

In the first activity, the students list what they have heard and the questions they have about the greenhouse effect. Their lists provide insight into the prior knowledge that students bring into the classroom. At various points throughout the unit, review the list with the students and have them comment on what ideas have changed and what questions they have answered. (Outcomes 1, 2, 3, 4)

A Review of the Greenhouse Effect

Sessions 2–5 explore various aspects of the greenhouse effect in the atmosphere. Each session ends with questions about that particular topic. At the end of Session 5, review the questions from previous chapters so that students can articulate the information they have learned, orally or in writing. An effective approach is to have small groups of 2–4 students discuss key questions and report back to the class. (Outcome 1)

The Effects Wheel

In Session 7, the students create an Effects Wheel in which they speculate about a chain of cause-and-effect relationships that might occur from global warming of five degrees Fahrenheit. The teacher can examine the students' work for evidence of their understanding of the ideas presented in the previous lesson. (Outcome 2)

**GLOBAL WARMING
AND THE GREENHOUSE EFFECT**
Grades 7–10
Eight Sessions

Students explore this controversial topic through a wide variety of formats, from hands-on science activities and experiments, to a simulation game, analysis of articles, a story about an island threatened by rising sea levels, and a world conference on global warming. This GEMS guide has two major aims: to present the scientific theories and evidence surrounding the controversial environmental issue of global warming, and to help students see environmental problems from different points of view—from people who live on islands in the Pacific to those who work in the lumber and auto manufacturing industries.

Skills
Observing, Measuring, Recording Data, Interpreting Graphs, Experimenting, Drawing Conclusions, Synthesizing Information, Role Playing, Using Simulation Games, Problem Solving, Brainstorming Solutions, Critical Thinking

Concepts
The Atmosphere, Visible and Infrared Photons, The Greenhouse Effect, Sources of Carbon Dioxide, Climate and Weather, The Effects of Climate Change, the Interaction of Light, Heat, and Matter

Themes
Systems and Interactions, Models and Simulations, Stability, Patterns of Change, Evolution, Scale, Structure, Energy, Matter

---

World Conference

In the last session of the unit, the students conduct a World Conference. They then stop the role play to express and solidify their own ideas. At this point, ask the students to write essays to express their own opinions and formulate plans for action. The conference, the discussion, and the essays all provide the teacher with insights into the students understanding of global warming and the greenhouse effect. (Outcomes 1–4)

This activity is a Case Study on page 175.

Additional Assessment Idea

Global Warming Newsletter

As a class project, have your students create a newsletter that discusses what is known and what is controversial about global warming, and what all citizens need to know about this important topic. (Outcomes 1–4)

Global Warming and the Greenhouse Effect

Global Warming and the Greenhouse Effect

GROUP SOLUTIONS

Selected Student Outcomes

1. Students develop mathematical language, deductive reasoning, and logical thinking as they work together to solve problems, and articulate their problem-solving processes. They communicate as well as gain respect for each other's ideas.

2. Students demonstrate the ability to identify, sort, classify, and distinguish objects according to their attributes.

3. Students demonstrate spatial visualization skills as they follow pictorial and written directions to arrange objects in a line or group.

4. Students gain familiarity with number properties, place value, and our money system.

5. Students enhance their map-reading skills.

Built-In Assessment Activities

Stand Up! Sit Down!

This introductory activity to the Searches section is an excellent pre-assessment. Students stand up and sit down according to attributes. The teacher observes the extent to which the students recognize attributes and how well they are able to sort themselves accordingly. (Outcome 2)

Draw a Picture

As they solve a problem in the Searches section, groups of students are asked to draw a picture that fits all the clues in their envelope. The teacher will be able to identify how well the group has listened to all the clues, and how well the members are able to isolate the attributes of the solution to the problem. (Outcomes 1, 2)

Student Line-Up

As a pre-assessment in the Bear Line-Up section, students place themselves in a line according to specific directions. The teacher can use this activity to assess students' understanding of directional and spatial vocabulary. (Outcomes 1, 2, 3)

Chart Patterns

As a pre-assessment in the Secret Number section, students work with 50's and 100's charts to find, record, and describe number patterns. The teacher gains information about students' familiarity with patterns and properties of numbers, and their readiness level for the ensuing activities. The teacher could use this activity again at the end of the section to measure students' growth of knowledge as a result of working with the problems in the section. (Outcome 4)

Map a Journey

This activity may be used as a pre-assessment to the Maps section. Students use pre-made maps to trace their paths as they tour their classroom, school

---

> **GROUP SOLUTIONS**
> Grades K–4
>
> The more than 50 highly involving cooperative logic activities in this guide are designed for groups of four students. Each student receives a clue to a problem and needs to share the information with the other group members to find the solution. The entire group is responsible for finding the solution, and it can ONLY be figured out by connecting the information from ALL the clues. The games, puzzles, and problems are clearly stated and cleverly illustrated with easy-to-use, fun manipulatives. Introductory sections explain how to use the book and discuss cooperative learning and logic in the classroom. Many key elements in mathematics and science are naturally explored, leading to student questions such as "Are we really doing math?" "Can we do this again, soon?"
>
> **Skills**
> Visual Discrimination, Counting, Sorting, Classifying, Using the Process of Elimination, Using Deductive Reasoning, Communicating, Sequencing, Spatial Visualization, Recognizing Shapes and Colors, Using Charts, Comparing Amounts, Map Reading
>
> **Concepts**
> Numeration, Computation (Fractions), Directionality, Ordinal Numbers, Money, Mapping
>
> **Themes**
> Patterns of Change, Models and Simulations, Systems and Interactions, Stability, Structure, Scale
>
> **Mathematics Strands**
> Number, Measurement, Geometry, Pattern, Functions, Statistics and Probability, Logic, Algebra

site, or neighborhood. They then describe their journeys. The teacher can assess students' familiarity with maps and the vocabulary associated with maps, and use this information to plan the unit. (Outcome 5)

Create Your Own

During any of the sections, the teacher may want to challenge older students to create their own cooperative logic problems. This may be done as a longer-term group project. Students' work will demonstrate their ability to apply problem-solving skills, use mathematical language, and work collaboratively. (Outcomes 1, 2, 4, 5)

Additional Assessment Ideas

Self-Assessment

Throughout the guide, teachers can ask students to evaluate their group dynamics. Students list ways that their group worked well together, as well as difficulties that they had. Teachers can use this information to gain insight into students' feelings about group work as well as to assess each group member's level of self-awareness.

This activity is a Case Study on page 196.

Design a Line-Up

As a Going Further activity in the Bear Line-Up section, students create and draw their own line-ups. The teacher will be able to assess the students' use of mathematical vocabulary and logical-thinking skills. (Outcome 1, 3)

Number Search

As a Going Further activity at the end of the Secret Number section, students choose a number and write a list of clues that might help a classmate guess the number. The teacher can assess how well the student is able to use mathematical vocabulary and knowledge of number properties to solve the problem. (Outcomes 1, 4)

Bear Line-Ups from Group Solutions

Record the Coins

As a Going Further activity in the Coin Count section, students record their solutions to problems using coin stamps. Or, students make their own combination using stamps, and describe the result. The teacher can use the students' work to assess their knowledge of the properties of our money system. (Outcome 4)

Smart Shoppers

In this Going Further activity in the Coin Count section, students explore advertising flyers from supermarkets and make statements about what they've found. They could also be given specific challenges (for example., make a balanced meal for under $10). The teacher will notice students' ability to work together to solve real-world problems associated with money. (Outcomes 1, 4)

Young Cartographers

As a Going Further activity in the Maps section, students create a fictional place and a map of it, complete with directional statements. Through reading the students' work, the teacher, can assess their ability to use mapping language, spatial skills, and logical thinking. (Outcomes 1, 2, 5)

Dream Animal

Students draw or construct a fictitious animal. They then list the attributes of that animal. If they wish, they may write a story about the animal. (Outcome 2)

Hidden Picture

Students draw a picture in which there is a hidden or camouflaged object. They then write clues for a classmate to use to find the object. (Outcomes 1, 2, 4)

Design a Coin System

Students design an imaginary coin system. They describe the value of each coin, and list equivalent values of the coins—for example, two GLEEPS = 1 GLOP. (Outcome 4)

Treasure Hunt

A group of students hide a treasure in the classroom. They make a map of the room, and clues to the location of the treasure. They then challenge another group to find their treasure. (Outcomes 1, 4)

HEIGHT-O-METERS

Selected Student Outcomes

1. Students apply geometry skills to build and "zero" an instrument that measures degrees of altitude.

2. Students articulate the difference between angular and linear distance.

3. Students use a graphical method to triangulate the height of an object.

4. Students use words and/or diagrams to articulate why measuring the base line and angle are sufficient to determine the height of an object.

Built-In Assessment Activities

Building Height-O-Meters

During Sessions 1 and 2, students construct and "zero" the scale of Height-O-Meters (clinometers) and learn how to use them to measure angular heights. At the end of the activity, they test their instruments to measure the altitude of some point in the classroom.

HEIGHT-O-METERS
Grades 6–10
Four Sessions

Students are introduced to the principle of triangulation by making simple cardboard devices called Height-O-Meters. Students measure angles to determine the height of the school flagpole, and compare how high a Styrofoam ball and a rubber ball can be thrown. *Height-O-Meters* is a prerequisite for GEMS rocketry activities in *Experimenting With Model Rockets*. Going Further activities relate triangulation to the real-life activities of forest rangers and astronomers and also introduce the tangent function of trigonometry.

Skills
Predicting, Estimating, Making and Calibrating Scientific Instruments, Measuring in Degrees, Graphing, Calculating, Interpreting Data

Concepts
Angular and Linear Measurement, Triangulation with Scale Drawings, Metric System

Themes
Systems and Interactions, Models and Simulations, Stability, Scale

---

The teacher can ask each student for their measurement and immediately determine which students may have incorrectly constructed or adjusted their instrument. With this information, the teacher can provide extra assistance as needed. (Outcome 1)

Measuring the Height of a Flagpole

In Session 3, students use their Height-O-Meters to measure the angular height of the flagpole or some other tall object in or near their school. Prior to the activity, the teacher has measured the object physically, and placed the measurement in an envelope. After the students calculate the height of the flagpole with the base line and the angles they measured, the teacher graphs the results of the class and opens the envelope. At this point, teachers and students can evaluate how accurately they have determined the height of the flagpole. (Outcomes 2, 3)

Applying the Concept of Triangulation

In Session 4, the students apply the technique of triangulation to complete an experiment and determine how different kinds of balls can be thrown. The teacher can look at each team's results, and pose questions during the activity to determine the degree to which students are able to describe the technique and explain why it works. (Outcomes 2, 3, 4)

Additional Assessment Idea

Where's the Fire?

In a Going Further, students assume the role of forest rangers who use triangulation to find the distance to a forest fire. Provide the equipment the students will need, have them proceed on their own, and observe whether or not they are able to meet the challenge (the triangle in the model is horizontal rather than vertical). Note the problems they encounter, and provide assistance when necessary. After the activity, ask students why our measurements did not determine the distance to the fire without additional information. (Students must also know the distance between the two ranger stations). In addition, ask students to describe in their own words how the triangulation method works. (Outcomes 2, 3, 4)

HIDE A BUTTERFLY

Selected Student Outcomes

1. Students can explain why a butterfly is protected from a hungry bird when it is hidden on a flower of the same color.

2. Students are able to create a paper model of a butterfly that can be camouflaged so it cannot be seen by a hungry bird puppet.

3. Students demonstrate their understanding of the predator-prey relationship through dramatic play with butterflies and birds.

Built-In Assessment Activities

The Butterfly Play

In Session 2, students watch a short play about a butterfly that is hidden from a bird when its butterfly wings are closed, yet quite visible to the bird when the butterfly's wings are open. Teachers can reenact the play and pause to ask questions to check for understanding.

HIDE A BUTTERFLY
Preschool–K
Three Sessions

Children create camouflaged butterflies, hungry birds, and a meadow of flowers to enact "The Butterfly Play" and learn basic concepts of protective coloration.

During the activities, children identify parts of a flower, make flowers and grass for the mural, then talk about small animals they've seen in real grass or on flowers. They decorate paper butterflies and make bird puppets, then act out the behavior of birds and butterflies. Children also learn more about real butterflies and their various means of protective coloration.

Skills
Observing, Communicating, Comparing, Matching, Role Playing, Using Scissors (optional)

Concepts
Biology, Entomology, Butterflies, Protective Coloration, Predator/Prey Relationships

Themes
Systems and Interactions, Models and Simulations, Scale, Energy, Diversity and Unity

---

Questions might include:
"Why is this butterfly hidden from the bird?"
"Can the bird see the butterfly now?"
" Why?"
Students' responses can indicate the degree to which they understand the concept of camouflage — animals can hide if they match the color of their surroundings. (Outcome 1)

Butterfly, Butterfly

Also in Session 2, the students assist the teacher to create a butterfly with coloration on the inside of its wings. They then design their own butterfly to complement their flower and bird. As students work, the teacher can ask them why they have selected particular colors for their butterfly or why they have added (or decided not to add) color to its wings. Students further demonstrate the degree to which they understand protective coloration when they use their creations in the butterfly play. (Outcomes 1, 2)

The Butterfly and Bird Dramas

Session 2 ends as each student performs "The Butterfly Play" with the flower, butterfly, and bird they made. The teacher can watch for sequences of events that depict the camouflage concept as well as for descriptive language and new vocabulary as appropriate. Spontaneous and cooperative dramas will occur if students are allowed ample free time with the puppets. (Outcomes 1, 3)

Additional Assessment Ideas

Butterflies in the Wild

Students can search for real butterflies that may or may not be camouflaged during a class hike or at home. (Outcome 1)

Butterflies Fly Home

Send the flower, butterfly, and bird home with the students. Ask families to watch and listen to the dramatic play, and to describe what was presented in a note to the teacher. (Outcomes 1, 3)

HOT WATER AND WARM HOMES FROM SUNLIGHT

Selected Student Outcomes

1. Students demonstrate their ability to conduct controlled experiments in which only the test variable is different and all other possible variables are kept the same.

2. Students are able to measure, record, and graph accurate temperature measurements.

3. Students compare graphs of temperature changes and interpret the data to form a hypothesis about the effects of solar heating.

4. Students articulate the value of solar energy as a potential source for home heating.

Built-In Assessment Activities

Introductory Activity

The unit begins with a "paper experiment" to illustrate how plants grow with different amounts of

---

HOT WATER AND WARM HOMES FROM SUNLIGHT
Grades 4–8
Five Sessions

Students build model houses and hot water heaters to discover more about solar power. They conduct experiments to determine the effects of size, color, and number of windows on the amount of heat produced from sunlight. Information on the greenhouse effect connects to the GEMS guide on *Global Warming and the Greenhouse Effect*. The introductory activity, Controlled Experimentation, is an on-paper experiment about growing plants that helps define terms such as controlled experiment, variable, and experimental outcome.

Skills
Experimenting, Controlling Variables, Measuring and Recording Data, Graphing, Drawing Conclusions

Concepts
Models and Systems, Solar Energy, Using Sunlight to Heat Homes and Water, the Greenhouse Effect, Home Energy Use, Conducting Science Experiments

Themes
Energy, Models, Systems and Interactions, Equilibrium

---

fertilizer. Questions are posed to reveal students' understanding of controlled experimentation. Teachers can ask the same questions after the unit to determine how much students have learned about controlled experimentation. (Outcome 1)

Students' Solar Home Experiments

In Sessions 1–3, students conduct experiments with the solar houses they've constructed. In Sessions 4 and 5, they conduct experiments with solar water heaters. Teachers can observe how the students' skills improve from the first experiment to the second as they measure and record data, graph and analyze results, and change only one variable. (Outcome 2)

Compare Experiments

Teachers can compare students' performance on the solar home with their design of the solar water heater experiments. Look for gradual improvement in students' abilities to interpret experimental results in terms of an initial hypothesis. (Outcome 3)

Additional Assessment Idea

Creative Writing

Ask your students to write a manual on how to build a new house with an explanation of how the reader might save energy if the house is planned carefully. Student work should include a discussion of why it is important to utilize solar energy whenever possible. The manual should include references to the results of experiments performed during the class, such as the color of the house, the presence or absence of windows, and the orientation of the house. Manuals should also contain advice on how to construct a solar water heater, as well as details of the water heater construction, such as its color and whether or not it is covered. (Outcomes 1, 2, 3, 4)

IN ALL PROBABILITY

Selected Student Outcomes

1. Students use statistical and mathematical vocabulary and logical-thinking skills to record and interpret data.

2. Students gain an intuitive understanding of probability by using concrete objects. They are able to make predictions, formulate hypotheses, and draw conclusions based upon statistical analysis.

3. Students improve their ability to effectively communicate their thinking, orally and in writing. They learn to support their conclusions with charts, graphs, or pictorial analysis of data.

Built-In Assessment Activities

Flip a Penny/Predict 30 Rolls

In this pre-assessment to the Penny Flip and Roll A Die investigations, students are asked to predict results of 20 penny flips or 30 die rolls. The teacher

---

IN ALL PROBABILITY
Grades 3–6
Five Activities

Students play games that involve coins, spinners, dice, and Native American game sticks. They investigate chance and probability with concrete materials, learn how to gather and analyze data, make predictions, and draw conclusions. As they gain direct experience, they also build confidence in their ability to explore probability and statistics. These activities provide a solid basis for the development of much-needed (and often neglected) real-life understandings and skills. Cooperation is stressed and students learn that mathematics is fun!

Skills
Predicting, Describing, Comparing, Estimating, Drawing Conclusions, Working with a Partner

Concepts
Probability, Statistics, Prediction

Themes
Patterns of Change, Models and Simulations

Mathematics Strands
Number, Pattern, Statistics and Probability, Logic

---

may observe students developing ideas about probability. (Outcome 2)

Write About 10 Flips

After they have conducted the Penny Flip activity, students are asked to describe in writing the results of the investigation. They are asked to analyze the class data. The teacher can observe how accurately students interpreted the data in this investigation. (Outcome 1)

Predict 100 Flips

After the Penny Flip activity, students are asked to predict what they think would happen if a penny were flipped 100 times. Students articulate their predictions and reasons in writing. The teacher gains insight into the students' ability to generalize from previous information. (Outcomes 2, 3)

Make True Statements

During the first session of the Track Meet activity, students are asked to make "true" statements about the graph of the race results from the class. The teacher can observe how accurately students are able to interpret data. (Outcome 1)

Design Spinners

After participating in the Track Meet activity, students are asked to design two spinners, one fair and one unfair, and to describe how they are fair or unfair. The teacher will be able to assess how well students understand and can construct models of equal and unequal probability. (Outcome 2)

Predict the Winner

As a pre-assessment to racing the horses in the Horse Race game, students are asked to predict results of the game, which uses two dice. The teacher can glean some insight into students' early thinking about this type of probability, especially in light of the preceding session, in which students have used one die. (Outcomes 1, 2)

Write about the Horse Race Game

After they have played the game and analyzed the results, students are asked to write about which horses are most likely, and least likely, to win the race, and why. The teacher will observe the students' mathematical reasoning and their ability to understand and make sense of combinations of sums of dice. (Outcomes 1, 2, 3)

This activity is a Case Study on page 45.

Write About Game Sticks

At the conclusion of the Native American Game Sticks activities, students write about the game results in light of what they know about probability. They are encouraged to extend the results of the two-stick and four-stick game to analyze the six-stick game. The teacher will notice the level of sophistication in students' thinking about the patterns of probability as they relate to this game. (Outcomes 1, 2, 3)

Additional Assessment Ideas

Change the Rules

In the Going Further extension to the Horse Race activity, students are asked to change the rules of the game, so that another horse or horses have a better chance of winning. The teacher will notice how well the students understand the concept of probability. (Outcomes 2, 3)

Describe Another Game

As a Going Further activity for the Game Sticks sessions, students find and describe another game as it relates to probability. The teacher will observe the students' ability to generalize probability rules. (Outcome 2)

Make Dice

Students are challenged to design a die, or dice, of their own. They may use cubes or they may create the dice from heavy construction paper. They may construct "fair" or "unfair" dice, depending on how they label each face of the die. They predict what will happen if the dice are rolled 200 times and explain the reasons for their prediction. They could make up rules for a fair and unfair dice game. (Outcomes 2, 3)

In All Probability

INVESTIGATING ARTIFACTS

Selected Student Outcomes

1. Students demonstrate their understanding that objects have a variety of attributes, and can be sorted and classified in many ways. Students are able to differentiate natural from non-natural objects/materials.

2. Students are able to distinguish evidence from inference and demonstrate progress in making logical inferences based on partial evidence.

3. Students are able to create, in drawing and/or writing, a story or legend that helps explain or model natural phenomena.

4. Students demonstrate their ability to keep track of archaeological findings and map the location of objects as they work in teams in a simulated archaeological investigation.

5. Students gain insight into, and increased respect for, elements of diverse Native American and world cultures.

INVESTIGATING ARTIFACTS
Grades K–6
Six Sessions

This guide weaves together three activities related to anthropology, archaeology, and diverse Native American and world cultures. Students sort and classify natural objects found on a class walk. They make their own masks. They create their own stories to explain natural phenomena and learn how ancient peoples evolved myths to explain and represent the natural world. Students learn that a midden is an archaeological term for deposits earlier peoples left behind, including utensils, garbage, and other artifacts. Teams of students carefully sift through "artifacts" in shoebox-middens. Possible extensions raise important social issues. A major scientific thread in all three activities concerns inferences that can be drawn from varying evidence. Resource sheets provide information on Native American and world masks, myths, and archaeological sites. An annotated list of related young people's literature is included.

Skills
Observing, Recording, Sorting and Classifying, Finding and Making Patterns, Mapping and Diagramming, Making Inferences, Designing Models, Writing, Relating, Communicating, Drama and Role Playing, Working Cooperatively, Analyzing Data

Concepts
Anthropology, Archaeology, Cultural Diversity and Similarity, Art, Language, Culture, Myths, Legends, Storytelling

Themes
Patterns of Change, Models and Simulations, Systems and Interactions, Structure, Scale, Unity and Diversity

Mathematics Strands
Functions, Measurement, Number, Pattern, Logic

Built-In Assessment Activities

Yarn Loop Sort

Teachers can observe the development of students' sorting and classification skills in Session 1 through the yarn loop sort and its extension into an open-ended sort. These skills are also applied during the Secret Sort game at end the session. (Outcome 1)

Sharing Stories and Class Discussion

In Session 4, students share the stories/myths they have created. The story explains some natural phenomena and the teacher can observe how well student teams worked together to originate and present the story. Class discussion of the story of "How the Stars Came to Be" can help teachers assess growth in students' ability to make inferences. Additional evidence/inference information is provided as students share and discuss a myth or legend from their own culture. (Outcomes 2, 3, 5)

Midden Excavation, Mapping, and Task Cards

As students excavate the simulated middens, the teacher can observe how well teams cooperate, assess students' understanding and performance of the archaeological tasks, and observe the groups' level of accuracy and care. Older students should be able to note which objects are found at different layers, make a grid to precisely record their findings, and demonstrate an understanding of soil layers as gradations in time. The "midden map" and the Archaeological Checklist Task Cards provide information on students' accuracy and attention to detail, their understanding of archaeology and their ability to develop inferences. (Outcomes 1, 2, 4)

Midden Class Discussion/Data Chart

The class discussion of artifacts in Session 6 provides an opportunity for teachers to assess students' observation and recording skills, as well as growth in their ability to make inferences from partial evidence. As students place artifacts in categories, teachers can listen to discussion and debate about the plausibility and accuracy of inferences. Students' oral comments provide information about how well they have developed these key thinking skills. (Outcomes 1, 2, 4)

Additional Assessment Ideas

Mystery Objects

In a Going Further activity for middens, teachers bring in an object that is unfamiliar to students (for example, a slide rule or a part of a machine) and present it as a mystery object from the past. Students are asked to make inferences about the object's function and importance to the culture it represents. (Outcome 2)

This activity is a Case Study on page 129.

Motel of the Mysteries

Read *Motel of the Mysteries* by David Macaulay (Houghton Mifflin, Boston, 1979). Have students write/draw their own versions of the story, using the classroom and its related "artifacts" as an excavation site unearthed at an imagined time several thousand years in the future. Ask students to include at least two misinterpretations—wrong inferences about actual artifacts—that could possibly be thought to be true if little else were known. (Outcome 2)

Going Further with Masks

In Going Further activities for Sessions 1 and 2, students feature their masks in stories and plays and bring in pictures of real masks. To create a display of masks from different cultures, students select a mask, report on it, list its materials, describe what they can infer from it, and sketch how the mask was used by the particular culture. These stories/plays/reports can be used to assess how students apply the skills and content they have gained from the mask activities. (Outcomes 1, 2, 5)

Controversial Issues

Many of the Going Further suggestions provide excellent assessment possibilities for midden activities. One option further develops the shopping mall/Native American cultural site controversy. For older students, the shopping mall scenario can provide an underlying theme for the classroom midden activity. Team presentations can be assessed to determine how well students demonstrate understanding and sensitivity to Native American concerns, depict the role of archaeologists in preserving culture, and consider multiple opinions about complex social issues. (Outcomes 2, 4, 5)

Newspaper Article

The teacher reads aloud a scenario about a possible arson. With a written version of the scenario, the students are asked to identify the unfair inferences made in a newspaper article about the situation and then to rewrite the article to better reflect the facts and avoid unfair inferences. (Outcome 2)

This activity is a Case Study in *Mystery Festival* on page 72.

Famous Finds

Devise a "What's Hidden in a Real Midden" assignment, to build upon and extend the Famous Finds page. Each team can research a famous find and select five artifacts unearthed at the site. Other teams can ask questions to attempt to figure out more about the discovery and determine the exact location and culture. (Outcomes 2, 4, 5)

Favorite Legends

Have students select two of their favorite stories, legends, or myths. In a brief essay, students should state at least two inferences about the culture of the people who originated each story. Students can also discuss ways the stories are similar and different. (Outcomes 2, 3, 5)

Indigenous Peoples

Conduct a class project or assign teams of students to visit with and/or research a Native American tribe or tribes from your region. Have students make a presentation of what they've learned. (Outcome 5)

INVOLVING DISSOLVING

Selected Student Outcomes

1. Students articulate that some solids dissolve, while others don't; and some solids dissolve quickly, while other solids dissolve over days.

2. Students explain that though a dissolving solid *seems* to disappear, it actually remains in the liquid.

3. Students improve their ability to observe and describe substances.

4. Students demonstrate increased confidence in predicting/guessing what might happen in an unknown situation.

5. Students improve their ability to describe changes that take place after solids and liquids are mixed.

Built-In Assessment Activities

Regularly Making Predictions

During each activity in the unit, students make predictions about what they think will happen when a solid is dissolved in a liquid and where they think the solid has gone once it disappears. The teacher can observe students' willingness to make predictions/guesses, and whether they become more confident over the course of the unit. (Outcome 4)

What Happened?

In each of the four sessions, students have the opportunity to comment on their final "product," such as the Gel-O, Gelatin disks, or Starry Night papers. The students explain what happened in the experiment or describe the changes that took place. The teacher can note how the students articulate their responses and how the responses improve in clarity and detail over the four sessions. (Outcome 5)

Additional Assessment Ideas

Dissolving Other Substances

In the Going Further activity described at the end of Activity 1: Homemade Gel-O, students dissolve other substances such as powders, crystals, and various solids. The teacher can observe how well students draw or write about what they did, what they saw, and what happened. (Outcomes 1, 3)

INVOLVING DISSOLVING
Grades 1–3
Four Activities

Students learn about the concepts of dissolving, evaporation, and crystallization. Using familiar substances, they create homemade Gel-O, colorful disks, and crystals that emerge on black paper to make a Starry Night. Does the substance disappear? If not, where did it go? As young students ponder these ideas and gain experience mixing and observing differing solutions, they enjoy very positive early experiences with chemistry.

Skills
Observing, Comparing, Describing, Measuring, Recording, Predicting, Drawing Conclusions

Concepts
Chemistry, Liquids and Solids, Dissolving, Solutions, Evaporation, Crystals

Themes
Systems and Interactions, Patterns of Change, Structure, Matter

---

Involving Dissolving

A Story About a Mystery Solid

In another Going Further activity for Homemade Gel-O, students create stories about a mystery solid that is dissolved in a mystery liquid. They tell what happens to the solid as it dissolves and what dissolving it does to the liquid. They then illustrate the story. These stories may reveal students' concepts about where a solid goes after it seems to disappear, or a student's understanding that some solids dissolve while others do not. Some descriptions can demonstrate richness and detail. (Outcomes 1, 2, 3)

Mystery Solution

Give your students a mystery substance such as Kool-Aid powder or Jello powder. Have them think of words to describe the mystery substance, using as many senses as they can. Ask them to predict what might happen when the substance is mixed with cold water, and then let them test the predictions. (Outcomes 3, 4, 5)

Write a Letter

Students can write or dictate a letter to a younger student explaining what happens to salt when it dissolves in water. (Outcome 2)

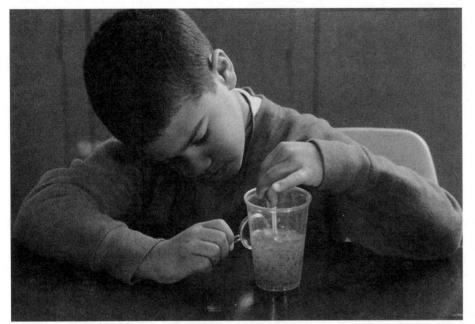
Involving Dissolving

Involving Dissolving

LADYBUGS

Selected Student Outcomes

1. Students become familiar with ladybug structure and behavior as they observe and care for live ladybugs.

2. Students create models of ladybugs and enact their behaviors through dramatic play.

3. Students become familiar with the different life stages of a ladybug.

4. Students model predator-prey relationships through dramatic play.

5. Students gain an intuitive understanding of symmetry as they study the symmetrical external features of ladybug and human bodies.

LADYBUGS
Preschool–1
13 Sessions

This unit, with five main activities, takes off from childhood delight with ladybugs to present key science and mathematics concepts to young children, including basic information relating to animal life and ecology. The children engage in a series of activities that help them learn more about ladybug body structure and symmetry, life cycle, defensive behavior, and foods. Mathematics is an integral part of this unit and role-playing is interwoven in the activities. Colorful posters of ladybugs are included. In the last session, "Ladybugs Rescue the Orange Trees," children learn important lessons about the environmental role of ladybugs and the interdependence found in nature.

Skills
Observing, Identifying, Creative and Logical Thinking, Communicating, Comparing, Matching, Role Playing

Concepts
Ladybugs (Body Structure, Life Cycle, Defenses), Symmetry, Predator/Prey, Environmental Role of Ladybugs

Themes
Systems and Interactions, Patterns of Change, Models and Simulations, Evolution, Scale, Structure, Diversity and Unity

Mathematics Strands
Geometry (Symmetry), Pattern, Number, Measurement, Logic

Built-In Assessment Activities

Live Ladybugs in the Classroom

In Activity 1, Getting to Know Ladybugs, students observe live ladybugs and study their structure, symmetry, and behaviors. Through questions and discussions, the teacher can see how students describe and compare what they observed about ladybugs. (Outcome 1)

Predict the Spots

In Activity 1, students paint a few spots on one half of a paper ladybug body. They then fold the body on the line of symmetry and predict how many spots will appear on the other half. Teacher can ask students to state their prediction and explain their reasoning. Through this process, students will demonstrate the degree to which they understand and can apply the concept of symmetry. (Outcome 5)

Making Models and Role Playing

In Activity 2, Ladybugs Eating Aphids, students feed live aphids to their ladybugs. They pretend they are ladybugs as they eat aphid popsicles. They also draw an aphid on a leaf for their ladybug model to eat. During these activities, the teacher listens for descriptive language, detailed stories, explanations, and role plays. Student drawings and paper models can also be evaluated for detail and inclusion of body structures. (Outcomes 1, 2, 4)

Ladybugs

The Life Stages of a Ladybug

Activity 3, Eggs and Baby Ladybugs and Activity 4, Ladybug Pupae and Life Cycle introduce students to the life stages of the ladybug. They watch a drama of the life cycle and then make models of young ladybugs. The models are used to dramatize the ladybug life sequence. The teacher can observe how the students build the models, and enact the dramas and role plays. The teacher should watch for role plays (told in words or through dramatics) that use new vocabulary and concepts that relate to the ladybug life stages. Some students may be able to demonstrate the life cycle process. (Outcome 2, 3)

Additional Assessment Ideas

Writing Ladybug Stories and Plays

Students can write or dictate stories about ladybugs and add illustrations. Teachers can assist students to create a play from their stories and perform it for classmates and families. (Outcome 2, 3, 4)

Ladybugs at Home

Send the ladybug projects home with a piece of paper. Ask families to help the student write down a story—by the student—that describes an aspect of ladybug life. (Outcomes 2, 3, 4)

More Creatures in the Classroom

Bring in other small creatures such as meal worms, earthworms, and pillbugs for your class to observe and care for. Have the students compare their structure, behavior, and life stages to those of the ladybug. (Outcome 1)

Symmetry Hunt

Have students find symmetrical objects in the classroom or at home. Students can draw pictures or dictate words to record their discoveries. Compile a class list of student responses. (Outcome 5)

Ladybugs

Ladybugs

LIQUID EXPLORATIONS

Selected Student Outcomes

1. Students describe and compare the qualities that make one liquid different from another, and those that make them similar.

2. Students improve their ability to classify substances according to their attributes.

3. Students can articulate that some liquids mix while others do not.

Built-In Assessment Activities

Classifying Liquids

In Activity 1, Liquid Classification, students play a Guess My Rule classification game. If this activity is repeated at the end of the unit or later in the school year, teachers can look for improvements in students' ability to observe, compare, and classify liquid attributes. (Outcomes 1, 2)

LIQUID EXPLORATIONS
Grades 1–3
Five Activities

In this series of fun and engaging activities, students explore the properties of liquids. They play a classification game, observe how food coloring moves through different liquids, create secret salad dressing recipes, and an "ocean in a bottle." The Rain Drops and Oil Drops activity can prompt discussion of environmental issues such as oil slicks. The Rain Drops and Oil Drops activity was used in the Alaska schools as part of their efforts to educate students in relation to the 1989 Exxon oil spill.

Skills
Observing, Comparing, Describing, Classifying, Recording, Drawing Conclusions

Concepts
Properties of Liquids, Simple Definitions, Classifying, Observing Attributes, Comparing, Mixtures

Themes
Systems and Interactions, Stability, Patterns of Change, Structure, Matter

---

Some Liquids Mix; Others Don't

In the opening demonstrations of Session 4, Ocean in a Bottle and Session 5, Secret Salad Dressing, students guess whether the various liquids might mix. After the liquids are poured together, the children are encouraged to explain what happened. The teacher can see how students articulate their guesses and explanations. (Outcome 3)

Additional Assessment Ideas

Classifying Other Things

A Going Further activity for Liquid Classification has students classify various materials such as leaves, attribute blocks, fruits, vegetables, or shoes. This gives the teacher an opportunity to observe how students can apply classification skills in new situations. (Outcome 2)

Mystery Liquids

In the Going Further activity for Swirling Colors, students observe how drops of color move through mystery liquids. The teacher can observe how students use the results from the initial experiment to determine the identity of the mystery liquid. (Outcome 1)

Shipwrecked!

Students are asked to help a pirate determine which liquids are saltwater and which are freshwater without tasting them. (Outcome 1)

Imaginary Liquids

Ask students to draw an imaginary liquid and to think of a name for it. Tell them that they are the only people who know the special properties of their liquid. First have the students in small groups each tell you about their liquids; then, ask them to tell you how the liquids are similar to each other, and how they are different. (Outcome 1)

MAPPING ANIMAL MOVEMENTS

Selected Student Outcomes

1. Students are able to apply sampling techniques to observe and record animal behavior during an investigation.

2. Students can create graphs to represent the mapped data from their investigation.

3. Students compare, analyze, and interpret the graphs of different animal investigations.

4. Students are able to articulate the importance of animal-mapping research to the preservation of certain animal species and their habitats.

Built-In Assessment Activities

Sampling Movement Patterns

In Session 1, Modeling the Sampling System, students participate in a whole-group investigation of an animal's behavior (a student) in response to its habitat (the classroom). The whole class works as a team to practice the sampling technique to map the student's movements. Later, in Session 3, Mapping Animal Movements, teams conduct the sampling procedure with different animals. During these activities, the teacher can circulate among the teams to observe how well they use the technique and how effectively they cooperate with each other. The teacher can also review the team's data sheet and ask for explanations. (Outcome 1)

Interpreting the Data

In Session 4, Identifying Movement Patterns, students construct bar graphs of their mapped data, interpret their results, and compare their results to other team's research. The teacher reviews the student bar graphs, observes how each team reports their findings, and how they have interpreted the results and bar graphs. The teacher should listen for ideas that are supported by the graphs and mapped data, and evaluate the quality of questions and responses asked of other teams. (Outcomes 2, 3)

MAPPING ANIMAL MOVEMENTS
Grades 5–9
Four Sessions

Students apply field biology techniques, using a sampling and mapping system, to quantify and compare the movements of hamsters and crickets. Students plan and conduct experiments, and graph changes in movement patterns when food and shelter are added to the environment. There are also sections on mapping the movements of Tule Elk, animal care, food, housing, handling, and the NSTA Code of Practice on Use of Animals in Schools. This guide makes an excellent extension to the GEMS *Animals in Action* unit.

Skills
Observing, Classifying, Mapping, Analyzing Data, Experimenting, Making Inferences

Concepts
Biology, Animals, Insects (Crickets), Hamsters, Treatment of Animals, Habitat Requirements, Research Techniques of Biologists

Themes
Systems and Interactions, Stability, Patterns of Change, Evolution, Structure, Diversity and Unity

---

Mapping Animal Movements

A Mapping Study

In Session 1, students are asked to read an overview of a mapping study done on a reintroduced species to a grassland habitat in California. Use this assignment after Session 4 as a real-life situation to discuss in light of the student's investigations. The teacher should listen for student description of using mapping activities to study threatened species and their habitats. As a final scenario, the teacher can observe if students can relate components of the study to their own mapping investigations. (Outcomes 3, 4)

Additional Assessment Ideas

Mapping At Home

Have students design and conduct another animal mapping investigations in the classroom and at home with their own family, pets, backyard animals, etc. (Outcomes 1, 2, 3)

Mapping Fish

Students can conduct the activities in the *Mapping Fish Habitats* GEMS guide and compare terrestrial and aquatic research methods. (Outcomes 1, 2, 3)

Research in the Wild

Students can view videos of animal research, such as the movie, "Never Cry Wolf," or the 1987 National Geographic Special, "The Grizzlies." Discuss how their own investigations compare with the research methods used in the videos. (Outcomes 3, 4)

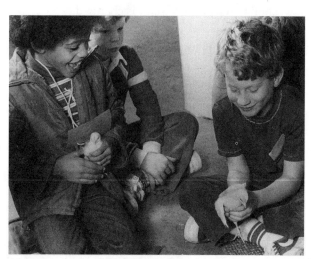

Mapping Animal Movements

Mapping Animal Movements

MAPPING FISH HABITATS

Selected Student Outcomes

1. Students can use a sampling system to map the movements of fish within an aquarium habitat.

2. Students are able to plan an experiment and make predictions about how fish behavior will change when the habitat is changed.

3. The students improve their ability to work co-operatively as a team to conduct the mapping investigations.

4. Students articulate the relationship between physical structures of fish and their habitat needs.

MAPPING FISH HABITATS
Grades 6–10
Four Activities

Students learn about and apply the field-mapping techniques of aquatic biologists as they chart the movements of fish in a classroom aquarium. Students plan experiments to determine the effects of an environmental change on the home ranges of the fish. An aquarium becomes a habitat for a variety of fish that move in different areas of the tank. Students use a simple technique to map and observe the movements of individual fish as they feed, defend themselves, and establish their territory within the aquarium.

Skills
Observing, Classifying, Mapping, Analyzing Data, Experimenting, Making Inferences

Concepts
Biology, Fish, Habitat Requirements, Home Range, Animal Territories, Research Techniques of Biologists, Monitoring An Aquarium Ecosystem, Humane Treatment of Animals

Themes
Systems and Interactions, Stability, Patterns of Change, Evolution, Structure, Diversity and Unity

---

Built-In Assessment Activities
Mapping Fish Movements

In Sessions 2 and 3, students learn mapping techniques and how to analyze data. They also make predictions of what behavioral changes they might observe when something is changed in the aquarium. In Session 4, Daily Experiments in the Aquarium, students plan and conduct their own investigations. The teacher can ask each team to write a description of the investigation. The description should include any habitat changes, predictions, and procedures. The teacher can review these descriptions and ask students to explain each component. The final acetate map can also be evaluated and compared to the demonstration map. Additionally, it is important to assess students' cooperation with teammates and their level of effort. (Outcomes 1, 2, 3)

Adaptations to Habitat

At the end of Sessions 3 and 4, teams are asked to analyze their maps and to relate their findings to the physical structures fish have evolved to adapt to their habitat. For example, catfish have feelers and are flat on the bottom. These structures enable them to gather food from the bottom of the tank. The teacher should listen for other evidence that students understand how fish have adapted to their environment. (Outcome 4)

Additional Assessment Ideas
Mapping Other Animals

Students can conduct the activities in the GEMS guide *Mapping Animal Movements*. The teacher can look for improvements in the students' abilities to design and conduct experiments, to interpret data, and to cooperate as members of a team. (Outcomes 1–4)

Aquatic Research

Encourage students to find out about aquatic research done in the wild with animals such as whales, sea otters, or sea lions. Hold a class discussion to determine how well the students are able to compare the experimental designs and the particular mapping techniques used by the marine biologists in their investigations. (Outcome 4)

MOONS OF JUPITER

Selected Student Outcomes

1. Students gain understanding and improve their ability to make inferences about the moons of Jupiter and their revolutions.

2. Students are able to identify distinguishing features of impact craters, such as rays and raised rims, and refer to their own experiments to explain how these physical features were formed.

3. Students improve their ability to visualize the huge scale of the Earth-Moon system and the even more massive system of Jupiter and its moons.

4. Students can describe distinguishing features of Jupiter's moons and how they differ from Earth's moon.

5. Students can imagine and articulate what it might be like to live on one of Jupiter's moons.

Built-In Assessment Activities

Tracking Jupiter's Moons

In Activity 1, Tracking Jupiter's Moons, the students observe a slide simulation of the movement of Jupiter's moons over a period of nine nights. They work in small groups to determine how long it takes each moon to circle Jupiter. Students collect data and work together to interpret the results. In this pre-assessment, the teacher can listen for explanations of why the moons seem to "jump" to a new position each night. (Outcome 1)

Looking at Craters On the Moon

In Activity 2, Experimenting with Craters, the students experiment with impact craters in the classroom. They then look at a slide of the Moon and a close-up of a crater. The teacher asks the students to describe what they see and to identify physical features. Students should notice a raised rim around the larger craters and rays of material ejected by the impact of the meteor. (Outcome 2)

A Scale Model of the Jupiter System

After Activity 3, A Scale Model of the Jupiter System, teachers ask questions to determine whether the students grasp the huge scale involved.

"Could we see people on this scale?"

"Could we see the largest mountains on Earth?" To further apply the concept of scale, students can use a smaller scale to create a paper model and describe how that model differs from physical models. (Outcome 3)

Grand Tour

Look at the students' drawings of the moons after they view the slide presentation in Activity 4, A Grand Tour of the Jupiter System. These drawings will provide information about how closely the students observed the features of the moons. The teacher can

---

> **MOONS OF JUPITER**
> Grades 4–9
> Five Activities
>
> In this unit your students become modern day Galileos as they recreate, through viewing beautiful slides (provided with the guide) Galileo's historic telescopic observations of Jupiter's moons. They observe and record orbits of the moons over time and learn why these observations helped signal the birth of modern astronomy. In subsequent sessions, students model moon phases of Earth's Luna and the moons of Jupiter, experiment to learn how craters are formed, take a grand tour of the Jupiter system as viewed by the Voyager spacecraft, and make scale models to better understand size and distance. In the final session, students work in teams to create, from an assortment of common materials, a settlement on one of the moons of Jupiter. Fascinating background information is also provided.
>
> **Skills**
> Creating/Using Models, Synthesizing, Visualizing, Observing, Explaining, Recording, Measuring, Using a Map, Evaluating Evidence, Inferring, Drawing Conclusions, Creative Designing
>
> **Concepts**
> History of Astronomy, Systems of Planets and Satellites, Revolution and Rotation, Comparing Surface Features, Crater Formation, Geocentric and Heliocentric Models of the Solar System, Relative Sizes and Distances of Solar System Bodies, Space Settlements
>
> **Themes**
> Systems and Interactions, Stability, Models and Simulations, Patterns of Change, Energy, Scale, Structure

also ask questions about how the moons differ from each other and from Earth's moon. (Outcome 4)

Moon Settlements

Students report on their moon settlements in Activity 5. Teachers can look for ways that students have considered conditions on the moon and human needs.

- Have they provided air, food, water, and shelter?
- Have they kept features of their assigned moon in mind? (Outcome 5)

Additional Assessment Ideas

Letter Writing

Ask your students to write a letter home from their moon base, describing the craters or other features they have seen, and what it is like to work there. (Outcomes 2, 3, 4, 5)

Lunar Real Estate

Create a real estate convention of lunar settlements for prospective settlers of Jupiter. Students can act as tour guides for other classes who will visit the convention to select their ideal lunar home on one of the moons of Jupiter. Teachers can observe how students communicate what they have learned during the unit. (Outcome 5)

Moons of Jupiter

Moons of Jupiter

MORE THAN MAGNIFIERS

Selected Student Outcomes

1. Students are able to recognize that lenses have properties that can be measured.

2. Students learn that some lenses are better for some purposes than others.

3. Students are able to recognize that, with just two lenses, many optical instruments can be made.

Built-In Assessment Activities

Magnifiers

By feeling the curvature of the surfaces of two lenses, students will be able to predict which will be a more powerful magnifier. They are also able to describe what is meant by the terms *magnifying power* and *field of view*. (Outcomes 1, 2)

Cameras

Students use a lens to project an image, and explain how this is like a camera lens. They measure the approximate focal length of a lens and explain how the focal length (short or long focus) determines the size of the projected image. (Outcomes 1, 2)

MORE THAN MAGNIFIERS
Grades 6–9
Four Activities

Using the same two lenses, students find out how lenses are used in magnifiers, simple cameras, telescopes, and slide projectors. They learn that lenses have certain measurable properties that can help determine which lenses are best for specific purposes. The background section includes information on lenses, optics, the human eye, and how the instruments made in class work. (Class sets of inexpensive lenses for doing this activities are available by separate purchase from the GEMS project.)

Skills
Observing, Comparing, Measuring, Graphing

Concepts
Lenses, Images, Focal Length, Focus, Magnifiers, Cameras, Telescopes, Projectors, Field of View

Themes
Systems and Interactions, Models and Simulations, Patterns of Change, Scale, Energy, Matter

---

Telescopes

Students demonstrate how to use two lenses to create a telescope, and determine whether a short or long focus lens is best for the eyepiece and objective lens of the telescope. They describe how the objective lens functions in a camera and in a telescope, and how the eyepiece lens functions in a magnifier and in a telescope. (Outcomes 1, 2, 3)

Projectors

Students explain how slide projectors work, and how they are, in a sense, "cameras that operate backwards." (Outcomes 1, 2, 3)

Wrap-Up Discussions

At the end of each session, the teacher asks for the students' results and explains how the particular optical device works. Questions are suggested to assess the students' understanding up to that point. For example, students can be asked to predict the effect if lenses of shorter or longer focal lengths are used in the same activities. (Outcomes 1, 2, 3)

Additional Assessment Idea

Predictions

Bring a variety of cameras, telescopes, magnifiers, and projectors into class. Have the students locate each of the lenses and explain each of their functions. Invite them to use the instruments to observe distant objects or project images. Challenge the students to predict how the effects of the instruments would be different if shorter or longer focal length lenses were used. (Outcomes 1, 2, 3)

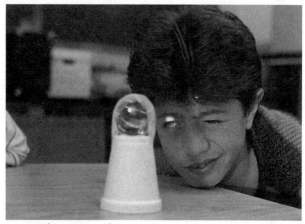

More Than Magnifiers

MYSTERY FESTIVAL

Selected Student Outcomes

1. Students improve their ability to make careful observations.

2. Students are able to compare known samples to unknown clues.

3. Students improve their ability to distinguish evidence from inference, make logical inferences based on partial evidence, and evaluate whether various inferences are plausible or implausible.

4. Students improve their ability to draw conclusions.

5. Students demonstrate an increased understanding of how scientific methods are used to solve crimes.

Built-In Assessment Activities

Active Observers

In the introductory A Note About Pre-Teaching, several activities are suggested to encourage your students to be active observers. These activities (Sharp Eyes, Find the Change, and Composite Drawing) challenge students to notice small changes. If used as a pre- and post-unit assessment, they will provide students with an opportunity to hone their observation skills and offer teachers an opportunity to see students' observation skills in action. (Outcome 1)

Footprint Activities

A number of footprint activities appear in A Note About Pre-Teaching. Find that Print and Footprint Concentration offer opportunities to observe students as they match known and unknown clues (footprints). Footprint Mysteries and Student Footprint Mysteries enable the teacher to observe students as they draw conclusions based on evidence. All of these activities can be used before and/or after the unit. (Outcomes 2, 4)

Solving the Mystery

Session 5, Solving the Mystery, offers the teacher three options to have students evaluate their findings and attempt to solve the mystery. To assess students' abilities to think logically and distinguish evidence from inference, listen carefully to the reasons they use to support their conclusions. If no written work is involved, teachers may need to interview students to discern the reasons why they believe a particular suspect is guilty. (Outcomes 3, 4)

MYSTERY FESTIVAL
Grades 2–8
10 Sessions
(five sessions for each mystery)

This GEMS festival guide features two imaginative and compelling mysteries, one for younger and one for older students. Students observe a "crime scene," then conduct crime lab tests on the evidence at classroom learning stations, analyze the results, and try to solve the mystery. Whether it be Who Borrowed Mr. Bear? or The Mystery of Felix, students are intensely involved throughout—debates and new insights continue long afterward. The important distinction between evidence and inference is emphasized. Crime lab tests include thread tests, powder tests, DNA, chromatography, fingerprinting, and many more. Fun and excitement are combined with careful experimentation, logical thinking, and real-life connections to forensic science. Student understanding of the nature of science is deepened as they experience the ways that science is like the process of detection. The guide suggests modifications for presenting the Mr. Bear mystery to first grade.

Skills
Observing, Comparing, Relating, Sorting, Classifying, Analyzing and Evaluating Evidence, Making Inferences, Distinguishing Evidence from Inference, Problem Solving, Drawing Conclusions, Communicating, Describing, Working in Teams, Logical Thinking, Organizing Data, Role-Playing, Debating, Drawing and Mapping

Concepts
Forensic Science, Evidence, Fingerprints, Footprints, Chromatography, Acids, Bases, Neutrals, pH Testing, Powder Testing, Thread Comparison Testing, Crystals, Dissolving, DNA

Themes
Systems and Interactions, Matter, Patterns of Change, Models and Simulations, Stability, Scale, Structure, Diversity and Unity

Mathematics Strands
Number, Pattern, Logic, Measurement, Algebra

Additional Assessment Ideas

Newspaper Article

The teacher reads aloud a scenario about a possible arson. With a written version of the scenario, the students are asked to identify the unfair inferences made in a newspaper article about the situation and then to rewrite the article to better reflect the facts and avoid unfair inferences. (Outcome 2)

This activity is a Case Study on page 72.

Science In Action

Invite local detectives, criminalists, or forensic experts to visit your classroom. Have students prepare questions to find out how these investigators use scientific techniques (for example, fingerprinting, chromatography, DNA analysis, etc.) to solve crimes. Students can then write a summary of what they learned through the interview. (Outcome 5)

Mystery Festival

Mystery Festival

Mystery Festival

OF CABBAGES AND CHEMISTRY

Selected Student Outcomes

1. Students develop functional definitions of acids (as substances that will cause cabbage juice to turn pink); bases (as substances that will cause cabbage juice to turn green); and neutrals (substances that don't significantly alter the color of cabbage juice).

2. Students demonstrate an intuitive knowledge of the concept of neutralization—a substance can be mixed with another, changing whether it is acidic, basic, or neutral.

3. Students demonstrate and explain that some acids are more powerful than others, and some bases are more powerful than others.

4. Students are able to articulate that there are safe acids and dangerous acids; safe bases and dangerous bases.

5. Students learn to identify acids, neutrals, and bases in their everyday lives.

OF CABBAGES AND CHEMISTRY
Grades 4–8
Four Sessions

This series of activities offers students a chance to explore acids and bases using the special indicator properties of red cabbages. The color-change game Presto Change-O helps students discover the acid-neutral-base continuum. Students discover that chemicals can be grouped by behaviors; and relate acids and bases to their own daily experience. The guide includes an Acid and Aliens from Outer Space extension activity. The activities in this unit are an excellent lead-in to the GEMS guide *Acid Rain*.

Skills
Observing, Recording Results, Comparing, Classifying, Experimenting, Titrating, Drawing Conclusions

Concepts
Chemistry, Acid, Base, Neutral, Indicators, Pigments, Safety, Neutralize, Concentration, Titration, Continuum

Themes
Systems and Interactions, Stability, Patterns of Change, Scale, Matter

---

Built-In Assessment Activity
Acid, Base, or Neutral?

In Session 4, Household Mysteries, students use cabbage juice to determine whether a substance is acidic, basic, or neutral. The teacher can observe whether students grasp the functional definitions of acid, base, and neutral as they analyze the color that results when a substance and cabbage juice are mixed. (Outcome 1)

Additional Assessment Ideas
Acid and Aliens from Outer Space

In Acid and Aliens from Outer Space, a Going Further activity, students neutralize a variety of mystery liquids. In this challenge, the teacher can observe how students apply what they learned in the unit and as they play the game. To extend the activity, students can write a letter for publication in the *Neutral News*, an intergalactic newspaper, to articulate their strategy for neutralizing mystery liquids. (Outcomes 1, 2, 3)

Testing Mystery Solutions

Have pairs of students use cabbage juice to test whether two mystery solutions are acid, base, or neutral. Have them record their results, explain how they were obtained, and predict which chemical could be used to neutralize the mystery solutions, and test their predictions. If the prediction is incorrect, ask students to come up with an explanation of why it was incorrect and to make a new prediction. (Outcomes 1, 2)

Powerful Acids I Have Known

Ask students to reflect on and then write about the least powerful acid (normal rain? saliva?) and the most powerful acid they know (toilet bowl cleaner? stomach acid?). Have them explain why that particular acid is powerful (or not) and the ways each acid can be useful. (Outcomes 3, 4)

My Chemical Day

Ask students to recount the points in a typical day when they encounter acids, bases, or neutrals. The teacher can see whether students recognize orange juice, soap, water, and other everyday substances as chemicals. (Outcome 5)

OOBLECK: WHAT DO SCIENTISTS DO?

Selected Student Outcomes

1. Students improve their ability to observe, hypothesize, and experiment with a new substance to determine its properties.

2. Students are able to critically discuss, analyze, and modify their initial list of properties in light of comments and questions from other students.

3. Students recognize that substances cannot simply be classified as a solid or liquid, and that a given substance may exhibit solid or liquid properties under different conditions.

4. Students apply their understanding of a substance's properties to design a spacecraft that will land on an ocean of Oobleck.

5. Students learn about the fields of science and engineering and become aware of the many processes and skills used by scientists and engineers.

Built-In Assessment Activities

Lists of Properties

In Session 1, student teams investigate Oobleck and list its properties. This provides information about whether or not students understand the concept of a property, and the degree to which they have analyzed their list to assure its accuracy. (Outcome 1)

Scientific Convention

In Session 2, students critically discuss and compare the properties of their substances. During the discussion, the teacher can notice whether students move beyond their initial statements to listen to each other, consider various points of view, and try to reach consensus about the truth. (Outcomes 2, 5)

OOBLECK: WHAT DO SCIENTISTS DO?
Grades 4–8
Four Sessions

Students investigate and analyze the properties of a strange green substance, Oobleck, said to come from another planet. The class holds a scientific convention to critically discuss experimental findings. Students design a spacecraft to land on an ocean of Oobleck. In the final session, the methods the students used to analyze Oobleck are compared to those of professional scientists, such as those on the Mars Viking Project. A large poster illustrating the Viking project is included with the guide. One of the most popular GEMS guides, *Oobleck: What Do Scientists Do?* is not only a great hands-on experience for all ages, the unit also provides students with authentic insight into the real work of science.

Skills
Experimenting, Recording Data, Engineering, Critical Discussion, Communicating, Group Brainstorming, Decision Making

Concepts
Scientific Methods, Solids and Liquids, Properties, Space Probes, Designing Models

Themes
Systems and Interactions, Models and Simulation, Stability, Patterns of Change, Structure, Matter

Oobleck: What Do Scientists Do?

Is Oobleck a Liquid or Solid?

During the convention, teachers can look for statements that describe the liquid or solid properties of Oobleck. They can observe whether students can articulate the conditions which cause Oobleck to act as a solid or as a liquid. (Outcome 3)

Designing a Spacecraft

During Session 3, teachers can observe whether students apply the information they know about the properties of Oobleck as they design a spacecraft to land on an ocean of Oobleck. (Outcome 4)

Additional Assessment Ideas

What Do Scientists and Engineers Do?

Have students pretend they are applying for a job in a science or engineering firm. Have them write a detailed letter to the personnel director and explain how they gained experience as scientists and engineers when they investigated Oobleck. The letters will help illustrate students' level of awareness of the some main processes of science, such as experimenting, observing, and inferring. (Outcome 5)

Properties of Sand

Substitute sand in all of the activities in the guide. Ask students if sand is a liquid or solid. Have them justify their point of view. (Outcomes 1, 2, 3, 4, 5)

This activity is a Case Study on page 139.

Oobleck: What Do Scientists Do?

Oobleck: What Do Scientists Do?

PAPER TOWEL TESTING

Selected Student Outcomes

1. Students improve their ability to design and conduct controlled experiments.

2. Students identify fair and unfair elements of a test.

3. Students can collect objective, quantifiable results from their experiments.

4. Students are able to analyze results from their experiments and draw conclusions based on objective data.

5. Students use experimental results to convince consumers to purchase a particular product.

PAPER TOWEL TESTING
Grades 5–9
Four Sessions

In a series of experiments, students rank the wet strength and absorbency of four brands of paper towels. Based on their findings and the cost of each brand, they determine which brand is the best buy. These activities provide a stimulating introduction to both consumer science and the concept of controlled experimentation.

Skills
Designing Controlled Experiments, Measuring, Recording, Calculating, Interpreting Data

Concepts
Consumer Science, Absorbency, Wet Strength, Unit Pricing, Cost-Benefit Analysis, Decision Making

Themes
Systems and Interactions, Models & Simulations, Stability, Patterns of Change, Structure, Matter

---

Built-In Assessment Activity
Follow-up Experiments

In Sessions 2 and 3, students plan and conduct experiments to further explore the comparative qualities of paper towels. The teacher can observe growth in students' ability to design controlled experiments. (Outcome 1–4)

Additional Assessment Ideas

The following Going Further activities are featured at the end of the unit and are well suited for assessment.

Test Other Qualities of Paper Towels

Students design and conduct fair tests to evaluate other attributes of paper towels, such as softness or durability. This activity provides the teacher with an opportunity to observe students' abilities to identify variables and design controlled experiments. The teacher can also see how students justify their claims about a particular brand of towel. (Outcomes 1–5)

Analyze Advertisements

Students evaluate the advertising claims from magazine or television ads. They suggest experiments that could be done to test those claims. This activity provides the teacher with another opportunity to observe students' abilities to identify unfair tests and design fair tests. (Outcomes 1, 2)

Write a Sales Pitch

Students write a television or magazine ad for the brand of paper towel they think is best. A teacher can observe how students incorporate experiment results to support their claims. (Outcomes 4, 5)

This activity is a Case Study on page 61.

Design Other Experiments

Challenge your students to devise a controlled experiment to investigate something they're interested in. You may wish to provide options from various GEMS guides or other science books. Observe how your students apply what they've learned about how to design and evaluate controlled experiments. (Outcomes 1–5)

PENGUINS AND THEIR YOUNG

Selected Student Outcomes

1. Students gain experience with the concepts of freezing, melting, and floating through their exploration of ice and water.

2. Students are able to compare their own size, shape, and body structures to those of an emperor penguin.

3. Students are able to create a paper model of a penguin and use it to explain penguin feeding, parenting behaviors and locomotion.

4. Students are able to role-play behaviors that help penguins survive in a cold environment.

Built-In Assessment Activities

Ice Play

In Activity 1, Session 2, An Ice Home, students are given their cups of water from the day before that have now frozen in the freezer overnight. Teachers guide an exploration of the ice in and out of a tub of water by asking the following questions.

"What happened to the water in our cups?"
"What does the ice feel like?"
"What does the ice look like?"
"What is happening to the ice now?"
"What is happening to the ice in the water?"

Teachers can observe the spontaneous play and conversation that occurs as children explore. Responses to questions provide information on the degree to which students understand the concepts of freezing, melting, and floating. (Outcome 1)

As Tall as a Penguin!

In Activity 1, Session 3, Making Comparisons, students are shown a full-size emperor penguin poster. In kindergarten, the teacher asks, "Do you think you are taller or shorter than the emperor penguin?" The teacher can listen to their guesses and observe their responses when they come up to the poster to measure themselves. Students can compare their height, size, and body structures to the penguin, as teachers again note verbal and physical responses to questions. (Outcome 2)

The Penguin Dramas

In Activity 2, Session 2, Making Paper-Bag Penguins and Session 3, Penguin Families, students make a model of a penguin, listen and participate in a drama enacted by the teacher, and use the paper-bag penguins in a variety of real-penguin life dramas. As students create their own dramas, the teacher can watch for feeding, parenting, locomotion, and keeping-warm behaviors. The spontaneous dramas will also

---

PENGUINS AND THEIR YOUNG
Preschool–1
Four Activities
(14 sessions)

Penguins And Their Young features the emperor penguin. Children learn about its body structure, its cold home of ice and water, what it eats, and how emperor penguin parents care for their young. Using a life-size poster, children to compare their heights and body structures to those of this four-foot-tall bird. The other side of the poster shows different kinds of penguins and their diverse nesting behaviors. Children experience a penguin's icy home by playing with cork penguins in a tub of "icebergs" and water. Using paper-bag penguins, the youngsters create dramas on a paper ocean scene complete with floating ice. Role playing continues when baby penguins hatch from plastic eggs. Important mathematics concepts and skills are introduced when children pretend to be hungry penguins and "catch" fish crackers to eat in a fun series of multi-sensory math games. Children learn how penguins stay warm, then finish their explorations with ice investigations and tasty ice treats. Throughout the unit, life science, mathematics, and physical science are integrated with language activities.

Skills
Observing, Comparing, , Communicating, Creative and Logical Thinking, Role Playing

Concepts
Penguin Habitat, Body Structure, Parenting, Feeding Strategies, Heat and Warmth, Melting, Freezing, Ice, Floating, Size, Shape

Themes
Patterns of Change, Scale, Structure, Energy, Systems and Interactions, Diversity and Unity, Models and Simulations

Mathematics Strands
Measurement, Number, Pattern, Logic

evoke new vocabulary and language usage. (Outcome 3)

I'm a Penguin

In Activity 2, Session 3, Penguin Families and Session 4, A Penguin Parent, students role play being part of a penguin family on an icy shore. They later dress-up as penguins using a dark jacket and pillow. The teacher can observe the behaviors of the student "penguins," including whether the behavior includes keeping warm in a cold environment. (Outcome 4)

Penguins And Their Young

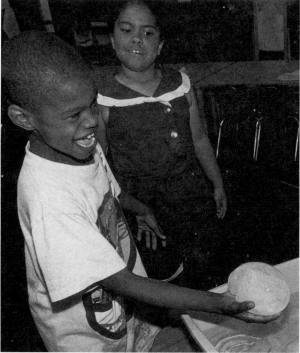
Penguins And Their Young

Additional Assessment Ideas
Penguin Ice Festival

Later in the year, conduct an ice fair or festival that uses all of the ice activities from the unit. Observe students' responses to the activities again, and look for their usage of new language that explains ice and water concepts. (Outcome 1)

Penguins at Home

Send the paper-bag penguins, eggs, poster, and other props home with the students. Ask families to watch and listen to the dramas and role plays, and describe what was presented in a note back to the teacher. (Outcomes 2, 3, 4)

Penguins And Their Young

QUADICE

Selected Student Outcomes

1. Students improve their ability to think and talk about mathematical relationships.

2. Students develop and refine problem-solving strategies and improve their ability to do mental arithmetic.

3. Students gain an understanding of fractions and basic operations.

4. Students increase their understanding of probability.

Built-In Assessment Activities

Student Discussion

At the beginning of Session 2, Review and Analysis, the students engage in a discussion about alternatives in playing QUADICE asking question such as "Which patterns of combinations are better in order to win the game?" Students begin to articulate strategies. The teacher observes students' understanding of mathematical combinations and of strategies for this game. (Outcomes 1, 2)

QUADICE
Grades 4–8
Five Sessions

This challenging and fun mathematics game encourages students to perform mental calculations, handle fractions with greater confidence, and explore probability. Teams of three students, using a special set of four dice play 12 rounds that involve the arithmetic skills of addition, subtraction, division, and multiplication. A cooperative version of the game helps students work together to solve problems. The guide also contains mystery puzzles to solve and encourages players to create mystery puzzles of their own!

Skills
Mental Arithmetic, Basic Operations (Addition, Subtraction, Division), Fractions

Concepts
Mathematics, Probability, Strategy Development, Problem Solving

Themes
Systems and Interactions, Models and Simulations

Report Strategies

After students have played Cooperative QUADICE in Session 3, they discuss their strategies to win. They then play again incorporating their shared strategies. The teacher observes the relative success of the students and watches to see if the students' scores increase. (Outcomes 1, 2, 3)

Report How Many Ways

In Session 4, students explore combinations; make systematic lists of possible sums, differences, and quotients; and interpret the data to help to organize their thinking about how to win the game. The teacher observes each group's written work and their verbal articulation to the whole group. The teacher observes how students organize the data, interpret the data, understand mathematical combinations, and make sense of probability. (Outcomes 3, 4)

Mystery Puzzles

After the students solve the QUADICE Puzzles in Session 5, they make up their own mystery puzzles. The teacher observes the students' problem-solving skills and their abilities to articulate strategies. (Outcomes 1, 2, 3)

Additional Assessment Ideas

Write About Strategies

After the students have had ample chance to play QUADICE, ask them to write about their strategies. You may want to give the whole class the same set of simulated dice rolls, and ask individuals to discuss what they might do to combine the numbers to win, depending on whether they were the adder, subtracter, or divider. Ask students to share their strategies with one another. (Outcomes 1, 2, 3)

Extend the Game

After students have played the cooperative version of QUADICE, challenge groups to make up an extension for the game. For example, they might add a rule that the divider's score gets doubled. Ask students to discuss and write about how their extension might change the team's strategy in playing the game. Have the students write their new version for another group to try. (Outcomes 1, 2, 3, 4)

Whom Would You Rather Be

After students have participated in the How Many Ways? activity, give them a set of numbers which represent a fictitious roll of the dice. Ask individuals to write whether they'd rather be the adder, subtracter, or divider. Have them articulate the reasons for their choice, using mathematical combinations and probability. (Outcomes 3, 4)

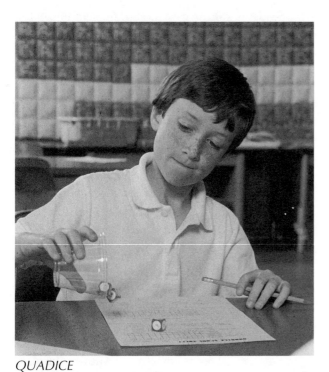

QUADICE

QUADICE

QUADICE

RIVER CUTTERS

Selected Student Outcomes

1. Students demonstrate an increased understanding of rivers as dynamic, changing systems that evolve over time.

2. Students gain further knowledge of erosion as one of the main ways that the surface of the Earth is shaped, and gain an awareness that some erosion can pose serious environmental problems.

3. Students demonstrate their ability to use models to simulate a flowing river with its various geological features, and to accurately record, draw, or map the results.

4. Students improve in their ability to use accurate river-related and geological terminology to describe geological features.

5. Students improve in their ability to design, conduct, and evaluate experiments.

6. Students gain an increased understanding of the intersection between science and technology and social/environmental issues.

Built-In Assessment Activities

River Model and Student Data Sheet

Throughout the unit, the students' river models and data sheets provide information about their knowledge of river features and their ability to accurately draw/record results of the river model. The same data sheets, if used for optional sessions, will provide information about students' ability to design controlled experiments and/or student understanding of the possible impact of dam construction and toxic waste pollution on river systems. (Outcomes 1–6)

River Features and Erosion Discussion

In Session 3, Discussing River Features, the class discussion of river model results, data sheets, and erosion provides information about the level of student knowledge, additional questions to explore, initial understandings of erosion. (Outcomes 1, 2, 3, 4)

River Features Flags

Students use small flags to label river features on their model rivers as they begin Session 4, The Life and Times of Your River. Their labeling and placement of the flags in Session 4 and any subsequent sessions can provide information about their understanding of terminology and knowledge of geologic features. (Outcomes 3, 4)

Design A Travel Brochure

This activity is noted in the acknowledgments and is a Going Further activity and assessment in later editions of the guide. Students design a promotional brochure to advertise the natural beauty, geologic features, and tourist attractions of their own river area. The teacher can review these brochures for use of terminology, descriptive detail, understanding of river systems, and human impact. (Outcomes 1, 4)

This activity is a Case Study on page 54.

RIVER CUTTERS
Grades 6–9
Seven Sessions

Geological time passes quickly in *River Cutters*. Students build a model of a river and simulate the creation of a river system in minutes. Using diatomaceous earth and a simple dripping system, students create rivers, observing and recording their results. They acquire geological terminology and begin to understand rivers as dynamic, ever-changing systems. By "running" many rivers, young "river-ologists" are introduced to the sequence of geological events and to differences between old and young rivers. The concepts of erosion, pollution, toxic waste, and human manipulation of rivers are also introduced. With *Acid Rain* and *Global Warming and the Greenhouse Effect*, *River Cutters* can be used in a curriculum unit on environmental issues and human impact.

Skills
Recording Data, Experimenting, Communicating, Decision Making, Designing and Refining Models

Concepts
Geology, Rivers, Erosion, Sequencing of Geological Events, Pollution, Human Impact on Environment

Themes
Systems and Interactions, Models and Simulations, Patterns of Change, Evolution, Scale, Structure, Energy, Matter

---

Additional Assessment Ideas

Describe A Real River Visit

Have students write a paragraph about a river area they have visited. Students should be able to make use of vocabulary introduced throughout the unit to describe river and geologic features. After they have finished their descriptions, students can compare their own river model with the real river area. (Outcomes 1, 4)

Create-A-River-Legend

Have students write an imaginary legend or story that explains why the Earth's surface is shaped as it is. The story can have whatever characters and events the students decide, but it must include a character who represents the power of water. (Outcome 2, 4)

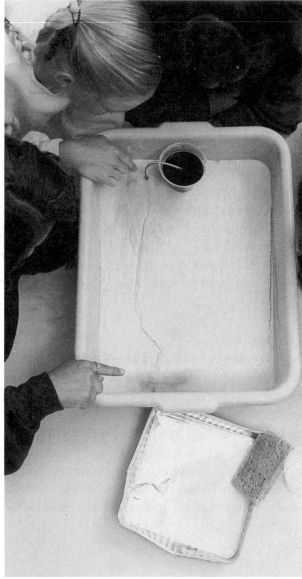

River Cutters

Dialogue

Students can write an imaginary conversation between a young river and an old river. As the two rivers talk to each other, they can compare their features. For example, the young river might say: "I'd really like to be able to meander around like you do. Do you think I ever will?" The students' dialogues can be incorporated into a skit. (Outcomes 1, 4, 5)

Group Design Challenge

Assign student teams to design a different dripper system to model the dripping of raindrops onto the soil. Teams can draw their own dripper system and use any materials and mechanisms. The one condition is that the system should drip. Pose the following challenges.

➤ In your system, can the rate of the drip be adjusted from slower to faster?

➤ Can you design a system that is more like a rainstorm?

➤ Give your dripper system a name and write a few sentences to describe the river you think your dripper system might create. (Outcome 3)

Letter to the Editor

Have students write a letter to the editor of a local newspaper to take a position on a controversial river-related issue. Here is an example.

> You live on the shore of a large river. Two previously unknown toxic waste dumps have been unearthed 25 miles upstream from your home, both about 200 yards away from the river's shoreline. Meanwhile, a small dam project to bring water to several new housing developments is being planned about 20 miles upstream. You are concerned that there has not been enough discussion about the toxic waste dumps and, furthermore, that no one even seems to question whether or not the dam construction might make matters worse. (Outcomes 1, 4, 6)

TERRARIUM HABITATS

Selected Student Outcomes

1. Students articulate that an animal's habitat provides air, water, food, and shelter.

2. Students understand the concept of adaptation and are able to describe the structures and behaviors of an animal that help it survive in its habitat.

3. Students can explain how small animals that live in the soil help break down plant and animal material to return the nutrients to the soil.

4. Students improve their ability to make careful observations.

5. Students are able to identify changes that occur in the terrarium and can determine when those changes are part of a larger cycle.

Built-In Assessment Activities

A Terrarium Habitat

In Activity 2, teams of students design and build a habitat for small animals that live in or on the soil. During the project, the teacher can ask each team to explain why they add soil, water, plants, seeds, and bark. If students have terrarium journals, they can describe how their habitat provides water, air, shelter, and food for small animals. (Outcome 1)

Animals in the Terrarium

In Activities 3–5, students observe earthworms, pillbugs, sow bugs, and snails. They note physical characteristics and behaviors that will help the animals survive in the terrarium. Over many weeks, the students observe how the animals behave in their new habitat. As students study the animals, the teacher can pose questions that will reveal students' observation skills and their developing knowledge about animal behavior. For example, the teacher can ask students how an earthworm's shape and movements help it burrow in the soil. Students can write down these ideas in their journal and later add behaviors they observe to support their ideas. The teacher can review journal entries or have students share their observations with the whole class. (Outcomes 1, 2, 4, 5)

Decomposers

As students continue to observe the changes in their terrarium, they will begin to understand how small creatures help to recycle nutrients in the habitat. The students observe how animals eat leaves, seeds and other plant material. Even a dead cricket will "disappear" in the terrarium! Students observe waste left by the animal and a build up of soil. The teacher can ask students to explain the relationship between these events in their journal or during a class discussion. (Outcomes 3, 4, 5)

TERRARIUM HABITATS
Grades K–6
Five Activities

Bring the natural world into your classroom and deepen understanding of, and connections to, all living things. The guide begins with an exploration of soil and has an optional soil profile test. Teams of students design and construct terrariums for the classroom. Sow bugs, earthworms, and crickets are placed in the terrarium habitat, and students observe and record changes over time. There are detailed instructions on setting up and maintaining the terrariums, along with concise and interesting biological information on a number of possible small organisms that can become terrarium inhabitants. Another section tells how to maintain the terrariums.

Skills
Observing, Comparing, Describing, Measuring, Communicating, Organizing, Experimenting, Recording, Drawing Conclusions, Building Models

Concepts
Soil and Ground Habitats, Ecology, Life Cycle, Food Webs, Nutrient Cycle, Decomposition, Recycling, Adaptation, Animal Structures and Behavior

Themes
Systems and Interactions, Patterns of Change, Structure, Energy, Matter

Mathematics Strands
Pattern, Number, Measurement

Additional Assessment Ideas

An Isopod's Journal

Have students imagine they are a pill bug or sow bug that lives in a terrarium. Ask them to them to write about what they would experience in one day of their life. (Outcomes 1, 3, 4, 5)

This activity is a Case Study on page 35.

More Animals in the Terrarium

Invite students to bring in other small creatures to add to the habitat. Have them explain why they think the animals will survive in the terrarium. Challenge them to keep their terrarium animals alive through the school year and to continue to record observations and ideas in their journal. (Outcomes 1, 3, 4, 5)

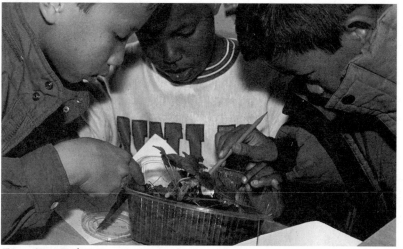

Terrarium Habitats

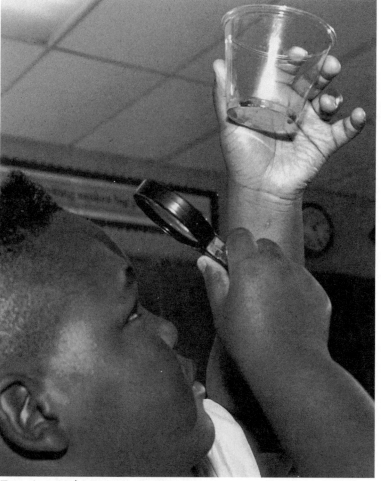

Terrarium Habitats

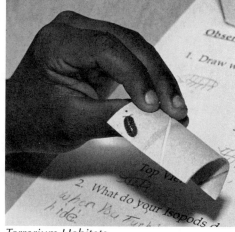

Terrarium Habitats

TREE HOMES

Selected Student Outcomes

1. Students gain familiarity with trees as they observe a live tree and compare it to a cardboard tree they build.

2. Students demonstrate their knowledge about animal homes as they participate in role plays of different animals that live in tree holes.

3. Students describe the behaviors that help animals stay warm, feed, protect themselves, and raise their young in trees.

4. Students improve their ability to use a variety of attributes (size, color, features) to sort, classify, and compare animals and objects.

TREE HOMES
Preschool–1
Six Activities

The activities in this guide encourage appreciation for trees and animals that live in tree homes, stimulating children's interest in the world around them and the biological need for warmth and shelter. Children become familiar with a living tree, then build a child-sized tree from cardboard boxes, paper, and cardboard tubes. The class role-plays dramas about a mother bear and her cubs, raccoons, and a family of owls and their tree homes. Students make paper models of raccoons and owls. Sorting, classifying, and measurement are also emphasized.

Skills
Observing, Comparing, Matching, Sorting and Classifying, Communicating, Role Playing, Creative and Logical Thinking

Concepts
Animal Shelter and Habitat, Heat and Warmth, Friction, Size, Shape, Tree Structure

Themes
Patterns of Change, Stability, Scale, Structure, Energy, Systems and Interactions, Diversity and Unity

Mathematics Strands
Measurement, Number, Pattern, Logic

Built-In Assessment Activities

Getting to Know Trees

In Activity 1, A Tree and Its Holes, students observe live trees or tree branches and compare them to a cardboard box tree they build. The teacher observes the children's understanding of the parts of a tree when the children compare the living tree to the cardboard tree. (Outcomes 1, 4)

A Tree Home for Bears

In Activity 2, Black Bears, students learn that black bears can use a large hole in a tree to keep warm and to raise their cubs. Children watch a drama about bears and their young, and pretend that they are bears who keep warm in a tree. The role plays and dramas allow students to demonstrate their understanding of a bear's need for a tree-hole home. The teacher can observe how students communicate these concepts to friends and family when activities are repeated at home and at school. (Outcomes 2, 3)

Sorting Bears

In Session 2, Activity 2, students sort toy bears by color, size, texture, type of bear, and other features. The Going Further activity has students sort and classify shoes. Through these activities, the teacher can observe each student's ability to select a particular characteristic and use it to group objects. (Outcome 4)

Keeping Warm

In Activity 3, Getting Warmer, children learn that people wear clothes, move around, and sip warm drinks to keep warm. The children compare how bears and humans keep warm. Teachers can observe students' insights and logical thinking as they watch the activities and listen to responses in discussions. (Outcomes 2, 3)

Making a Model

In Activity 5, Owls, children watch a short drama about a pair of owls who live in a tree. They make a model of an owl and build a paper bag nest. The teacher can observe the model of the owl and nest, and note how it is used in dramas and role plays. The teacher can look for descriptive language and new vocabulary used by the children as well as dramatics that describe the various behaviors of owls. (Outcomes 2, 3)

Other Animals That Live in Trees

In Activity 6, More Tree Homes, children bring specific toy animals to school that could live in trees. As an assessment opportunity, ask the children to think of another animal that could live in trees and to bring in a toy or picture of that animal. The children can present the animal and describe or act out where the animal would live. The teacher can observe the richness of the children's explanations as compared to their earlier responses to the bear, raccoon, and owl experiences. (Outcomes 1, 2, 3)

Additional Assessment Ideas

Writing About Tree Homes

Have your students write or dictate stories about their owl's, raccoon's, or toy bear's life in a tree. (Outcome 3)

Trees through the Seasons

Keep the cardboard tree in the classroom during the whole school year and change the tree (different colored leaves, fewer or more leaves, blossoms, fruit) to match the different seasons. Continue to observe the living tree outdoors. Introduce new animals and have children come up with new stories and role plays to act out. (Outcomes 1, 2, 3)

Tree Homes

Tree Homes

VITAMIN C TESTING

Selected Student Outcomes

1. Students demonstrate their ability to perform a titration.

2. Students are able to determine the relative vitamin C content in beverages.

3. Students can articulate why different people can conduct the same test on the same beverage and arrive at varying results.

4. Students improve their ability to control variables.

5. Students learn to use a histogram graph to display results from an experiment.

Built-In Assessment Activities

Conducting a Titration Test

In Session 4, Experimenting with Vitamin C Content, students conduct an experiment to determine how certain variables affect vitamin C content. The teacher can observe how well students use accurate techniques and procedures during the experiment. (Outcomes 1, 2, 3, 4)

Testing More Beverages

In Session 3, Testing More Beverages, students use the experiment from Session 1 to compare the vitamin C content in beverages they bring from home. The teacher can observe how students apply methods and procedures from Session 1 in new situations. (Outcomes 1, 2, 4)

Explaining Diverse Results

In the wrap-up of Session 3, Testing More Beverages, students again explain diverse results. The teacher can observe how well students are able to explain the same problem that arose when they analyzed the results from Session 1. (Outcome 3)

Additional Assessment Idea

Making Histograms

Ask students to display other kinds of data with the histogram graph that was used to compare vitamin C content in beverages. (Outcome 5)

VITAMIN C TESTING
Grades 4–8
Four Sessions

This guide is a stimulating introduction to chemistry and nutrition. The students perform a simple chemical test using a vitamin C indicator to compare the vitamin C content of different juices. They then graph the results. Older students can examine the effects of heat and freezing on vitamin C content.

Skills
Chemistry Laboratory Techniques, Experimenting, Analyzing Data, Graphing, Drawing Conclusions

Concepts
Chemistry, Nutrition, Vitamin C Content, Titration, Indicator, End Point, Conditions Causing Vitamin Loss

Themes
Systems and Interactions, Stability, Patterns of Change, Scale, Matter

---

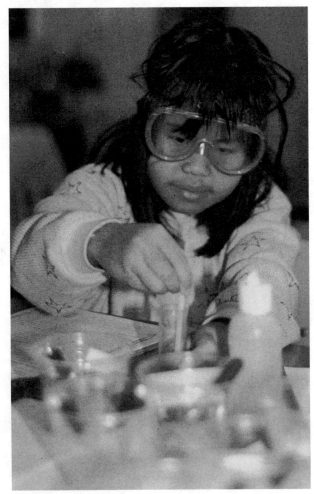

Vitamin C Testing

RESOURCES

Selected Resources in Assessment
of Activity-Based Mathematics and Science

Atkin, J. Myron; Karplus, Robert. 1962. "Discovery or Invention." *The Science Teacher*: September 1962.

Appalachia Educational Laboratory and Virginia Education Association. 1992. *Alternative Assessments in Math and Science: Moving Toward a Moving Target*. Charlotte, West Virginia.
    Available from:
    Appalachia Educational Laboratory
    Resource Center
    PO Box 1348
    Charleston, WV 24325

Armstrong, Thomas. 1987. *In Their Own Way: Discovering and Encouraging Your Child's Personal Learning Style*. New York: G.P. Putnam's Sons.

Armstrong, Thomas. 1994. *Multiple Intelligences in the Classroom*. Alexandria, Virginia: Association For Supervision and Curriculum Development.
    Available from:
    Association for Supervision and
    Curriculum Development
    1250 North Pitt Street
    Alexandria, VA 22314
    (703) 549-9110

California State Department of Education. 1992. *Mathematics Framework for California Public Schools*. Sacramento: California Department of Education.
    Available from:
    California State Department of Education
    PO Box 271
    Sacramento, CA 95802-0271
    (916) 445-1260

California State Department of Education. 1989. *A Question of Thinking: A First Look at Students' Performance on Open-ended Questions in Mathematics*. Sacramento: California Department of Education.
    Available from:
    California State Department of Education
    PO Box 271
    Sacramento, CA 95802-0271
    (916) 445-1260

California State Department of Education. 1991. *A Sampler of Mathematics Assessment*. Sacramento: California Department of Education.
    Available from:
    California State Department of Education
    PO Box 271
    Sacramento, CA 95802-0271
    (916) 445-1260

California State Department of Education. 1993. *A Sampler of Mathematics Assessment: Addendum*. Sacramento: California Department of Education.
    Available from:
    California State Department of Education
    PO Box 271
    Sacramento, CA 95802-0271
    (916) 445-1260

California State Department of Education. 1990. *Science Framework for California Public Schools*. Sacramento: California Department of Education.
    Available from:
    California State Department of Education
    PO Box 271
    Sacramento, CA 95802-0271
    (916) 445-1260

Cohen, Miriam. 1980. *First Grade Takes A Test*. New York: Dell.

Fiske, Edward B. 1992. *Smart Schools, Smart Kids: Why Do Some Schools Work?* New York: Simon & Schuster.

Gardner, Howard. 1983. *Frames of Mind*. New York: Basic Books.

Herman, Joan; Aschbacher, Pamela; and Winters, Lynn. 1992. *A Practical Guide To Alternative Assessment*. Alexandria, Virginia: Association For Supervision and Curriculum Development.
    Available from:
    Association for Supervision and
    Curriculum Development
    1250 North Pitt Street
    Alexandria, VA 22314
    (703) 549-9110

Jorgensen, M. 1993. *Assessing Habits of Mind: Performance-Based Assessment in Science and Mathematics*. Columbus, Ohio: ERIC Clearinghouse for Science, Mathematics and Environmental Education.

Available from:
ERIC Clearinghouse
1929 Kenny Road
Columbus, OH 43210-1080
(614) 292-6717

Kulm, Gerald and Malcolm, Shirley, ed. 1991. *Science Assessment in the Service of Reform*. Waldorf, Maryland: American Association for the Advancement of Science.

Available from:
American Association for the
Advancement of Science Books
PO Box 753
Waldorf, MD 20604
(301) 645-5643

Mathematical Sciences Education Board, National Research Council. 1993. *Measuring Up: Prototypes for Mathematics Assessment*. Washington, D.C.: National Academy Press.

Available from:
National Academy Press
2101 Constitution Avenue NW
Washington, D.C. 20418

Meng, Elizabeth and Doran, Rodney. 1993. *Improving Instruction and Learning Through Evaluation: Elementary School Science*. Columbus, Ohio: ERIC Clearinghouse for Science, Mathematics and Environmental Education.

Available from:
ERIC Clearinghouse
1929 Kenny Road
Columbus, OH 43210-1080
(614) 292-6717

National Council of Teachers of Mathematics. 1991. *Professional Standards for Teaching Mathematics*. Reston, Virginia: National Council of Teachers of Mathematics.

Available from:
NCTM
1906 Association Drive
Reston, VA 22091
(800) 235-7566

Perrone, Victor, ed. 1991. *Expanding Student Assessment*. Alexandria, Virginia: Association For Supervision and Curriculum Development.

Available from:
Association for Supervision and
Curriculum Development
1250 North Pitt Street
Alexandria, VA 22314
(703) 549-9110

Pierce, Lorraine Valdez and O'Malley, J. Michael. 1992. *Performance and Portfolio Assessment for Language Minority Students*. Washington, D.C: National Clearinghouse for Bilingual Education.

Available from:
National Clearinghouse for Bilingual Education
1118 22nd Street NW
Washington, D.C. 20037

Stenmark, Jean, ed. 1991. *Mathematics Assessment: Myths, Models, Good Questions and Practical Suggestions*. Reston, Virginia: National Council of Teachers of Mathematics.

Available from:
NCTM
1906 Association Drive
Reston, VA 22091
(800) 235-7566

Stenmark, Jean. 1989. *Assessment Alternatives in Mathematics*. Berkeley: Lawrence Hall of Science, Regents of the University of California.

Available from:
EQUALS
Lawrence Hall of Science
University of California
Berkeley, CA 94720
(510) 642-1910

Webb, Norman and Coxford, Arthur. 1993. *Assessment in the Mathematics Classroom*. Reston, Virginia: National Council of Teachers of Mathematics.

Available from:
NCTM
1906 Association Drive
Reston, VA 22091
(800) 235-7566

Wiggins, Grant. 1989. "A True Test: Toward More Authentic and Equitable Assessment." *Phi Delta Kappan:* May 1989, 703-713.

Dear GEMS

One day, I asked my students to bring stuffed animals to class. For language arts, I had the students complete job applications from the perspective of the animals. Though my initial intentions were to have a lot of fun as we wrote from another perspective, my students and I learned a message that was far beyond my expectations.

As we shared our completed applications, we realized that certain animals were better suited for particular jobs. A duck or crocodile would be great candidates for a lifeguard position, but would not do well in land-based occupations. The dog was quite appropriate for a companion to a child, but a porcupine would be better suited as a security guard.

In the midst of our discussion, Renae tearfully remarked, "Sometimes I feel like I'm the wrong animal for school. I'm not so good at math and reading. The things that I'm good at don't matter at school, especially on our report card. I'm like a rabbit who's trying out for a flying job." Renae's comment is still vivid in my mind. Although she was well below grade level in all academic subject areas, she provided brilliant insights during oral discussions and was the star of our school play and sports events.

However, our report card presented only a limited picture of each student, and in Renae's case, it did not validate her strengths. Since that time, I've tried to create evaluation tools that allow all students to shine.

—Teacher, Grade 4

George looked at the test. It said:
Rabbits eat

❑ lettuce

❑ dog food

❑ sandwiches

He raised his hand. "Rabbits have to eat carrots, or their teeth will get too long and stick into them," he said. The teacher nodded and smiled, but she put her finger to her lips. George carefully drew in a carrot so the test people would know.

First Grade Takes A Test
by Miriam Cohen
Dell Publishing. New York. 1980.

Dear GEMS

When the authentic assessment movement came along, I figured that this was just one more educational fad that would be imposed on me from the district. Though at first I was skeptical, now I'm convinced! My students have always worked best when they're engaged with a subject, and when they have a chance to bring their own experience to the learning situation.

For the first time in 25 years of teaching, my assessment program is directly connected to my goals and philosophy. This educational change is a welcome relief.

—Teacher, Grade 2

Send Us Your Letters!

Dear GEMS

Authentic assessment is not new. To get a driver's license, we are asked to drive a car in the middle of traffic. When students apply to art school, they submit portfolios of their work. To try out for baseball teams, athletes demonstrate their pitching, hitting, and fielding skills. Even teachers are evaluated on our performance in the classroom. So, how do we assess students? We give them tests and worksheets where they regurgitate facts; find the answers to problems but rarely explain them; and explore hypothetical situations which have little connection to what we teachers know is important. Ironically, authentic assessment is used everywhere in the real world, except for the field of education whose goal is to prepare students for tomorrow!

— Elementary School Principal

Dear GEMS

I think that teachers create cheaters. Through our textbooks and tests, we let students know that there is only one right answer, and their goal is to produce it for us. When a student knows he doesn't have the right answer, he has two choices. He can fail the test or he can locate the answer from someone else. The most resourceful students will get the answer from someone else! We call this cheating, but perhaps it's a form of cooperative learning!

— Teacher, Grade 7

Dear GEMS

I feel very fortunate that I grew up in a society that validated my strengths when I was a student. I succeeded in school because I was articulate, a good reader, and polite in class. Those were the values of my teacher and of the school. If the school's goal had been to produce students who were strong, agile, and athletic, I would have been a candidate for the most severe Special Day Class.

—Teacher, Grade 9